my **revisi⦿n** notes

OCR A Level

LAW

Clare Wilson
Craig Beauman

HODDER
EDUCATION
AN HACHETTE UK COMPANY

Although every effort has been made to ensure that website addresses are correct at time of going to press, Hodder Education cannot be held responsible for the content of any website mentioned in this book. It is sometimes possible to find a relocated web page by typing in the address of the home page for a website in the URL window of your browser.

Hachette UK's policy is to use papers that are natural, renewable and recyclable products and made from wood grown in sustainable forests. The logging and manufacturing processes are expected to conform to the environmental regulations of the country of origin.

Orders: please contact Bookpoint Ltd, 130 Milton Park, Abingdon, Oxon OX14 4SE. Telephone: +44 (0)1235 827827. Fax: +44 (0)1235 400401. Email education@bookpoint.co.uk Lines are open from 9 a.m. to 5 p.m., Monday to Saturday, with a 24-hour message answering service. You can also order through our website: www.hoddereducation.co.uk

ISBN: 978 1 5104 2632 0

© Clare Wilson and Craig Beauman 2018

First published in 2018 by

Hodder Education,

An Hachette UK Company

Carmelite House

50 Victoria Embankment

London EC4Y 0DZ

www.hoddereducation.co.uk

Impression number   5 4 3 2 1

Year   2022   2021   2020   2019   2018

Cover photo © imagineerinx/Shutterstock.com

Illustrations by Aptara

Typeset in India

Printed in Spain

A catalogue record for this title is available from the British Library.

Get the most from this book

Everyone has to decide his or her own revision strategy, but it is essential to review your work, learn it and test your understanding. These Revision Notes will help you to do that in a planned way, topic by topic. Use this book as the cornerstone of your revision and don't hesitate to write in it – personalise your notes and check your progress by ticking off each section as you revise.

Tick to track your progress

Use the revision planner on pages iv and v to plan your revision, topic by topic. Tick each box when you have:

- revised and understood a topic
- tested yourself
- practised the exam questions and gone online to check your answers.

You can also keep track of your revision by ticking off each topic heading in the book. You may find it helpful to add your own notes as you work through each topic.

Features to help you succeed

Exam tips

Expert tips are given throughout the book to help you polish your exam technique in order to maximise your chances in the exam.

Typical mistakes

The author identifies the typical mistakes candidates make and explains how you can avoid them.

Now test yourself

These short, knowledge-based questions provide the first step in testing your learning. Go online to check your answers at **www.hoddereducation. co.uk/myrevisionnotesdownloads**

Definitions and key words

Clear, concise definitions of essential key terms are provided where they first appear.

Key words from the specification are highlighted in bold throughout the book.

Revision activities

These activities will help you to understand each topic in an interactive way.

Exam practice

Practice exam questions are provided for each topic. Use them to consolidate your revision and practise your exam skills.

Exam summaries

Descriptions of the types of questions you can expect in the examination.

Online

Go online to check your answers to the Now test yourself and Exam practice questions at **www.hoddereducation.co.uk/ myrevisionnotesdownloads**

My revision planner

OCR A Level Law

REVISED   TESTED   EXAM READY

5 The nature of law

6 Human rights law

7 The law of contract

Countdown to my exams

1 The legal system

In the OCR A Level Law H415 specification, the English legal system and the nature of law are divided into three sections. The first section, *The legal system*, is assessed in Section A of the Component 1 exam paper.

This is a compulsory section which examines your ability to explain, describe or discuss:
- civil courts and other forms of dispute resolution
- criminal courts and lay people
- legal personnel/professions
- access to justice.

Make sure you do not regard this section and the other two English legal system sections (*Law making* and *The nature of law*) in isolation. They are complementary to each other, along with the **substantive law** sections. Drawing on these different sections will help you appreciate how the English legal system operates, which in turn can enhance your exam responses.

> **Substantive law:** legal rules which determine rights and obligations or how a society must behave, for example criminal, contract, tort or human rights law.

1.1 Civil courts and other forms of dispute resolution

This chapter looks at five key areas of civil law in the English legal system:
- civil courts: County Court and High Court – jurisdictions, pre-trial procedures and the three tracks
- appeals and appellate courts
- tribunals and alternative dispute resolution (ADR)
- online courts and online dispute resolution (ODR)
- evaluation of the civil courts and other forms of dispute resolution.

Civil courts

REVISED

The **civil courts** deal with non-criminal matters, such as contract, tort and human rights issues. They are designed to deal with disputes between individual citizens and/or businesses. There is some crossover with criminal courts, but generally they have separate courts.

> **Civil courts:** courts that deal with non-criminal matters.

Examples of disputes include disagreements arising under contract, family or employment law.

The civil justice system was largely reformed in the 1990s. There are two key civil courts of first instance: the County Court and the High Court.

> **Revision activity**
>
> Explain what is meant by tort law and why such disputes are dealt with under civil law.

> **Exam tip**
>
> You need a clear understanding of the civil courts' structures, procedures and appeals systems. It might help you to visit as many types of civil court as you can, to observe their workings in practice.

> **Revision activity**
>
> Identify which courts have both civil and criminal jurisdiction.

Reform of the civil justice system

In 1995, following historic public criticisms of the civil justice system, Lord Woolf reported that 'the key problems facing civil justice today are cost, delay and complexity'.

His report, *Access to Justice* (1996), suggested major reforms to the civil justice system, which were largely incorporated into the Civil Procedure Rules of 1999. The main objective of these rules was to enable the civil courts to deal with cases in a more just way.

As a result of these reforms:
- case management was handed to individual judges
- a 'track' system was introduced in the County Court, to put claims in a hierarchical order depending upon the value of the claim
- pre-action protocols were introduced
- other forms of dispute resolution were encouraged, including alternative dispute resolution (ADR).

Jurisdictions of the civil courts

Table 1.1.1 **Jurisdiction of the County Court**

Jurisdiction	Evaluation

• Deals with the majority of civil matters and the enforcement of previous judgments that have not been complied with
• Hears:
  – contract disputes, e.g. businesses recovering monies owed
  – tortious (civil wrong) actions, e.g. landowners seeking to prevent trespass issues
  – compensation claims for injuries to claimants
  – some bankruptcy and insolvency matters, and cases involving wills and trusts up to £30,000
  – disputes arising under the Equality Act 2010
  – defamation cases where all parties agree to County Court jurisdiction.
	• Simpler system of civil courts post-Woolf reforms
	• ADR is encouraged, but not always appropriate nor enforced by judges
	• Simpler DIY method of bringing a case, generally with a fixed fee and explained via leaflet or the internet
	• Small claims court is less formal than the main County Court, with a District Judge taking an active role setting time limits and asking questions
	• Solicitor not needed in many cases, unless the claim is contested
	• Appeal routes possible

Table 1.1.2 **Jurisdiction of the High Court (three divisions)**

Jurisdiction	Evaluation
Queen's Bench Division hears: • both civil cases (especially contract and tort) and criminal cases • common-law business cases in contract, unless under the Chancery Division's jurisdiction • tort cases involving defamation, trespass, negligence or nuisance • judicial review actions.	• Clear and distinct separation of types of law via the three divisions • Jury trial possible in tortious cases, including defamation and malicious prosecution • Expensive and time-consuming cases can prevent many claims from reaching the High Court • Simplified and single set of rules governing both the High Court and the County Court
Chancery Division hears: • specialist civil cases, which include company law, patents and contentious probate • professional negligence cases • competition-law cases.	
Family Division hears: • family-related cases • cases involving children under the Children Act 1989 • wardship cases involving the custody and day-to-day care of minors.	

Pre-trial matters and the three tracks

While some civil cases start in the Magistrates' Court, most civil cases start in the County Court.

If the claim value is for a specific amount, in some cases a claim can be made online. If the value is unspecified, a claimant fills in an N1 form and sends this, with the appropriate fee, to the HM Courts and Tribunals Service. Depending on the value of the claim, and whether the defendant denies liability, the service can allocate the claim to the most appropriate track:

- small claims track for straightforward claims of not more than £10,000 or personal injury of not more than £1,000
- fast track for claims between £10,000 and not more than £25,000
- multi-track for claims exceeding £25,000 and not more than £50,000
- High Court for more complex claims over £50,000.

Typical mistake

Do not muddle the three tracks when it comes to the financial limits and the key types of cases they hear. Exam questions might ask about which court(s) an appeal will go to after it is heard in one of the tracks – be clear on the differences.

Revision activity

Print out and complete an N1 form. This will help you appreciate the idea of simplicity and understand its requirements.

Appeals and appellate courts

REVISED

If either party in a case is dissatisfied with the decision made by the judge at first instance, then it is possible to appeal. Generally:

- A first appeal from a decision of the small claims court or the fast track is heard by a next-level judge. If the case was first heard by a District Judge, the appeal will be to a Circuit Judge. If first heard by a Circuit Judge, then the appeal is to a High Court Judge.
- It is possible for a second appeal from the decision of a Circuit Judge or High Court Judge to go to the Court of Appeal (Civil Division), but this would be in exceptional circumstances and only with the Court of Appeal's permission.
- An appeal from a decision of the multi-track, whether heard by a District or Circuit Judge, is to the Court of Appeal (Civil Division).
- An appeal from the High Court is to the Court of Appeal (Civil Division), or on rare occasion to the Supreme Court (called a 'leapfrog' appeal) where a point of general public importance is present.
- It is possible for a further appeal from the Court of Appeal (Civil Division) to the Supreme Court, but only if either court gives permission.
- A final appeal is possible for a case to be referred to the European Court of Justice, under Article 234 of the Treaty of Rome, if a point of European Union law is involved.

Revision activity

Draw a flow chart showing the civil courts' appeal routes from:
- the County Court, and
- the High Court.

Tribunals and alternative dispute resolution

REVISED

There are two main alternatives to the civil courts:
- **tribunals**
- **ADR** – negotiation, mediation, conciliation and arbitration.

Exam tip

Make sure you understand the advantages and disadvantages of tribunals and ADR, as questions are commonly set on this area.

Tribunals: an informal method of dispute resolution developed for issues arising under the UK's 'welfare state', for example education, health and employment.

ADR: alternative dispute resolution, one of the key Woolf reform recommendations.

Tribunals

Table 1.1.3 Outline and evaluation of tribunals

Structure	• Tribunals are separated at first instance into seven divisions dealing with specific areas of law and four divisions for appeals. • First-tier tribunals hear cases at first instance, and upper tribunals hear appeals from the first tier. • There is a possible appeal route to the Court of Appeal and from here an appeal route to the Supreme Court. • A separate first-tier tribunal and upper tribunal exist for disputes involving employment law.
Role	• The system of administrative tribunals runs alongside the civil courts system. • Tribunals were established to deal with specific areas of law generally concerning social and welfare legislation, e.g. employment rights.
Advantages	• Tribunals are cheaper, and in many cases quicker, than going to court. • They are an informal hearing of fact, in most cases heard in private. • Some legal aid is available, usually for human rights issues concerning immigration or mental health issues. • They are heard by a panel of three – in most cases consisting of a tribunal judge and two lay persons having expertise in the area in dispute.
Disadvantages	• Public funding is not available in most cases, and the individual has to bear the cost of using a tribunal. • The government department that the individual is in dispute with will generally use a lawyer to represent it. • They are more formal than alternative methods of dispute resolution, with an inquisitorial nature to the hearing. • Due to the huge volume of cases, especially those involving employment law, there can be a delay in hearing the case.

Negotiation

Negotiation: where an individual attempts to resolve an issue directly, privately and possibly face to face with the other party.

Revision activity

Using the internet, draw a flow chart to reflect the tribunals' structure in England and Wales.

Table 1.1.4 Outline and evaluation of negotiation

Description	The most basic form of ADR, where an individual attempts to resolve the issue directly, privately and possibly face to face with the other party
Advantage over litigation	Potentially the quickest, cheapest, most informal way of settling a dispute between parties, as no court or lawyers are involved
Disadvantages compared to litigation	• Requires confrontation with the other party • If the dispute is not settled, the case may go to court, which will involve costs and the court may insist the parties go back to negotiation before trial
Examples	• Noise caused by neighbours • Returning faulty goods to a shop • Receiving poor service from a tradesperson

Revision activity

Role play the following scenario. Your neighbour's son keeps playing his music very loud and in the early hours of the morning. You have asked him to stop, but he has ignored you. How could negotiation help resolve the dispute?

Mediation

Mediation: where a neutral third party attempts to resolve a dispute (possibly face to face) with both parties, without giving their opinion.

Table 1.1.5 Outline and evaluation of mediation

Description	• Slightly more formal than negotiation, but still a relatively informal method of dispute resolution • A neutral third-party mediator attempts to resolve the issue (possibly face to face) with both parties, without giving their opinion
Advantages over litigation	• The parties are, in effect, in control of proceedings and decisions • Based on common sense rather than decisive legal rules
Disadvantages compared to litigation	• Will only work if both parties agree and cooperate • Many decisions may not ultimately be binding on both parties
Examples	• Businesses negotiating or renegotiating contracts • Marriage guidance to avoid separation or divorce

Revision activity

Copy out and complete the following revision chart to evaluate negotiation and mediation.

Type of ADR	Advantages	Disadvantages
Negotiation	1 2 3	1 2 3
Mediation	1 2 3	1 2 3

Conciliation

Conciliation: a form of mediation where a third party is active in raising ideas for compromise between the parties in dispute.

Table 1.1.6 Outline and evaluation of conciliation

Description	Form of mediation, where a third party is active in raising ideas for compromise between the parties in dispute
Advantage over litigation	More formal version of mediation, where an impartial conciliator takes an active role in suggesting and advising the parties
Disadvantages compared to litigation	• Can require confrontation with the other party, but some cases are dealt with via telephone • The decision of the conciliator is not binding • The parties may still need to go to court if the decision is not followed
Examples	• Disputes access to goods and services by disabled people • Cases of alleged discrimination • Some employment disputes • Some family law matters involving the Family Division of the High Court

Typical mistake

Do not muddle up mediation and conciliation, or forget to support your definitions with examples (real or imagined) of organisations that operate in these areas of ADR.

Arbitration

Table 1.1.7 Outline and evaluation of arbitration

Description	Form of ADR where the parties to a dispute refer the case to an independent third party, known as an arbitrator, to decide
Advantages over litigation	• An agreement to arbitrate can be made at any time and is usually included in a contract by what is known as a *Scott v Avery* clause • The decision is binding and can be enforced through the courts
Disadvantages compared to litigation	• Requires confrontation with the other party • The use of a professional arbitrator can mean this process is more expensive than going to court
Examples	• Package-holiday contracts • Disputes between employees and employers using ACAS

Arbitration: a form of ADR where the parties to a dispute refer the case to an independent third party, known as an arbitrator, to decide.

Exam tip

You might be asked to assess the options a defendant would have if they wanted to resolve a dispute without going to court. This would require a discussion of tribunals and ADR.

Online courts and online dispute resolution

REVISED

ADR outside the courts has long been championed as saving both time and money for claimants. The Woolf reforms of the 1990s recommended ADR as a way of avoiding the overburdened courts.

Since 2015, the government has looked at ways of developing online courts and **online dispute resolution (ODR)**, in a more internet-focused and technically savvy world than at the time of the Woolf reforms.

The government tasked the Courts and Tribunals Judiciary Service with looking at ways that internet technology could be used to resolve disputes in low-level civil cases without parties having to attend court. Their proposals included:
- allowing senior judges to look at case and court papers and decide the outcome of a case online (a video or telephone conference with the parties could be used, but given the low-level nature of the cases, this would be rare)
- using an 'online facilitator'; this person would look to bring parties together 'virtually' online to negotiate, and act as a mediator to resolve the issue in cases that did not need to go to court and could be resolved as such.

The Civil Justice Council produced a report on ODR in 2015, which stated:

'ODR is not science fiction ... each year on eBay around 60 million disagreements amongst traders are resolved through ODR. This is a well-established way of resolving disputes, appropriate for the internet age.'

The Courts and Tribunals Judiciary Service's panel of judges took inspiration from around the world, notably the success of the Canadian online dispute resolution system in British Columbia. Head of the Panel, Professor Richard Susskind, said:

'This kind of technology will do two things. Firstly, it will increase access to justice because we believe more people will use the system. It will be cheaper, more convenient, less forbidding. And secondly ... it will lower the cost ... to individual participants in disputes and also the cost of the overall justice system.'

Online dispute resolution (ODR): a contemporary method of using digital means, for example the internet, to resolve disputes without having to use litigation.

Exam tip

This is a new topic in the OCR specification, relating to more modern methods of dispute resolution. Use the internet to identify up-to-date government proposals and implementation of online courts and ODR.

Revision activity

Use the following video clip to define, in basic terms, what is meant by online dispute resolution (ODR): www.youtube.com/watch?v=MQfLPpqiTFk.

The 2015 Civil Justice Council report recommended the establishment of a new internet-based court service (known as HM Online Court) to introduce ODR into the English legal system. This would be a three-tier service.

The full report can be found at: **www.judiciary.gov.uk/wp-content/ uploads/2015/02/Online-Dispute-Resolution-Final-Web-Version1.pdf**.

Using pages 6–7 of the report as a start (pages 19–21 provide further detail), complete the following table.

Recommended ODR tier service	Explanation
Tier One: Online Evaluation	
Tier Two: Online Facilitation	
Tier Three: Online Judges	

Now test yourself

TESTED

1 List three areas of law that would be dealt with in the civil courts.
2 List the three key problems Lord Woolf stated were facing the civil justice system by 1995.
3 Look at the chart below and complete the missing court or value of claim.

Court	Claim value
Small claims	
	Between £10,000 and £25,000
Multi-track	
	Over £50,000

4 Explain the purpose of tribunals in the civil justice system.
5 Explain one advantage and one disadvantage of the tribunal system.
6 Give three ways that alternative dispute resolution (ADR) is different from using the civil courts.
7 Explain what is meant by negotiation and mediation.
8 List two advantages and two disadvantages in using online dispute resolution (ODR) to resolve civil cases.

Answers online

Exam summary

In the exam, you MAY be asked to:
● explain the civil courts and other forms of dispute resolution, for example the jurisdiction of the County Court
● describe the civil courts and other forms of dispute resolution, for example the appeals process from the County Court
● discuss the advantages or problems associated with the civil courts and other forms of dispute resolution, for example the advantages of using mediation as a way of dealing with a civil dispute.

These types of questions will be worth a maximum of 10 or 15 marks each.

1.2 Criminal courts and lay people

This chapter looks at five key criminal areas in the legal system:
- criminal process: jurisdiction of the Magistrates' Court and the Crown Court, including classification of offences and pre-trial procedures
- appeals and appellate courts
- sentencing and court powers: aims, factors and types of sentence
- lay magistrates and juries: qualification, selection, appointment and their role in criminal cases
- evaluation of the different types of sentence and of using lay people in criminal cases.

> **Criminal courts:** there are two levels – the Magistrates' Court deals mainly with summary offences, and the Crown Court deals mainly with indictable offences.
>
> **Lay people:** in the criminal justice system, either magistrates or juries; 'lay' in this circumstance means legally 'unqualified'.

Criminal process

REVISED

The criminal courts system is designed to uphold laws which forbid certain types of behaviour. Indulging in those behaviours risks punishment, thereby maintaining a civilised society.

There are two key criminal courts of first instance: the Magistrates' Court and the Crown Court.

There are three key criminal processes in the criminal courts' system:
- **bail**
- jurisdiction in the Magistrates' Courts and/or Crown Court
- the Crown Prosecution Service.

> **Bail:** a form of security, either a sum of money or a promise in exchange for the freedom of an arrested person as a guarantee that they will appear in a criminal court when required.
>
> **Rebuttable presumption:** a conclusion that a judge will take in court unless the contrary is raised and proven.

Bail

There is a **rebuttable presumption** that bail should be granted under s 4 of the Bail Act 1976.

After being arrested and charged with an offence, a suspect can be released on bail at the police station. Bail can be issued by the police or any court before which the defendant appears, usually either the Magistrates' Court or the Crown Court.

Bail will remain in place until the court hearing. It can also be refused if there are sufficient grounds.

Conditions can be applied to the bail, for example:
- to reside at a particular address
- not to contact certain people, such as the victim or witnesses
- to surrender their passport to the police if considered a 'flight-risk'
- to report to a police station at specific, agreed times each week.

Failure to comply means the suspect can be arrested again and remanded in prison until their court hearing.

> **Revision activity**
>
> Read s 4 of the Bail Act 1976 and summarise succinctly the section's main constituent parts.

> **Revision activity**
>
> Consider any other conditions that could be attached to a person's bail.

> **Exam tip**
>
> You might be asked to explain the reasons for three conditions that could be attached to a suspect's bail. Make sure that you understand this. For example, a passport might have to be surrendered to make sure the suspect does not flee the country.

Jurisdiction in the Magistrates' Court

Around 97 per cent of all criminal cases are dealt with in a Magistrates' Court, with more than 90 per cent being concluded there. The court's key functions include:
- trying **summary offences** and most **triable-either-way offences**
- carrying out plea-before-venue hearings for either-way offences

> **Summary offences:** the least serious offences in terms of injury or impact, tried in the Magistrates' Courts, for example assault, battery and certain road traffic offences such as speeding.
>
> **Triable-either-way offences:** offences that can be tried in the Crown Court or in the Magistrates' Court, for example theft, s 47 ABH and s 20 GBH/wounding.

- sentencing defendants if found guilty – powers are limited but reflect the seriousness of the crimes under its jurisdiction
- dealing with the first hearing of **indictable offences** such as the granting of bail, or making reporting restrictions before being sent to the Crown Court
- dealing with ancillary matters, such as issuing 'bench' arrest warrants and granting or refusing bail in summary or either-way trials
- trying cases in the Youth Court for defendants aged 10–17.

Jurisdiction in the Crown Court

In 1971, a system of Crown Courts was established to deal with those criminal cases not tried fully in the Magistrates' Courts. The Crown Courts deal with the most serious, indictable offences.

The trial normally begins with a plea and case management hearing, where the defendant will plead either:
- guilty – and subsequently be sentenced, or
- not guilty – whereupon a full trial involving a jury of 12 citizens will commence.

Crown Prosecution Service

The Crown Prosecution Service (CPS) is responsible for prosecuting most criminal cases in England and Wales. It:
- decides which cases are to be prosecuted
- determines the most appropriate offences with which to charge the defendant
- prepares cases and presents them in court.

Under the Code for Crown Prosecutors, a decision to prosecute is made if the merits of the case pass a two-fold test:
1 the evidential burden test: there must be sufficient evidence to prosecute
2 the public interest stage test: the prosecution must be in the public interest.

Factors influencing the CPS to prosecute would include:
- a premeditated decision to commit a crime
- use of a weapon
- the defendant was in a position of authority or trust
- vulnerability of the victim
- the defendant has previous convictions.

> **Indictable offences:**
> the most serious, more complicated offences tried only and fully in the Crown Court, for example murder, manslaughter and robbery.

> **Revision activity**
>
> Identify the Magistrates' Courts in your local area and the geographical area each one serves.

> **Revision activity**
>
> Browse the CPS website (**www.cps.gov.uk**) and try to find out further information about the Code for Crown Prosecutors.

> **Exam tip**
>
> You might be asked to explain three factors influencing the CPS to prosecute a suspect, or to assess the likelihood of a suspect being prosecuted in an example scenario. You will need to remember these factors and be able to spot them in a scenario.

Classification of criminal offences

Table 1.2.1 Classification of criminal offences

Classification of offence	Trial court	Examples of offences	Sentencing powers of court
Indictable	Administrative hearing in the Magistrates' Court, then transferred to the Crown Court for trial	● Murder ● Manslaughter ● Robbery ● Section 18 wounding/GBH	Up to the maximum set for the specific offence by common law or statute
Triable either way	(Plea before venue) Magistrates' Court, or Crown Court	● Theft ● Section 20 wounding/GBH ● ABH	Up to maximum set for the specific offence (but see below for magistrates' maximum sentencing powers)
Summary	Magistrates' Court	● Common assault ● Driving without insurance or a licence	Up to six months' imprisonment for a single offence, or up to 12 months in total for two or more offences; and/or a fine, generally of up to £5,000

Revision activity

Create and illustrate a diagram on A3 paper identifying the three classifications of offence.

Pre-trial procedures

Table 1.2.2 Pre-trial procedures

Pre-trial procedure	Explanation
Summary offences	Most trials in the Magistrates' Court start with a first appearance at a trial. However, an adjournment of the trial could be needed, and bail set, if the: ● CPS requires more time to prepare the case ● defendant is unprepared and wishes to engage a solicitor ● magistrates request pre-sentence reports on a defendant who pleads guilty ● defendant pleads not guilty and wants to go to trial and, for example, witnesses need to be called.
Triable-either-way offences	● The magistrates will ask the defendant if they plead guilty or not guilty. ● Then a decision is made whether to hear the trial in that court or the Crown Court.
Indictable offences	After an early administrative hearing in the Magistrates' Court, the case is sent immediately to the Crown Court to be dealt with by (usually) a single Circuit Judge.

Appeals and appellate courts

REVISED

The criminal courts system provides appeal routes for defendants in all cases and to the prosecution in certain situations.

Table 1.2.3 Appeals from the Magistrates' Court to the Crown Court

Available to	Only the defence
Reason for appeal	Against sentence and/or conviction
Appeal heard by	Panel of a single Circuit Judge and two magistrates
Further appeal possible?	• Generally no, but possible to appeal to the Queen's Bench Divisional Court purely on a point of law • Possible further appeal to the Supreme Court (see below)
Result of appeal	Appeal quashed, confirm appeal or remit case back to the Magistrates' Court

Table 1.2.4 Appeals from the Magistrates' Court to the Queen's Bench Divisional Court (QBD)

Available to	The prosecution and the defence
Reason for appeal	On a point of law by way of case stated
Appeal heard by	Panel of two or three High Court Judges, which might include a Court of Appeal judge
Further appeal possible?	• Possible appeal by the prosecution or the defence to the Supreme Court on a point of law of general public importance • Must have leave to appeal by either the Supreme Court or QBD
Result of appeal	Appeal quashed, confirm appeal or remit case back to the Magistrates' Court

Table 1.2.5 Appeals from the Crown Court (1)

By whom?	Defendant
Reason for appeal	Rare, but possible – against sentence and/or (unsafe) conviction
Where heard?	• Court of Appeal (Criminal Division) within six weeks of conviction and must be granted permission • Fresh evidence can be heard at this appeal
Further appeal possible?	• Again, rare but possible, to the Supreme Court on a point of law of general public importance • Must have leave to appeal
Result of appeal	Appeal quashed or confirm appeal

Table 1.2.6 Appeals from the Crown Court (2)

By whom?	Prosecution
Reason for appeal	• Against the *acquittal* of the defendant if the prosecution is unhappy with the decision, or by the Attorney-General to clarify a point of law relevant to the acquittal • Against *sentence* if the Attorney-General considers the sentence to be unduly lenient
Where heard?	Court of Appeal (Criminal Division)
Further appeal possible?	• Rare, but possible • To the Supreme Court on a point of law of general public importance • Must have leave to appeal
Result of appeal	Appeal quashed or confirm appeal

Revision activity

Create a flow chart poster showing the different appeal routes from the Crown Court.

Sentencing and court powers

The term 'sentencing' means any punishment given to an offender who has been convicted. An adult offender is anyone aged 21 years or older who has been convicted of an offence.

> **Sentencing:** any punishment given to an offender who has been convicted.

Aims of sentencing

The aim of a sentence is what exactly it is trying to achieve. Under s 142 of the Criminal Justice Act 2003, there are five basic aims of sentencing for adult offenders, and any court dealing with an offender in respect of their offence must have regard to:

'(a) the punishment of offenders,

(b) the reduction of crime (including its reduction by deterrence),

(c) the reform and rehabilitation of offenders,

(d) the protection of the public, and

(e) the making of reparation by offenders to persons affected by their offences.'

Factors of sentencing

There are many factors which can influence the sentencing of adult offenders, including the:
- type of crime committed
- seriousness of the crime – for example, was someone injured or was there a fatality?
- circumstances of the crime – for example, was the victim vulnerable or was a weapon used?

> **Typical mistake**
>
> Do not use incorrect or out-of-date information. As part of your self-study or homework, make sure you research relevant websites, for example www.sentencingcouncil.org.uk.

Types of sentence

There are four main types of adult sentence:

1 Imprisonment: the offender's behaviour is so serious that none of the other sentences will suffice. Offenders serve half of their sentence in prison and the other half on licence in the community.
2 Community sentences: offenders are made to carry out between 40 and 300 hours of demanding work in the community or to undergo treatment for issues like drug addiction.
3 Fines: these are for less serious offences and, by far, the most common type of sentence. The amount depends on the severity of the crime.
4 Discharges: this is where the court feels that simply being brought in front of a judge or magistrate is enough punishment. Conditions can be set with a discharge, for example to stay out of trouble, and if the offender commits another crime, the first crime will be taken into consideration if sentenced.

Table 1.2.7 Evaluation of different types of sentence

Type of sentence	Advantages	Disadvantages
Imprisonment	• It removes an individual's liberty and is a strong deterrent. • Rehabilitation through training is possible to break the cycle of criminal behaviour.	• It offers little deterrent – serious crimes are continuously committed despite the threat of imprisonment. • Only half of a prison sentence is served, the rest is 'on licence' after the prisoner is released.
Community sentences	• The sentence can be fixed to address offender's reason for committing the offence, e.g. a drug treatment order. • Work is generally labour-intensive and arduous, with many hours of punishment available.	• Reparation is basic and minimalist. • Many offenders refuse to participate, and counter-punishments are rarely severe.
Fines	• Financial penalty allows the individual's liberty to continue. • There are generally set fees for committing specific offences.	• The cost to administer a fine can usually outweigh the fine itself. • Many fines go unpaid and are simply 'written-off'.

> **Revision activity**
>
> Consider the following scenario: William is a DJ in a nightclub. He has a disabled son, and in order to make some extra money he sells illegal drugs to some of the customers. One of the customers, Ryan, takes some of the drugs, but dies due to an overdose.
>
> Which type of sentence do you think is appropriate? Explain your answer.

> **Exam tip**
>
> You might be asked to explain three types of sentence available to adult offenders, or to assess which sentences would be available to a judge in sentencing an adult defendant in a scenario.

Lay magistrates and juries

REVISED

Lay people are the important 'legally unqualified' persons in the criminal justice system. They play a key role in the decision-making process.

There are two main types:
- **magistrates** – part-time, unsalaried judges
- **juries** – drawn from the electorate, they decide the guilt of offenders in the Crown Court.

Magistrates

Table 1.2.8 Magistrates: a summary

Qualification	• Aged between 18 and 65, but can retire at 70 • Must demonstrate six 'key qualities': good character; commitment and reliability; social awareness; sound judgement; understanding and communication; maturity and sound temperament • Must sit for at least 13 days/26 half-days each year (or 35 half-days if they also sit in the youth or family courts) • Must not have any serious criminal convictions or be an undischarged bankrupt

> **Magistrates:** volunteer citizens who work as unpaid (except for expenses) judges in the Magistrates' Court and the Youth Court. They deal with the vast majority of criminal cases.
>
> **Juries:** representatives drawn from the electorate who decide the guilt of offenders in the Crown Court.

Selection	• Recruited and selected by a network of 47 local advisory committees made up of serving magistrates and local non-magistrates • Satisfactory character references sought before appointment • Rigorous training if selected • Two interviews are held before a recommendation to appoint an individual is made to the Senior Presiding Judge
Appointment	Under the Crime and Courts Act 2013, and from 1 October 2013, the statutory power to appoint magistrates is by the Lord Chief Justice, who delegates the function to the Senior Presiding Judge for England and Wales

Role and powers

The role of magistrates is to:

- sit, most usually, in benches of three
- try summary and relevant either-way offences
- deal with mode of trial hearings for either-way offences
- sentence guilty defendants
- carry out preliminary hearings, such as early administrative hearings for indictable offences, remand hearings and applications for bail
- issue bench warrants
- sit in the Crown Court to hear appeals from the Magistrates' Courts (here, two magistrates will sit with a Crown Court Judge).

Specially qualified magistrates sit in the Youth Court to hear charges against 10–17-year-olds.

Table 1.2.9 **Evaluating the use of magistrates in criminal courts**

Advantages of using magistrates	• **Cost:** using magistrates is much cheaper than using the Crown Court, as magistrates are volunteers and can only claim basic expenses. • **Speed:** cases are dealt with quickly; most cases come to trial within a month of the alleged crime and are generally dealt with in a matter of minutes. • **Gender balance:** there is a near gender balance between male (51%) and female (49%) magistrates. • **Local involvement:** ordinary, local citizens are involved in local justice, meaning that decisions are not simply made by elite professional judges.
Disadvantages of using magistrates	• **Unrepresentative:** magistrates do not represent a true cross-section of society; in particular, those who work full time are under-represented. • **Ignorance of local area:** being unrepresentative, many magistrates have no real sound knowledge of the local area, especially the poorer, working-class neighbourhoods. • **Variety of sentencing:** there are huge variations in sentencing, depending upon geographical location. • **Unsympathetic:** case-hardened magistrates can become more rigid and less sympathetic with defendants the longer they serve.

Revision activity

Where possible, visit your local Magistrates' Court and observe a morning's worth of cases.

Exam tip

You might be asked to discuss the role of a lay magistrate in the criminal justice system, so knowing four or five key roles is crucial to success.

See earlier in this chapter for more information on the powers of magistrates in criminal courts.

Typical mistake

Do not confuse the role of magistrates with that of juries, or vice versa.

Juries

Table 1.2.10 Juries – a summary

Qualification	• Aged between 18 and 76 • Registered as a parliamentary or local government elector • Resided in the UK for any period of at least five years since age 13 • Not subject to provisions under the Mental Health Act 1983 • Not disqualified from jury service, e.g. persons on bail
Selection	• Jury summons issued by Jury Central Summonsing Bureau from the electoral register • Jury vetting can be used by the prosecution or defence pre-trial to challenge the appropriateness of individual jurors • Once a jury is sworn in, individual jurors, or the entire jury, can be challenged by the prosecution or defence
Appointment	• Individual court divides jurors into groups of 15, and 12 names are drawn at random from the 15 to sit on a jury • First name selected at random from each 15 appointed foreperson of the jury

Role of juries in criminal courts

Only around two per cent of criminal trials use juries. Juries:

- sit in the Crown Court as a panel of 12 persons
- decide the verdict only for the defendant – guilty or not guilty
- decide the facts of the case, while the judge directs them on points of law
- are independent and without fear of pressure from the judge to either convict or decide a verdict quickly – see *Bushell's Case* (1670)
- are allowed a majority (11–1, 10–2) rather than a unanimous decision (12–0).

> **Revision activity**
>
> Research the facts, decision and impact of *Bushell's Case* (1670).

Table 1.2 11 Evaluating the use of juries in criminal courts

Advantages	• **Public confidence:** this is instilled due to the traditional idea of being judged by ordinary members of society rather than professional judges. • **Jury equity:** this upholds democracy and freedom of will – see *R v Ponting* (1985) and *R v Grobbelaar* (1997). • **Open system of justice:** the process is public and assumes no legal knowledge of jurors as points are explained. • **Privacy of decision-making process:** juries decide the verdict in private, without outside pressures. • **Random selection process:** this allows a cross-section of the community to be picked from. • **Neutrality:** a jury should be impartial and, as a panel of 12, any individual prejudices should be cancelled out.
Disadvantages	• **Slow and expensive:** having to explain points of law increases the time taken and cost of the judges and legal personnel. • **Unpopular:** the compulsory nature means many jurors would rather not serve due to its impact on their working or family life. • **Outside influences:** arguably, media and social media coverage can influence jurors, or jurors can be 'nobbled' – see *R v Twomey* (2010). • **No explanation of verdict:** the decision is made in secret and no reason is given behind the decision, or bizarre methods are used to reach decision – see *R v Young* (1995). • **Failure to understand the case:** due to the complex nature of the law, it is possible juries do not follow the issues clearly. • **Lack of neutrality:** a complete cancelling of bias, especially racism, is speculative at best and highly unlikely – see *Sander v UK* (2000).

Exam tip

Use cases to complement answers to a question on the advantages and disadvantages of juries. Keep up to date with new cases in law journals and magazines that your college might subscribe to.

Now test yourself

TESTED

1 Give a simple definition of bail.
2 Explain any three factors that would influence the CPS to prosecute a suspect.
3 List the key functions of a Magistrates' Court as a criminal court.
4 Identify and explain one of the types of punishment for adult offenders.
5 Explain the term 'lay people' with regard to criminal cases.
6 Name the different sentencing powers of a magistrate.
7 List three advantages of using a jury.

Answers online

Exam summary

In the exam, you MAY be asked to:
- explain the criminal courts and lay people, for example the jurisdiction of the Magistrates' Court
- describe the criminal courts and lay people, for example the appeals process from the Magistrates' Court
- discuss the advantages or problems associated with criminal courts and lay people, for example the advantages of using magistrates in the criminal courts.

These questions will be worth a maximum of 10 or 15 marks each.

Revision activity

Research the case of *R v Twomey* (2010). What is meant by jury 'nobbling'?

Revision activity

Using paper or card, create a domino set for the advantages and disadvantages of using juries in criminal courts.

1.3 Legal personnel

Types of legal personnel

REVISED

Barristers

Barristers at the Bar are self-employed advocates who practise out of chambers, sharing administrative staff. Their work can include:

- when required, being briefed by a solicitor on behalf of a client or approached directly in certain civil matters
- rights of audience in all courts to represent clients, particularly the Crown Court or higher courts
- acting as a specialist legal advisor, giving clients independent and objective advice and opinion on the merits of a case, called 'counsel's opinion'
- if appointed as Queen's Council (QC), handling very serious or complex cases
- drafting legal documents for court.

Some barristers work for the CPS or large businesses which have legal departments.

> **Legal personnel:** a collective term which includes barristers, solicitors and legal executives.

> **Exam tip**
>
> You might be asked to explain three important roles that a member of the legal profession might carry out or assess the function of a member of the legal profession in assisting a suspect in a scenario.

Table 1.3.1 **Barristers – a summary**

Qualification	Academic stage – qualifying law degree/other degree supplemented by Common Professional Examination (CPE) or Graduate Diploma in Law (GDL)
Training	• Vocational stage – Bar Professional Training Course (one year full time or two years part time) • Professional stage – Pupillage (one year full time with six months non-practising and six months practising) • Continued CPD

Solicitors

Solicitors' roles largely depend on what type of firm they are employed by. The work can include:

- acting as a first contact with clients needing legal advice
- acting as advocates for clients, generally in the lower courts such as the Magistrates' Court or County Court
- giving legal advice to clients on a range of specialist areas, for example conveyancing or family matters
- organising a barrister for their client if the case goes to Crown Court or a higher court (some solicitors have rights of audience in all the courts)
- writing letters on their client's behalf on legal matters
- drafting contracts or other legal documents such as wills
- generally, working in private practice, but they can also work for large businesses which have a legal department or local authorities.

Table 1.3.2 Solicitors – a summary

Qualification	Academic stage – qualifying law degree/other degree supplemented by CPE/GDL
Training	<ul><li>Vocational stage – Legal Practice Course (one year full time or two years part time)</li><li>Professional stage 1: two years of recognised training (reduced if the trainee solicitor has previous, relevant legal experience)</li><li>Professional Stage 2: Professional Skills Course – 12 days of full-time attendance centring on core solicitor skills</li></ul>

Legal executives

Legal executives are qualified lawyers and usually specialise in one particular area of law. They generally work alongside solicitors and provide a similar role.

The work can include:
- acting as a first contact with clients needing legal advice in straightforward cases
- limited rights of audience acting as advocates for clients, generally in lower courts such as the County Court
- giving legal advice to clients on a range of specialist areas, for example personal injury and debt recovery
- handling legal aspects of a property transfer
- drafting contracts or other legal documents such as wills.

Table 1.3.3 Legal executives – a summary

Qualification	Academic stage – CILEx Level 3 Professional Diploma in Law and Practice and CILEx Level 6 Professional Higher Diploma in Law and Practice; or, if holding a qualifying law degree, CILEx Graduate Fast-track Diploma
Training	<ul><li>Professional stage – a minimum of three years' training through qualifying employment under the supervision of a solicitor or chartered legal executive</li><li>Complete a portfolio of evidence of qualifying employment</li></ul>

Regulation of legal personnel

REVISED

Regulation of the legal profession is vital in order to ensure a safe, secure and responsible environment for lawyers and their clients.

If there were no specific regulation, lawyers could act unprofessionally or negligently without recourse, and their clients would have little redress against them.

Regulation: a process whereby the actions of individuals or a collective are overseen and governed by an authorised organisation.

Table 1.3.4 Summary of the regulation of legal personnel

	Barristers	Solicitors	Legal executives
Governing body	Bar Council	Law Society	Chartered Institute of Legal Executives (CILEx)
Regulatory body	Bar Standards Board	Solicitors' Regulatory Authority	CILEx Regulation
Duties of regulatory body	• Sets education and training requirements • Sets standards of conduct • Monitors the service provided • Handles complaints against barristers, taking disciplinary action where required	• Sets the standards for qualifying • Monitors performance • Sets the rules for professional conduct • Handles complaints • Operates a compensation fund for clients who have lost money as a result of a solicitor's dishonesty	• Oversees the education, qualification and practice standards • Takes action against legal executives who do not meet those standards
Powers of regulatory body	• Fine • Individual sanctions • Suspension • Disbarment from working	• Fine • Written rebuke • Reprimand • Severe reprimand	• Reject a complaint • Impose conditions on future work • Exclude from membership • Fine • Order to pay costs of the case
Client liability	No contractual liability but can be sued for negligence – see *Hall v Simons* (2000)	Contractual liability and can be sued for negligence – see *White v Jones* (1995)	Contractual liability and can be sued for negligence

Legal Services Board

The Legal Services Board was created under the Legal Services Act 2007 and oversees the regulation of lawyers in England and Wales. It operates as a second check to the regulatory bodies of the three types of legal personnel.

It suggests reform and recommendations to modernise the legal services market.

Legal Ombudsman

If the dispute between client and lawyer cannot be resolved between themselves or the relevant regulatory body, then the case could be referred to the Legal Ombudsman. This is an independent scheme that resolves complaints about lawyers from clients in a fair and effective way. It helps to drive improvements to legal services.

> **Revision activity**
>
> Using the internet, research the governing body websites for each type of legal personnel.

Changes and trends in legal services

Globalisation

While there is clear resistance to globalisation, there has been a consistent movement through the legal professions to embrace this concept:

- Law firms show a willingness to deal with international disputes.
- Trade barriers, which used to complicate the trade of goods and provision of services, have been reduced or removed, although Brexit has raised new challenges for those firms inside and outside the UK.
- Advancements in technology allow law firms a greater opportunity to communicate and provide online or virtual services.
- A more global culture with less national or border-controlled isolation is encouraged.

Benefits of globalisation to the legal profession

- Globalisation allows law firms to expand internationally.
- Law firms must adapt and change to the demand and the needs of changing international markets.
- Lawyers must be aware of international law and other countries' domestic laws in order to operate.
- Mergers between law firms in different countries allow the pooling of resources and expertise. This can reduce operating costs and, in consequence, costs to the consumer.
- England is seen as having a truly impartial judiciary, and international companies are keen to settle disputes in the UK, where possible.
- Shared laws, such as those affecting terrorism, trade and climate, can be addressed in a homogenous way so firms can tackle global issues together.

Legal education and globalisation

Alongside the globalisation of the legal profession, there is a concurrent requirement for legal education to become homogenised, or to work in parity with other legal systems' education. Law students will have to:

- appreciate how law operates in an international context
- understand how certain laws, for example contract law, are comparable within different jurisdictions
- have knowledge of different legal systems
- appreciate differences in legal ethics and cultural diversity
- understand other languages and methods of communication – especially electronic communication.

Technology

Modern technology has many advantages, as it shapes the future of the legal profession. It:

- enables those in the legal profession to become more efficient and accurate in research and case construction
- allows online dispute resolution
- reduces labour cost by swapping employees with machine-read or artificial-intelligence systems
- creates ideas for further process innovation
- produces work around cyber-security, data protection and new technology laws
- simply supports and follows changes to consumer demand and purchasing-expectation behaviours.

> **Revision activity**
>
> Using the internet, research why the Law Society is sceptical about online courts.

Using the internet, complete the following table by identifying how each type of technology enhances the provision of legal services.

Technology	Method of enhancing legal services
Smartphones and tablet computers	
Cloud storage	
e-Discovery	
e-Libraries	
Anti-virus software	
Social media	

The judiciary

The **judiciary** is split between the civil courts and the criminal courts. However, the further up the hierarchy, the more likely judges can sit in either civil or criminal cases, depending upon where they are needed. Their main role is to adjudicate either over transgressions of the law in criminal trials or in disputes in civil cases.

> **Judiciary:** collective term for all the different types of judge in the English legal system.

Type and role of judges

Table 1.3.5 **Type and role of judges**

Court	Type of judge	Role of judge
Supreme Court	• Justice of the Supreme Court • Head of the Supreme Court: President of the Supreme Court	Hear appeals on points of law in both civil and criminal cases
Court of Appeal	• Lord Justice of Appeal • Criminal Division Head: Lord Chief Justice • Civil Division Head: Master of the Rolls	• Hear appeals in criminal cases against conviction and/or sentence • Hear appeals in civil cases on finding of liability and/or amount awarded
High Court	• High Court Judge (Puisne Judge) • Head of Chancery Division: Chancellor of the High Court • Head of Family Division: President of the Family Division • Head of the Queen's Bench Division: President of the Queen's Bench Division	• Judges sit in one of three High Court Divisions • Hear large-value, first-instance civil cases to decide liability and remedy • Hear appeals from lower courts in both civil and criminal cases

Court	Type of judge	Role of judge
Crown Court	• High Court Judge (for serious cases) • Circuit Judge • Recorder (part time)	• Hear complex and serious criminal cases • Hear appeals from Magistrates' Courts • Try criminal cases with a jury • Decide the law • Assist the jury on points of law • Pass sentences
County Court	• Circuit Judge • Recorder (part time) • District Judge (small claims court)	• Hear civil cases • Decide liability and remedies
Magistrates' Court	District Judge (Magistrates' Court)	• Hear low- to medium-level criminal cases • Decide verdict • Pass sentences • Hear civil cases: some family work, licensing appeals
Tribunals	• Tribunal Judge • Head: Senior President of Tribunals	Hear cases on specific civil issues, such as employment disputes

Qualification, appointment and dismissal of judges

Judges can be divided into two types, according to the courts in which they sit:

• inferior (Crown Court and below), and
• superior (High Court and above).

There are differences in their qualification, appointment and how they are dismissed.

Table 1.3.6 Qualification, appointment and dismissal of inferior judges

Type	Court(s)	Qualification	Appointment	Dismissal (security of tenure)
Circuit Judge	• Crown Court • County Court	• Presently a Recorder • Crown Court or County Court advocate for ten years • District Judge for three years	Advertisement/ open competition and appointment by the monarch on the advice of the Lord Chancellor	By the Lord Chancellor on grounds of incapacity or misbehaviour
Recorder/ assistant Recorder	• Crown Court • County Court	Crown Court or County Court advocate for ten years	As above	As above
District Judge	County Court	Seven years' general advocacy qualification	As above	As above
District Judge (Magistrates' Court)	Magistrates' Court	Seven years' general advocacy qualification	As above	As above

Table 1.3.7 Qualification, appointment and dismissal of superior judges

Type	Court(s)	Qualification	Appointment	Dismissal (security of tenure)
Lord of Appeal in Ordinary	● Supreme Court ● Privy Council	● Held a high judicial appointment (e.g. Court of Appeal) for two years, or ● Fifteen years' advocacy in the Supreme Court	Appointment by the monarch on the advice of the Prime Minister, Lord Chancellor and Minister for Justice	● By the monarch following a vote by both Houses of Parliament ● (Act of Settlement 1700) + incapacity
Lord Justice of Appeal	Court of Appeal	● Presently a High Court Judge for two years, or ● High Court advocate for ten years	As above (NB: the Lord Chancellor consults senior judges)	As above
High Court Judge (Puisne Judge)	● High Court ● Crown Court (serious cases only)	● Circuit Judge for two years, or ● High Court advocate for ten years	● Appointment by the monarch on the advice of the Lord Chancellor ● Assigned to one of the three divisions	As above

Training

In England and Wales, direct responsibility for the training of judges and members of tribunals is overseen by the Judicial College, under the Tribunals, Courts and Enforcement Act 2007.

The Judicial College is also responsible for management of the training of magistrates. The idea of a Judicial College is that the training is under direct judicial control.

Security of tenure: retirement and removal

It is a long-established principle in the English legal system that:
● judges should not be under the control of the government (the executive) – see below regarding separation of powers
● judges should not be removed as a government changes, in order to serve a new government's purpose or desire
● individual judges are not criticised in parliamentary debates
● any judicial removal mechanisms and the length of tenure should be firmly established in law.

There is no minimum age to be appointed as a judge, but:
● in most cases, judges must be able to serve for a 'reasonable length of service', which in practice is for a minimum of five years
● judges must retire by the time they are 70 years old (some judges can work longer, but no judge is allowed to serve after they reach 75 years of age).

Judges hold office 'during good behaviour' and can be removed if there is an allegation of misconduct:
● For High Court Judges and Court of Appeal Judges, removal is by petition to the Crown following an address presented to both Houses of Parliament by virtue of the Act of Settlement 1701.

- There is a similar process to remove Supreme Court Judges, but this kind of judge can appear before a tribunal before any parliamentary motion is tabled (Constitutional Reform Act 2005).
- Circuit and District Judges can be removed by the Lord Chancellor on the grounds of misconduct or incapacity, but this can only happen if the Lord Chief Justice agrees.

Revision activity

Using the internet, research any instances where judges have been dismissed and for what reasons.

Immunity from suit

On the grounds of public policy, judges are given **immunity from suit** – see *Sirros v Moore* (1975). This means that they are free from any legal action while serving correctly in their capacity as a judge.

However, this does not prevent a complaint being raised against a judge because of their behaviour, language or conduct. It is therefore possible for a judge to be removed from office in certain circumstances.

Immunity from suit: free from any legal action.

Separation of powers

REVISED

Originating from the writings of the French philosopher Baron de Montesquieu, the theory of **separation of powers** refers to a tripartite model of governance in a democratic society. In Montesquieu's model, there must be a separation of the three main sources of power:

- the executive – the government
- the legislature – the parliament or equivalent
- the judiciary – judges in courts and those holding judicial office in tribunals.

Separation of powers: the three main sources of power (executive, legislature and judiciary) must be separate and not held by one specific person or body.

These powers must be separate and not held by one specific person or body. This is to ensure that no single person or body of persons can hold all the power in a society. In having separate bodies, each can work independently and be challenged in their operation.

Independence of the judiciary

In court, judges have to be independent from any external pressures, so that the defendant is seen to have a fair trial. The doctrine of separation of powers states that the judiciary must remain separate from the government and Parliament.

It is important that the public see that judges are independent. Judges must be impartial and free from any political bias or influence.

The judiciary should ignore pressure from the executive to:

- manoeuvre or coerce a judge into making certain pro-government decisions
- force a judge to rule against those who oppose the executive's policies or plans.

Other influences judges must ignore are:

- Parliament (the legislature)
- other judges, particular senior judges, unless bound by law such as precedent
- pressure groups
- their own self-interest, opinions and beliefs – see *Re Pinochet* (1998)
- the media.

Typical mistake

Do not avoid questions on the independence of the judiciary because of new and complicated terminology. If you learn the terms and understand the basic politics involved, this topic is fairly straightforward.

Reasons for judicial independence

Judicial independence is important to:
- ensure that the verdict, or decision in the case, is only decided upon by evidence of the facts and the law as it stands
- ensure that in jury trials, juries decide the verdict based on facts and not on any other influence
- deliver fair and impartial justice
- protect citizens and their rights against unlawful actions of government, state-run agencies, or any person or organisation that tries to infringe or remove their rights.

Methods for achieving judicial independence

Some argue that judges are above the law. Nevertheless, judicial independence is protected in several ways:
- Judges have immunity from being prosecuted for any acts they perform while carrying out their judicial function.
- Judges have immunity from being sued for defamation from anything they say about anyone involved in the court case, for example comments they may make about the defendant or witnesses.
- As a precaution, any errors made by a judge can be appealed against rather than being a rigid, permanent decision.
- Judges' salaries and pension rights are not set by the executive but by independent bodies.

Evaluation of the legal professions and the judiciary

REVISED

Table 1.3.8 Evaluation of the legal professions and the judiciary

	Advantages	Disadvantages
Legal profession	• The Legal Services Board oversees the bodies that effectively regulate the legal professions. • Extensive education and training mean legal professionals are highly skilled and objective. • There are advances in the availability of online legal services, as well as price-comparison websites. • Public access to barristers removes the need for 'referral' from solicitors. • Larger solicitors' firms offer a wealth of services, including those offered by legal executives and paralegals, as well as employing in-house barristers. • Solicitors can become advocates and have enhanced rights of audience. • Gender balance is even on entry for solicitors.	• The profession is slow to change and conservative in outlook. • As a barrister is self-employed, they might earn nothing but still have to pay overheads for their place in chambers. • The traditional monopoly on right of audience of barristers being eroded by solicitor advocates and associate prosecutors might threaten the identity of the profession. • It is very expensive to train, and therefore class and background issues still remain. • High-street firms are closing or amalgamating as the Legal Services Board opens up new types of law firm – good for the consumer as it gives choice and competition, but this might be at the expense of the profession's traditions, skills and quality. • The workload is inconsistent with family life, so the profession does not progress and retain a significant number of its female entrants.

	Advantages	Disadvantages
Judiciary	• The judiciary is independent of the state and politicians, and so not under pressure to impress an electorate. • Judges are legal professionals and so are quicker and more efficient than lay people. • Gender and ethnic balance is improving.	• Lack of transparency remains in appointment and disciplinary issues. • There are problems in the higher courts with gender and ethnic balance, as it will take years to filter through. • Class and background issues still remain. • There are arguably issues of inconsistency, particularly in sentencing in the lower courts.

Now test yourself

TESTED

1 Explain three roles undertaken by a barrister.
2 Explain three roles undertaken by a solicitor.
3 Explain three reasons why it is important to have regulation of legal personnel.
4 Explain three key differences between a barrister and a solicitor.
5 Look at the following chart in relation to legal personnel and decide whether the statement is true or false by placing a tick in the correct column.

	True	False
Barristers, and not solicitors, generally have rights of audience in the Crown Court or higher.		
Barristers cannot be approached directly by clients. Only a solicitor can speak directly to a barrister.		
Solicitors can work for small high-street firms, larger city firms and large multi-national businesses.		
Legal executives have the same rights of audience as barristers.		
Legal executives are not allowed to draft legal documents such as wills, only solicitors are allowed to carry out this task.		

6 Explain the role of a judge in the Supreme Court.
7 Explain the role of a judge in the Court of Appeal.
8 Discuss what is meant by the term 'security of tenure' in relation to the judiciary.
9 Discuss what is meant by the term 'immunity from suit' in relation to the judiciary.
10 Look at the following chart in relation to the judiciary and decide whether the statement is true or false by placing a tick in the correct column.

	True	False
District Judges sit in both the Crown Court and the High Court.		
Inferior judges include those of the Supreme Court.		
Superior judges can be removed by the Lord Chancellor, provided the Lord Chief Justice consents to the dismissal.		
It is important that the executive has control over the judiciary, or else judges might make decisions which go against government policy.		

Answers online

Exam summary

In the exam, you MAY be asked to:

- explain:
  - different types of legal personnel, for example the role of a barrister or the qualification of a solicitor
  - changes and trends in legal services, for example the impact of technology
  - the judiciary, for example the role of a judge
- describe:
  - different types of legal personnel, for example the regulation of legal executives
  - changes and trends in legal services, for example the impact of globalisation on legal education

- the judiciary, for example judicial independence
- discuss the advantages or problems associated with the:
  - different types of legal personnel, for example the problems associated with the training of barristers
  - changes and trends in legal services, for example the advantages of globalisation
  - judiciary, for example the advantages of an independent judiciary.

These types of question will each be worth a maximum of 10 or 15 marks.

1.4 Access to justice

This topic is about going to court to resolve cases but with specific reference to how it is paid for.

One of the central beliefs of the English legal system is that there must be equality before the law:

- This means that guilt or liability in a court is proved or disproved on the basis of the facts and the relevant law.
- This must be irrespective of a person's status or wealth, and therefore an inability to pay for legal services must never bar citizens from bringing an action or defending themselves in court.

However, going to court is an expensive matter, and many people cannot afford the high costs of lawyers. On many occasions, even if citizens can afford to go to court, they cannot afford the best lawyers, such as Queen's Council.

Typical mistake

Do not confuse access to justice with alternative dispute resolution (ADR). Access to justice is about access to the courts for people with less financial means, not looking for alternative ways to settle disputes.

Government funding for civil and criminal cases

REVISED

The Legal Aid Agency was created by the Legal Aid, Sentencing and Punishment of Offenders Act 2012 (LASPO). The agency runs the legal aid scheme in England and Wales, which provides civil and criminal legal aid and advice.

The Legal Aid Agency:

- ensures that legal aid services from solicitors, barristers and the not-for-profit sector are available to the general public
- funds the Civil Legal Advice Service
- publishes evidence about decisions made on whether or not to fund a case
- runs the Public Defender Service.

Table 1.4.1 The Civil Legal Advice Service and Public Defender Service, with evaluation

	Civil Legal Advice Service	Public Defender Service
Role	Provides free and confidential advice in civil-law matters, such as debt, housing and domestic abuse	Provides: • a range of services within the criminal defence market • free, full representation of defendants from the police station through to the courts, even on appeal • free advice and assistance when a person is under arrest at any time • an advocacy service with access to 25 advocates, including seven QCs
Merit tested?	Yes, via the **www.gov.uk** website	Yes
Advantages	• Funding of cases for those on no income or low income • Fundamental right to the agency's services as part of the welfare state in England and Wales • A stepped contribution process, allowing fairer access to justice for those unable to pay or those on low to mid-range salaries	
Disadvantages	• Penalises those in employment who have to contribute or are refused legal aid because of moderate to high wages • Very strict means test • Funding capped by government, which traditionally results in criminal funding taking priority over civil funding due to potential loss of liberty in criminal cases • Less attractive to qualified solicitors as fee rates are lower than private clients • Arguably seen as a quick entry into the profession by new, inexperienced solicitors • Civil legal aid unavailable for employment tribunal cases	

Private funding

Private funding requires citizens to pay for legal services themselves.

Own resources

Using their own resources to pay legal fees or raising the funds via a loan or remortgaging a home can put people into financial difficulties or prevent many people from pursuing a case.

Insurance

It is not uncommon for people to take out insurance to pay for court costs in civil cases and, in some situations, in anticipation of criminal cases.

There are two types of insurance for advice and representation:
- 'before the event' – in anticipation of fighting or defending a legal case
- 'after the event' – to insure against losing a case and having to pay the other side's costs as well as damages.

Examples can be found under household insurance and motor insurance policies as optional extras.

Some **conditional fee agreements** insist on insurance being taken out.

> **Exam tip**
>
> You might be asked to explain or compare three types of private funding of legal services, or to assess the ways in which private funding could be used to fund a civil case in a scenario question.

> **Conditional fee agreements (CFAs):** 'no win, no fee' arrangements.

Conditional fee agreements (CFAs)

Table 1.4.2 Outline of conditional fee agreements, with evaluation

Purpose	• CFAs were introduced as an alternative way to privately fund a civil case. • The client only pays the solicitor's fees if they win and pays nothing if they lose.
Method	• An agreement is struck between the client and their solicitor that any costs are paid from the compensation received if they win the case, along with a 'success fee'. • Until 2013, the 'success fee' could be recovered from the losing party, but this was stopped and instead it will be taken from the client's compensation.
Advantages	• They offer a further alternative to private funding of a case. • They remove the anxiety of having to pay huge costs. • Any deductions for costs are set at 25%. • Insurance can be taken out to compensate for any losses. • They are widely available. • There is no payment up front or in advance to begin a case.
Disadvantages	• Solicitors generally charge a higher fee to cover the risk of losing the case. • Court costs may still need to be paid that are not covered in the arrangement. • Certain firms are contracted to take on certain publicly funded cases, such as clinical negligence, restricting the pool of potential firms available. • They encourage the 'cherry-picking' by solicitors of those cases that stand a greater chance of winning. • Arguably lawyers might use tactics to win at all costs, including tactics of a dubious nature. • Lawyers will generally insist on insurance being taken out, precluding many poorer clients from accessing CFAs.

> **Exam tip**
>
> You might be asked to explain or compare three advantages (or disadvantages) of a conditional fee agreement, or you might be asked to assess the merits of using a conditional fee agreement to fund a civil case in a scenario question.

Other advice agencies

Sometimes free legal advice is available to members of organisations via a subscription to a general service, as outlined in the table below.

Table 1.4.3 Alternative sources of legal advice

Alternative source of legal advice	Method of assistance	Examples
Charitable organisations	Specific, targeted advice on issues relevant to the charity	MIND (mental health); Shelter (homelessness and housing); Sense (deafblind persons)
Helplines	Via telephone or online access direct to an operator qualified to provide advice	RAC/AA (motoring organisations); Disability Law Service (advice for many organisations and people with disabilities)
Citizens Advice Bureaux (CAB)	Town-centre-based legal advice agency providing general legal advice face to face, via telephone or online	Over 3,500 locations throughout the country and at **www.citizensadvice.org.uk**
Law centres	Free access to legal advice from solicitors	45 locations in England and at **www.lawcentres.org.uk**
Trades' unions	Specific, targeted advice on issues relevant to the trades' union – generally on employment issues	National Union of Teachers; British Medical Council (doctors); National Union of Journalists

Now test yourself

TESTED

1. Explain three advantages of using a conditional fee agreement.
2. Explain three disadvantages of using a conditional fee agreement.
3. Explain how Citizens Advice Bureaux can be considered alternative sources of legal advice.
4. Look at the following chart in relation to the private funding of legal services. Read each statement carefully and decide to which type of private funding it refers, then write your answers in the spaces provided.

Statement	Type of private funding
Client remortgages home to pay for legal services	
No win, no fee	
Offered by companies, e.g. motoring companies	

Answers online

Exam tip

You might be asked to explain or compare three alternative sources of legal advice, or you might be asked to assess the ways in which an alternative source of legal advice could help the claimant or defendant in a scenario.

Exam summary

In the exam, you MAY be asked to:
- explain access to justice, for example government funding for civil and criminal cases
- describe access to justice, for example private funding or advice agencies
- provide a discussion on the advantages or problems associated with access to justice, for example conditional fee agreements.

These types of question will each be worth a maximum of 10 or 15 marks.

Exam practice

Questions 1–4 could appear on either the AS or A Level exam paper.
Questions 5–8 could appear on the A Level exam paper only.

1 Discuss the advantages of using tribunals as a way of dealing with a civil dispute. [15 marks]

2 Explain conciliation as a form of alternative dispute resolution. [10 marks]

3 Describe the role of lay magistrates in criminal matters. [10 marks]

4 Discuss the disadvantages of using juries in criminal cases. [15 marks]

5 Describe the graduate routes to qualifying as a barrister. [10 marks]

6 Discuss the main challenges facing a graduate wishing to become a barrister. [10 marks]

7 Discuss the importance of judicial independence. [15 marks]

8 Discuss the disadvantages of conditional fee agreements as a method of funding civil disputes. [15 marks]

ONLINE

2 Criminal law

Criminal law is one of the four main substantive areas of law in the OCR A Level Law H415 specification, and it is assessed in Section B of the Component 1 exam paper. It comprises a series of topics examining common-law rules and statutes relevant to the English legal system which define conduct that is prohibited in our society because it threatens or causes harm to public safety or loss of property.

You need to be able to:
- define and explain the principles of criminal law relevant to the OCR specification
- apply these principles
- understand the rules and general elements of criminal law before examining criminal offences and defences in relation to offences against the person and offences against property.

2.1 Rules and theory

This chapter provides background material for what will be assessed in Section B of the Component 1 exam paper.

Outline of the rules of criminal law

Defining crime

Lord Atkin defined crime in *Proprietary Articles Trade Association v Attorney-General for Canada* (1931) as 'the act prohibited with penal consequences'. Therefore, there are two features to a crime:
- the act must be prohibited, i.e. it must be *forbidden* by the state
- the act must attract penal consequences, i.e. it must be *punished* by the state.

There are many different types of crime, but all will have these two points in common.

'Punished' means that the state must have provided a maximum or mandatory sentence to be imposed if a person is convicted of a criminal offence.

Usually, the state will create a crime by passing an Act of Parliament in the manner shown in Chapter 3.1, for example the Coroners and Justice Act 2009. Sometimes, crimes are created by the common law using the doctrine of precedent as shown in Chapter 3.4; for example the law of murder has never been set down by Parliament but has been developed over time by judges.

> **Typical mistake**
>
> When answering a scenario question, do not forget to identify the source of the offence.

> **Revision activity**
>
> Find an example of a fatal offence against the person, a non-fatal offence against the person and an offence against property. For each, find both the source (the relevant Act or common law) and the maximum sentence.

Criminal liability

The fundamental principle of English criminal law was stated by Edward Coke in the seventeenth century as '*actus non facit reum nisi mens sit rea*'. This means 'an act is not guilty unless the mind is also guilty'.

As a consequence, most crimes will have both:
- an *actus reus* (AR) – a guilty act, and
- a *mens rea* (MR) – a guilty mind.

These two elements must, generally, occur at the same time in order for a crime to have been committed.

> **Actus reus:** the guilty act.
>
> **Mens rea:** the guilty mind.

> **Revision activity**
>
> Create a table for every offence you have studied in this course, showing the source, the *actus reus*, the *mens rea* and the sentence (see the example below).
>
> | Offence | Source | Actus reus | Mens rea | Sentence |
> |---------|--------|-----------|----------|----------|
> | Theft | Section 1(1) of the Theft Act 1968 | A person appropriates property belonging to another | Dishonesty with the intention of permanently depriving the other of it | Maximum seven years' imprisonment |

Defending crime – removing liability

Although the defendant may have committed the *actus reus*, without the appropriate *mens rea* they generally cannot be guilty. So, if someone kills another person but does not, or cannot, intend to kill them, they cannot be guilty of murder.

In addition, there are a number of general defences that may be available even if the defendant has both the *actus reus* and *mens rea*. These will lead to a 'not guilty' verdict.

Defences can be split into two categories known as:
- mental capacity defences – insanity, automatism and intoxication
- general defences – self-defence, duress by threats or of circumstances, necessity and consent.

These are discussed in greater detail in Chapters 2.6 and 2.7.

> **Revision activity**
>
> Create a defence checklist, where each defence above is broken down into its constituent parts. Keep this handy to apply to an essay or scenario question.

Proving criminal liability

Burden of proof

A defendant is innocent until proven guilty. This means that it is the prosecution's responsibility to provide evidence in court that the defendant had both the *actus reus* and *mens rea* of the offence with which they have been charged.

Standard of proof

The prosecution must provide evidence of the defendant's guilt 'beyond all reasonable doubt'. This means that the jury or magistrates – depending on how serious the offence is and the type of court dealing with the case – should only convict if they are satisfied on the evidence that they are sure of the defendant's guilt.

This is a higher standard than in civil law, as here a person's liberty is at stake.

> **Burden of proof:** a defendant is innocent until proven guilty.
>
> **Standard of proof:** the defendant's guilt must be proved 'beyond all reasonable doubt'.

Overview of the theory of criminal law

The following section revises the theory of criminal liability. Specific elements and crimes are dealt with in detail in Chapters 2.2–2.5.

Theory of criminal liability

Harm as the basis for criminalising conduct

This concept is explored more thoroughly in Chapter 5.2, where the topic of law and morality is discussed.

The idea that harm to others is the only justifiable basis for imposing criminal liability is associated with the work of John Stuart Mill, *On Liberty* (originally published in 1859).

The idea that the law should protect us from harming ourselves as well as others is known as **paternalism**.

The view that behaviour which is offensive but not harmful could be criminalised was developed and explored by Joel Feinberg in *The Moral Limits of the Criminal Law* (1984–88). As society progresses and attitudes change, previous crimes can be decriminalised (such as homosexuality), as well as new crimes defined and outlawed (such as those related to computers).

Criminalising conduct on the basis of its lack of morality – without the need to establish harm or offensiveness – is known as **legal moralism**. In his book *The Enforcement of Morals* (1965), Patrick Devlin argued that a society's shared morality holds it together, and so it is proper to criminalise immoral conduct for the sake of social cohesion and preservation.

> **Paternalism:** the state is justified in protecting individuals from harm.
>
> **Legal moralism:** immoral conduct is criminalised for better social cohesion.

> **Typical mistake**
>
> Do not forget to mention, where necessary, these key terms and theorists throughout. It will show a deeper understanding of the underlying principles.

> **Revision activity**
>
> Create a list of the theorists and their theories as mentioned above. Make sure you can discuss in summary how they apply to the criminal law.

Autonomy and individual responsibility

This concept is closely linked to fault.

In a legal context, autonomy means being solely responsible, independent and able to speak for oneself, free of influences. This means most adults who are not suffering from debilitating illness or under oppressive and constricting conditions (see the defences in Chapters 2.6 and 2.7) are considered to be **autonomous** – and therefore responsible for their own actions and their consequences.

> **Autonomous:** legally capable of making one's own decisions, and therefore legally responsible for their consequences.

Principles in formulating rules of criminal law

This concept is closely linked to the rule of law (see Chapter 5.1).

There are a number of ideals that should be adhered to when new criminal laws are introduced.

Table 2.1.1 Principles in formulating rules of criminal law

Principles	Explanation

Fair labelling	• Crimes should be defined to reflect their wrongfulness and severity. This is essential in securing public confidence in the law and a sense of justice.
	• Fair labelling has two functions:
	  – properly describing the crime
	  – differentiating a crime from other crimes, particularly in relation to fault and social condemnation (e.g. the difference between murder and manslaughter).

Correspondence principle	• The result which the defendant intends or foresees should match the result which actually occurs. They should not be held liable for an act unless they meant to do it, or at least knowingly ran the risk of it. • The Law Commission in 2015 criticised the current laws of actual bodily harm (ABH, s 47 of the Offences Against the Person Act 1861) and grievous bodily harm (GBH, under s 20) as they do not conform to the 'correspondence principle'.
Maximum certainty	• This is key to the rule of law (see Chapter 5.1) – decisions are made according to legal rules, i.e. they are lawful. • This means providing citizens with the ability to organise their behaviour in such a way that does not break the law, as well as protecting them from arbitrary use of state power.
No retrospective liability	• A person cannot be guilty of committing a crime before that act was criminalised – the law does not apply backwards in time. • Parliamentary laws should not apply retrospectively, but it is possible by virtue of the doctrine of parliamentary sovereignty (see Chapter 3.2). • An example of retrospective criminal law is the Criminal Justice Act 2003, which allows the retrial of people acquitted of murder if there is 'new, compelling, reliable and substantial evidence' that the acquitted person is guilty. As a result, the defendants who were acquitted in the murder of Stephen Lawrence were allowed to be retried – see *R v Dobson and Norris* (2012).

Now test yourself

TESTED ☐

1 What are the two ways in which new crimes can be created?
2 Which two features are common to all crimes?
3 Why are there two elements to most crimes?
4 What is the impact of a successful defence?
5 Is the burden of proof in criminal law higher or lower than in civil law? Why is this?
6 What did Devlin mean by 'social preservation'?
7 When might a defendant not be considered autonomous?

Answers online

Exam summary

In the exam, you MAY be asked to:
• respond to a scenario question by advising a defendant, or defendants, whether they:
  – are criminally liable for their actions
  – can raise any defences to offences they may have committed
• discuss in a full-length essay question a key topic or topics relevant to the criminal law.

These types of question will each be worth a maximum of 25 marks.

Fair labelling: crimes should be defined to reflect their wrongfulness and severity.

Correspondence principle: the result which the defendant intends or foresees should match the result that actually occurs.

Exam tip

Once you have read this chapter, refer to the others it makes reference to, and ensure you are confident in using the terminology, concepts and issues when writing about those areas.

2.2 General elements of criminal liability

Most crimes require contemporaneously occurring *actus reus* and *mens rea*. This chapter will identify the key elements of, and explain, *actus reus* and *mens rea*.

Actus reus

Conduct and consequence crimes

Actus reus refers to the unlawful act or omission. This element therefore relates to what the defendant is 'doing', and that conduct must cause a consequence. However, sometimes it can also relate to what the defendant *omits* doing, or that they are simply 'being' rather than actually 'doing' anything.

Consequences

A crime can be an 'action', for example speeding, or it can be a 'consequence', for example murder where the consequence is a dead human being.

Most offences against the person – crimes where someone is injured or killed – are 'consequence' crimes.

Where the consequence is not directly caused by the defendant's action, i.e. there is another factor involved, the rules of causation apply (see below).

Voluntary acts (and involuntariness)

In carrying out the *actus reus*, the defendant must be acting voluntarily. Consider the cases of *R v Mitchell* (1983) and *R v Larsonneur* (1933). It cannot be as a consequence of an involuntary action such as a fit or reflex action.

In *Hill v Baxter* (1958), Devlin J in *obiter dicta* gave an example of a driver being attacked by a swarm of bees and consequently driving dangerously as not being liable for a subsequent accident as his actions would not be voluntary.

> **Revision activity**
>
> In which other part of this revision guide will you find the case of *Hill v Baxter* (1958)? Make the link.

Omissions

An omission means a failure to act. There is a general rule in English law that a failure to act does not amount to an *actus reus*. This is often referred to as the lack of a 'Good Samaritan' law: i.e. the law does not place an obligation on you to act in any situation.

However, in order to achieve justice, there are a number of exceptions to this rule where there *is* a duty to act:

- statutory duty to act, for example s 1 of the Children and Young Persons Act 1933 (as amended) or s 170 of the Road Traffic Act 1988
- duty arising from special relationship – *R v Gibbons and Proctor* (1918)
- duty arising from the assumption of care for another – *R v Stone and Dobinson* (1977)
- duty arising from contract of employment – *R v Pittwood* (1902)
- duty arising from official position – *R v Dytham* (1979)
- duty to avert a danger of one's own making – *R v Miller* (1983).

> **Exam tip**
>
> It is essential to make the link between the facts of the case and the point it is making.

> **Typical mistake**
>
> Do not write too much about the facts of the cases – practise summarising the key points in ten words or fewer.

State of affairs

In some circumstances, a defendant can commit an offence by simply 'being' rather than 'doing' – these are known as 'state of affairs' offences.

Having an offensive weapon in a public place is an example (s 1 of the Prevention of Crime Act 1953). The defendant does not have to do anything with the weapon, nor does it have to be visible. It is enough just to have it in one's possession in a public place.

Causation

Where a consequence must be proved, the prosecution has to show that the defendant's conduct was:
- the factual cause of that consequence, and
- the legal cause of that consequence.

Factual causation means but for the defendant's action, the victim would not have suffered that consequence.

However, on its own, the 'but for' rule is not enough. There has to be legal causation too – see the Supreme Court ruling in *R v Hughes* (2013). In basic terms, this looks at a theoretical percentage contribution by the defendant to the consequence.

Even where the rules on causation are established, the defendant may be excused criminal liability if there is a subsequent intervening act, known as a ***novus actus interveniens***, which breaks the chain of causation.

> **Revision activity**
>
> Compare the cases of *R v White* (1910) and *R v Pagett* (1983) to show how the rules on causation work.

> ***Novus actus interveniens***: where a subsequent intervening act breaks the chain of causation.

> **Revision activity**
>
> Complete the table.
>
> | Rule | Explanation | Case | Facts |
> |---|---|---|---|
> | 'De minimis' conduct was more than a 'minimal' cause | 'More than a slight or trifling link' between conduct and consequence | *R v Kimsey* (1993) | |
> | Thin skull | | | V refused a blood transfusion on religious grounds; D was responsible for her subsequent death. |
> | Intervening acts | • Act of a third party, or
• V's own act, or
• A natural but unpredictable event | • *R v Roberts* (1972)
• *R v Williams* (1992)
• *R v Marjoram* (2000) | |
> | Medical intervention | | • *R v Cheshire* (1991)
• *R v Jordan* (1956) | |
> | 'Operating' and 'substantial' cause | D's acts need not be the sole cause or even the main cause of death, provided that their acts contributed significantly to the death | • *R v Smith* (1959)
• *R v Jordan* (1956) | |

> **Exam tip**
>
> Look out for causation or omissions scenarios in the exam that are very similar to the cases in this topic and the revision activity above. You will be expected to use these as precedents and follow them.

Mens rea

Fault

Mens rea refers to the guilty mind. Most crimes require the defendant to have a degree of fault:

- An act without fault is generally regarded as an accident. So, in order to be criminal, an act generally has to be accompanied by a degree of fault – a level of *mens rea*.
- Different levels of *mens rea* are attached to crimes to indicate the level of fault required for a defendant to be guilty of that offence.
- These levels of fault tend to reflect how seriously the crime is viewed and its sentence – for instance, murder carries a *mandatory* life sentence, whereas gross negligence manslaughter only attracts a *maximum* life sentence (sentencing reflects fault rather than the outcome for the victim).

> **Intention:** a decision to bring about the criminalised act.
>
> **Direct intent:** it was the defendant's decision to bring about the prohibited consequence.
>
> **Oblique intent:** the prohibited consequence is virtually certain, and the defendant realises this.
>
> **Subjective recklessness:** the defendant commits an act knowing there is a risk of the consequence happening.

Intention and subjective recklessness

The highest level of fault is **intention**, and this can be further split into **direct intent** or **oblique intent**. There is also a lesser degree of *mens rea*, known as **subjective recklessness**.

Table 2.2.1 Types of intention

	Description	Key case
Direct intent	It was the defendant's decision to bring about the prohibited consequence (the *actus reus*). It was their aim and purpose.	*R v Mohan* (1976)
Oblique intent	There are two elements: • the prohibited consequence (the *actus reus*) is virtually certain, and • the defendant realises this.	• *R v Woollin* (1998) • *R v Matthews and Allleyne* (2003): the court has the option to find intention if these tests are satisfied, but is not obliged to do so
Subjective recklessness	The defendant appreciates the risk of the prohibited consequence (the *actus reus*) and continues anyway.	*R v Cunningham* (1957)

It is important to note that in the context of defences, crimes where only intent will satisfy the *mens rea* are known as '**specific intent crimes**'. Crimes where recklessness will suffice as the *mens rea* are known as '**basic intent crimes**'.

> **Revision activity**
>
> Create a bar chart, with degrees of fault on the y axis and types of *mens rea* on the x axis. Create bars for the types of *mens rea* and include their definitions and cases.

Negligence

Negligence is a failure to meet the standards of the reasonable person. It is rarely sufficient for a *mens rea* in criminal law, but there are exceptions such as gross negligence manslaughter. A key case in this area is *R v Adomako* (1994).

Strict liability

Offences requiring no fault are called **strict liability offences** (SLOs) and exist to regulate society and protect the vulnerable. Examples are given in Table 2.2.2 below.

> **Specific intent crimes:** crimes where only intent will satisfy the *mens rea*.
>
> **Basic intent crimes:** crimes where recklessness will suffice as *mens rea*.
>
> **Strict liability offences:** offences that require no fault for some or all of the *actus reus*.

Table 2.2.2 Examples of strict liability offences

Case	Facts	How the SLO protects society
PSGB v Storkwain Ltd (1986)	The appellant had allowed prescription drugs to be supplied on production of fraudulent prescriptions.	Supply of medicines must be carefully regulated.
Winzar v Chief Constable of Kent (1983)	D was 'found drunk on a highway', having been removed from a hospital by the police officers who then arrested him in their police car.	Drunken and anti-social behaviour must be deterred, especially as MR might not be able to be formed if drunk.
Callow v Tillstone (1900)	A butcher was convicted of selling unfit meat, despite the fact that he had had the meat certified as safe by a vet before the sale.	Food safety is paramount.
Harrow LBC v Shah (1999)	National Lottery tickets were sold to a person under the age of 16.	Gambling is a matter of social concern.
R v Prince (1875)	The appellant was charged with taking an unmarried girl under the age of 16 out of the possession of her father. He believed on reasonable grounds that the girl was aged 18.	Protection of children is a matter of social concern.
Alphacell Ltd v Woodward (1972)	A factory owner was convicted of causing polluted matter to enter a river. He was unaware of the pollution.	Safety and pollution is a matter of social concern.
R v Blake (1997)	D operated a pirate radio station without a licence.	Radio bands are used by emergency services and so any unauthorised use must be prevented.

As these offences are contrary to the normal rules of criminal law, judges treat them with caution. See the following key cases and note how they limit the application of strict liability offences: *Sweet v Parsley* (1970) and *Gammon Ltd v A-G of Hong Kong* (1985).

In *Sweet v Parsley* (1970), judges inserted the word 'knowingly' into the offence in order to prevent the defendant from being guilty.

However, despite this, strict liability offences are an important part of our legal system, as without them public standards and safety would drop.

In the case of *Gammon (Hong Kong) Ltd v A-G of Hong Kong* (1985), the judges stated that when determining whether an offence is one of strict liability, there is a presumption that *mens rea* is required. This presumption may be rebutted where:
- the crime is regulatory as opposed to a true crime, or
- the crime is one of social concern, or
- the wording of the Act indicates strict liability, or
- the offence carries a heavy penalty.

Transferred malice

Mens rea can be transferred from the intended victim to the actual victim where the defendant, for example, misses their intended target. Key cases here are *R v Latimer* (1886), *R v Mitchell* (1983) and *R v Gnango* (2011).

However, *mens rea* can only be transferred where the *actus reus* remains the same, for example aiming a punch at a victim, missing, but hitting another unintended victim; see *R v Pembliton* (1874).

> **Transferred malice:** where *mens rea* can be transferred from the intended victim to the actual victim.

Table 2.2.3 Key cases on transferred malice

Case	Facts	Point of law
R v Latimer (1886)	D got into a fight in a pub with another man. He took off his belt and hit the man with it. The belt ricocheted off and hit a woman in the face.	D was liable for the woman's injuries, despite not intending to harm her. The MR he had to cause harm to the man was transferred to the woman.
R v Mitchell (1983)	During an altercation in a post-office queue, D struck a man who fell against an 89-year-old woman, knocking her to the ground and causing her death.	Domino rally – application of *Latimer*
R v Gnango (2011)	V was walking through a carpark when she was killed during an exchange of fire between two gunmen, 'B' and D. V was killed by a bullet from B's gun, but he was never apprehended.	As D had intent to kill B, this MR was transferred to V.
R v Pembliton (1874)	D threw stones at a crowd of people. A stone hit and smashed a window.	D's MR for an offence against the person could not be transferred to a property offence, as they are entirely different.

Coincidence of *actus reus* and *mens rea* (contemporaneity rule)

REVISED

'Contemporaneity' means 'occurring at the same time'. Therefore, there is a general rule in English law that the *actus reus* and the *mens rea* must occur at the same time.

However, judges have shown themselves to be flexible with this rule in the interests of justice.

Contemporaneity rule: the general rule in English law that the *actus reus* and the *mens rea* must occur at the same time.

Table 2.2.4 Avoiding the need for contemporaneity

Case	Facts	How the rule was avoided
Fagan v MPC (1969)	D accidentally drove onto a police officer's foot. The officer shouted at him to get off. D refused to move.	Driving onto the foot and remaining there were part of a continuing act.
Thabo-Meli v R (1954)	When Ds formed the intention to kill, there was no AR as the man was still alive. When they threw him off the cliff, there was no MR as they could not intend to kill someone they believed was already dead.	The act of beating him and throwing him off the cliff was one continuing act/single transaction.
R v Church (1965)	During a fight, the appellant knocked the victim unconscious. He tried to wake her for 30 minutes to no avail. He believed she was dead and threw her body into a river. Medical evidence revealed that the cause of death was drowning.	The act of beating her and throwing her in the river was one continuing act/single transaction.

Exam tip

While exam questions may model themselves around established cases, this does not mean that the facts and therefore the decision will be exactly the same. Watch out for slight or significant differences that could affect the defendant's guilt in an exam scenario.

Now test yourself

1 Why is there generally no liability for a failure to act?
2 Why should a defendant be liable for the death of a victim who refuses life-saving medical treatment?
3 Identify both the objective and subjective elements of the definition of oblique intent.
4 Explain the *Cunningham* test of subjective recklessness.
5 When can *mens rea* not be transferred?
6 Why do *actus reus* and *mens rea* have to occur at the same time? Explain the exception to the rule.

Answers online

Exam summary

In the exam, you MAY be asked to:
- respond to a scenario question by advising a defendant, or defendants, whether they are criminally liable for their actions where:
  - there may be an omission or a break in the chain of causation
  - their *mens rea*, or lack of *mens rea*, is questionable
  - the issue of contemporaneity is in question
- respond to a scenario question by advising a defendant, or defendants, whether they can raise any defences to any offences they may have committed:
  - because of a lack of duty or a *novus actus interveniens*
  - where their *mens rea*, or lack of *mens rea*, is questionable
  - where the issue of contemporaneity is in question
- discuss in a full-length essay question a key topic or topics relevant to:
  - *actus reus*
  - *mens rea*
  - contemporaneity.

These types of question will each be worth a maximum of 25 marks.

2.3 Fatal offences against the person

This chapter looks at two specific homicide offences and two specific defences to murder:

- murder
- involuntary manslaughter
- voluntary manslaughter defences of loss of control and diminished responsibility.

Exam tip

When using cases in scenario/application questions, remember ILAC:
- **I**ssues – identify what has happened
- **L**aw – explain the relevant law
- **A**pply the point/case to the facts of the scenario
- **C**onclude – decide whether the defendant is, or is not, guilty.

Murder

REVISED

Murder is a common-law offence. The definition of murder originates from Edward Coke in the sixteenth/seventeenth century – 'the unlawful killing of a human being with malice aforethought'.

Murder: the unlawful killing of a human being with malice aforethought.

Actus reus of murder

The *actus reus* of murder is 'the unlawful killing of a human being'.

Table 2.3.1 Components of the *actus reus* for murder

Component	Explanation
Unlawful killing	This relates to the presence of a defence (see Chapter 2.7, as it is possible for a killing to be lawful if it is legally justified, such as in self-defence). Key case: *R v Clegg* (1995)
Causation	The usual rules and cases of causation apply. This could be via an act or omission, through direct or indirect actions.
Death	This is a medical test and not a legal one. It currently means 'brain stem death'. Key cases: *R v Malcherek and Steel* (1981) and *R v Inglis* (2011)
Human being	The test is 'when' is a human being, not 'what' is a human being: when is a human being capable of existence independent of the mother? This means being born alive and breathing through its own lungs. Key cases: *Rance v Mid-Downs Health Authority* (1991), *A-G Ref. No. 3 of 1994* (1997) and *CP v CICA* (2014)

Revision activity

Can you think of any reasons why the test for defining a human being may be controversial?

Typical mistake

In a scenario question, the victim will always be both human and dead, so do not waste too much time discussing these points. Concentrate on the causation/omission element and whether there is a defence.

Mens rea of murder

The *mens rea* of murder is 'malice aforethought'.

Lord Mustill said in 1998: 'The law of homicide is permeated by anomaly, fiction, misnomer and obsolete reasoning.' He was partly referring to the phrase 'malice aforethought'. What this actually means is 'intent to kill or cause grievous bodily harm'. This can be:

- direct intent to kill
- oblique intent to kill
- direct intent to cause really serious harm
- oblique intent to cause really serious harm.

Key cases here include *DPP v Smith* (1961), *R v Saunders* (1985) and *R v Janjua and Choudhury* (1998).

> **Revision activity**
>
> As you work through this chapter, make notes on and explore any issues of the law which you think may be open to criticism. You might be required to write about them.

Table 2.3.2 Key cases for *actus reus* and *mens rea* of murder

Case	Facts	Relevant area	*Ratio decidendi*
R v Clegg (1995)	A soldier used excessive force, killing a joyrider who failed to stop at a checkpoint.	AR – 'unlawful'	D's lack of 'wicked or evil' motive did not preclude his actions from being unlawful.
R v Malcherek and Steel (1981)	Doctors switched off life-support machines as neither victim was showing any activity in their brain stem.	AR – 'death'	Confirms 'brain stem' as the current medical test for death.
R v Inglis (2011)	D killed her son who was in a persistent vegetative state following an accident.	AR – 'death' and 'human being'	'A disabled life, even a life lived at the extremes of disability, is not one jot less precious than the life of an able-bodied person.'
A-G Ref. No. 3 of 1994 (1997)	A pregnant woman was stabbed in the abdomen. The baby was born alive but died 112 days later due to its premature and traumatic birth.	AR – 'human being'	'Murder or manslaughter can be committed where ... the child is subsequently born alive, enjoys an existence independent of the mother, thereafter dies.'
DPP v Smith (1961) *R v Saunders* (1985) *R v Janjua and Choudhury* (1998)	The wording is more relevant than the facts, but Janjua and Choudhury stabbed their V several times with a five-inch blade.	MR – 'intent to cause really serious harm'	*DPP v Smith* (1961): 'grievous means no more and no less than 'really serious'. *R v Saunders* (1985): the word 'serious' could safely be omitted. *R v Janjua and Choudhury* (1998): the trial judge should decide whether or not to include 'really'.

Voluntary manslaughter

Loss of control and **diminished responsibility** are defences, not offences, so there are no *actus reus* and *mens rea* elements. They are special, partial defences to murder only, i.e. they cannot be used for any other crime, and they reduce a murder conviction to one of voluntary manslaughter.

Loss of control

Loss of control is defined in s 54 of the Coroners and Justice Act 2009. There is a three-stage test:

- the defendant must lose control
- because of a qualifying trigger, and
- a person of their sex and age, with a normal degree of tolerance, might have reacted in the same way in the same circumstances.

A key case here is *R v Clinton* (2012).

> **Loss of control:** a special, partial defence to murder only, argued where an unlawful killing occurs following the defendant's loss of self-control.
>
> **Diminished responsibility:** a special, partial defence to murder only, argued where an unlawful killing occurs due to the defendant's abnormality of mental functioning.

Unlike diminished responsibility, which simply amended existing law (see below), this is a totally new defence. It replaced the previous defence of provocation. Be aware of Lord Thomas CJ in *R v Gurpinar and Kojo-Smith* (2015), who stated 'it should rarely be necessary to look at cases decided under the old law of provocation'.

Section 54(1)(b)

It does not matter whether or not the loss of control was sudden, but control must have been lost. It can still be put before a jury even where there has been delay between the trigger incident and the murder.

In *R v Jewell* (2014), Lady Justice Rafferty held: 'Loss of control is considered by the authors of Smith and Hogan 13th edition to mean the loss of an ability to act in accordance with considered judgement or a loss of normal powers of reasoning.'

> **Revision activity**
>
> Research the case of *R v Jewell* (2014) and see how the facts relate to the defence under s 54.

Section 55

This section defines what is meant by 'qualifying trigger':
- It can be the defendant's fear of serious violence from the victim, though this violence cannot be incited by the defendant – see s 55(6)(a). The defendant will have to show that they genuinely feared that the victim would use serious violence, whether or not that fear was reasonable. This is known as the 'fear trigger'.
- Alternatively, it can be something done and/or said by the victim that constituted circumstances of an extremely grave character (the breakdown of a relationship is not, by itself, sufficient – *R v Hatter* (2013)) and caused the defendant to have a justified sense of being wronged (in *R v Bowyer* (2013), D had no justifiable sense of being wronged, given that he was committing a burglary at the time of the offence). This is for the jury to determine, having applied an objective test. This is known as the 'anger trigger'.

The defence is not available to those who act in a considered desire for revenge (s 54(4)), even if the defendant loses self-control as a result of one of the qualifying triggers – see *R v Dawes* (2013).

Sexual infidelity cannot by itself qualify as a trigger, but it can be taken into account as part of a bigger picture – see *R v Clinton* (2012).

Also 'things said' can include admissions of sexual infidelity (even if untrue), as well as reports of it by others.

Section 54(1)(c)

This section requires that a person of the defendant's sex and age, with a normal degree of tolerance and self-restraint and in the circumstances of the defendant, might have reacted in the same or a similar way. This is a question for the jury to decide.

Additional characteristics may be relevant when assessing the circumstances of the defendant, and the impact on the defendant of sexual infidelity is not excluded, although under s 54(3) circumstances which relate to the defendant's general capacity to exercise tolerance and self-restraint are to be disregarded.

Burden of proof

Once the defence has been raised, the burden of disproof is on the prosecution.

Table 2.3.3 Key cases for loss of control

Case	Facts	Relevant area	*Ratio decidendi*
R v Clinton (2012)	D killed his ex-wife following taunts, revelations about affairs and mental illness.	All elements	Sexual infidelity can add to a defence where there exist other qualifying triggers. Aspects: ● whether things done or said amounted to extremely grave circumstances ● a justifiable sense of being wronged under s 55(4) ● examining the defendant's circumstances under s 54(1)(c).
R v Dawes (2013)	D attacked V with a bottle after finding him asleep with his estranged wife. V took the bottle and attacked D, who grabbed a kitchen knife and fatally stabbed V.	Qualifying triggers	Qualifying triggers based on s 55(3) (4) and (5) still apply despite D's bad behaviour, unless his actions were intended to provide him with the excuse or opportunity to use violence.

Diminished responsibility

Section 52 of the Coroners and Justice Act 2009 provides a four-stage test:
● whether the defendant was suffering from an abnormality of mental functioning
● if so, whether it had arisen from a recognised medical condition
● if so, whether it had substantially impaired their ability either to understand the nature of their conduct or to form a rational judgement or to exercise self-control (or any combination)
● and thus provide an explanation for their behaviour.

Where there is unchallenged medical evidence, the judge should withdraw the charge of murder from the jury – see *R v Brennan* (2014).

Abnormality of mental functioning

This means a state of mind so different from that of ordinary human beings that the 'reasonable person' would term it abnormal. It covers the ability to exercise willpower or to control physical acts in accordance with rational judgement. It is a question for a jury. See *R v Byrne* (1960).

Recognised medical conditions

These can be found in the World Health Organization's International Classification of Diseases. However, *R v Dowds* (2012) states that just because a recognised medical condition appears in the lists does not necessarily mean that it is capable of being relied upon to show an abnormality of mental functioning.

Impairment must be substantial

There must be evidence of this and it must be raised by the defence. The abnormality of mental functioning must have substantially impaired the defendant's ability to:
● understand the nature of the defendant's conduct, or
● form a rational judgement, or
● exercise self-control.

Key cases include *R v Golds* (2014), *R v Simcox* (1964) and *R v Lloyd* (1967). See the quote below (originally from *Simcox*, reiterated in *Golds*):

> 'Do we think, looking at it broadly as common-sense people, there was a substantial impairment of his mental responsibility in what he did? If the answer is "no", there may be some impairment, but we do not think it was substantial.'

Explanation for the behaviour

Abnormality of mental functioning provides an explanation for the defendant's behaviour if it was at least a significant contributory factor in causing the defendant to act as they did. It does not need to be the only cause or even the most important factor in causing the behaviour, but it must be more than a merely trivial factor.

The defence should not be able to succeed where the defendant's mental condition made no difference to their behaviour – when they would have killed regardless of their medical condition.

The effects of alcohol do not amount to an abnormality of mental functioning. However, the defendant may be able show diminished responsibility from brain damage caused by alcohol.

Key cases here include *R v Dietschmann* (2003), *R v Woods* (2008) and *R v Dowds* (2012).

Burden of proof

The evidential burden is on the defence on the balance of probabilities, i.e. the civil standard (in contrast to loss of control, see above).

Table 2.3.4 **Key cases on diminished responsibility**

Case	Facts	Relevant area	*Ratio decidendi*
R v Golds (2014)	D, who had a history of mental disorder, killed his partner by inflicting 22 stabs wounds on her following an argument.	Substantial impairment	The court should leave interpretation of the word 'substantial' to the jury but can advise that substantial means big or large.
R v Byrne (1960)	D, a sexual psychopath, was not guilty of murder when he strangled a young woman, and after her death mutilated her body.	Abnormality of mental functioning	Objective test: what would a reasonable person consider abnormal?
R v Dietschmann (2003)	D killed a friend who had broken his watch, which was a gift from a dead relative. D was medicated for suicidal thoughts relating to the relative's death.	Abnormality of mental functioning and alcohol	If D's mental abnormality substantially impaired his mental responsibility despite drinking alcohol, he is not guilty of murder but can be guilty of manslaughter.
R v Woods (2008)	D, an alcoholic, attacked V, stabbing him 37 times with a meat cleaver.	Effects of alcoholism	Alcohol dependency syndrome (ADS) is a recognised medical condition.
R v Dowds (2012)	D had been drinking heavily when he had an argument with his partner and killed her.	Voluntary acute intoxication	Voluntary acute intoxication is not capable of being relied upon to found diminished responsibility.

Involuntary manslaughter

Involuntary manslaughter is a common-law offence and so has an *actus reus* and *mens rea*:

- It has the *actus reus* elements of murder of causing the death of a human being.
- These offences are charged when the *mens rea* of murder cannot be satisfied, but a lower level of *mens rea* does exist.

Unlawful act manslaughter

Unlawful act manslaughter is where an unlawful and dangerous act causes the death of a human being.

> **Unlawful act manslaughter:** an offence requiring the death to have been caused by the defendant's unlawful conduct, rather than deliberately intending to kill.

Actus reus of unlawful act manslaughter

The killing must be the result of the defendant's act, not omission – see *R v Lowe* (1973).

The act must be unlawful (criminal), for example arson, robbery or assault – see *R v Franklin* (1883). However, the act need not be directed against the victim or any person. It can include assisting in the administration of a drug – see *R v Rodgers* (2003).

The unlawful act must be dangerous, which means all sober and reasonable people would realise it would subject the victim to the risk of physical harm, though not necessarily serious harm, whether or not the defendant realised this. It is irrelevant if the defendant had a mistaken belief that what they were doing was not dangerous. Key cases here include *R v Church* (1965) and *R v Ball* (1989).

The unlawful and dangerous act must cause the death, so the normal rules of criminal causation apply. Key cases here include *R v Williams* (1992) and *R v Carey* (2006).

Mens rea of unlawful act manslaughter

It is only necessary to establish the *mens rea* of the unlawful act. No additional *mens rea* is required for the subsequent death – see *R v Lamb* (1967).

Table 2.3.5 Key cases for unlawful act manslaughter

Case	Facts	Relevant area	*Ratio decidendi*
R v Lowe (1973)	The appellant's child died from neglect.	AR – 'act'	There must be an unlawful 'act'. It cannot be committed by omission.
R v Church (1965)	D knocked the victim unconscious and thought she was dead. He threw her body into a river. The cause of death was drowning.	AR – 'dangerous'	The unlawful act must be such as all sober and reasonable people would inevitably recognise must subject the other person to the risk of some harm resulting therefrom, albeit not serious harm.
R v Ball (1989)	D grabbed his gun and shot what he thought were blank cartridges at V. The cartridge was live and V died from her injury.	AR – 'dangerous'	The appellant's intention, foresight or knowledge is irrelevant.

Case	Facts	Relevant area	*Ratio decidendi*
R v Carey (2006)	V ran just over 100 metres away from B after a bullying incident but then collapsed and died of ventricular fibrillation, caused by the run. V had heart disease.	AR – 'causation'	X commits an unlawful act which is dangerous – it is recognised by reasonable persons as subjecting Y to the risk of some physical harm which in turn causes the death.
R v Lamb (1967)	One boy shot and killed another while playing with a gun, mistakenly thinking that the gun would not go off.	MR of the unlawful act	As there was no assault, there was no unlawful act manslaughter.

Gross negligence manslaughter

Gross negligence manslaughter is where the death is a result of a grossly negligent act or omission on the part of the defendant. Although it is a serious crime, it includes some civil-law tests.

The key case for this offence is *R v Adomako* (1994). The law has developed a four-stage test, known as the *Adomako* test:

1 The existence of a duty of care to the deceased:
  ○ This requires foreseeability, proximity, fairness, justice and reasonableness – see *Donohue v Stevenson* (1932).
  ○ The duty can arise from a contract of employment – see *R v Pittwood* (1902).
  ○ The duty can exist if the deceased and the defendant were engaged in an unlawful activity together – see *R v Wacker* (2003) and *R v Willoughby* (2004).
  ○ The risk must be a serious and obvious risk of death, not merely serious injury – see *R v Misra and Srivastava* (2005).

2 A breach of that duty of care which should be characterised as gross negligence, and therefore a crime:
  ○ This is an objective test and so is based upon what a reasonable person would do in the defendant's position at the time of the breach.
  ○ An unqualified person is not to be judged at a lower standard than a qualified person. Therefore, the lack of skill will not be a defence if the conduct is deemed negligent.
  ○ If, however, the defendant has particular skills and knowledge of a danger that the reasonable person would not have, their actions should be judged in the light of those skills or knowledge.
  ○ As it is an objective test, it does not matter that the defendant did not appreciate the risk (the foreseeable risk of death), only that the risk would have been obvious to a reasonable person in the defendant's position – see *R v DPP ex parte Jones* (2000) and *A-G Ref. No. 2 of 1999* (2000).

3 The breach must cause (or significantly contribute to) the death of the victim, so the normal rules of criminal causation apply.

4 The breach must be gross:
  ○ It is for the jury to decide whether the defendant's conduct was so bad, in all the circumstances, as to amount to a criminal act or omission.
  ○ In *R v Misra and Srivastava* (2005), the court decided that the term 'reprehensible' would be appropriate to describe the nature of the conduct.

> **Revision activity**
>
> Using A3 paper, draw a flow chart to explain the offence of unlawful act manslaughter.

> **Gross negligence manslaughter:** an offence requiring the death to have been caused by the defendant's gross negligence, rather than deliberately.

Table 2.3.6 Key cases for gross negligence manslaughter

Case	Facts	Relevant area	*Ratio decidendi*
R v Adomako (1994)	During an operation, an oxygen pipe became disconnected and the patient died. The anaesthetist appellant failed to notice or respond to obvious signs of disconnection.	The basis of the offence	The law of negligence applies to ascertain whether D has been in breach of a duty of care towards V. If breach is established, did it cause the death of V? If so, was it gross negligence and therefore a crime?
R v Misra and Srivastava (2005)	V was D's patient. V developed an undiagnosed and untreated infection in a wound, despite obvious symptoms.	Breach must be gross	Jury to decide whether D's behaviour was grossly negligent and consequently criminal.

Revision activity

Practise applying the law relating to these offences/defences to a given scenario. For example: 'Advise whether X is liable for the unlawful manslaughter of Y.'
- X has caused the death of Y by … *(identify the issues)*
- X will be charged with … *(identify the offences)*
- This comes from … *(identify the sources)*
- The *actus reus* of this offence is … *(state the actus reus, then use the ILAC method to work through each element of it – do not forget causation)*
- The *mens rea* of this offence is … *(state the mens rea, then use the ILAC method to work through each element of it – do not forget to look out for transferred malice here)*
- Conclusion *(your own)*.

Revision activity

To prepare for the exam, read the following summary reports from the Law Commission:
- *Legislating the Criminal Code: Involuntary Manslaughter* (Law Com No. 237)
- *Murder, Manslaughter and Infanticide* (Law Com No. 304).

Note the problems identified by the Law Commission, the extent to which they have since been addressed by Parliament and with what degree of success.

Now test yourself

TESTED ☐

1 What is the lowest *mens rea* possible for a murder conviction?
2 What does 'malice aforethought' actually mean?
3 For the purpose of the offence of murder, how is 'human being' defined?
4 What things will prevent a 'trigger' from qualifying?
5 What is the difference in the way that ss 52 and 54 of the Coroners and Justice Act 2009 treat the previous law?
6 How is abnormality of mental functioning determined?
7 What is the test for 'dangerous' in unlawful act manslaughter?
8 Why is the *mens rea* only for the unlawful act, not for the death?
9 Which tests are used to determine duty in gross negligence manslaughter?

Answers online

Exam summary

In the exam, you MAY be asked to:
- respond to a scenario question by advising a defendant, or defendants, whether they are criminally liable for their actions where:
  - an intentional death has occurred
  - a death has occurred as a result of an unlawful and dangerous act
- respond to a scenario question by advising a defendant, or defendants, whether they can raise any defences to any offences they may have committed where:
  - an intentional death has occurred
  - a death has occurred as a result of an unlawful and dangerous act
- discuss in a full-length essay question:
  - the *actus reus* and *mens rea* of murder
  - loss of control or diminished responsibility
  - unlawful act manslaughter.

These types of question will each be worth a maximum of 25 marks.

2.4 Non-fatal offences against the person

This chapter looks at four specific offences:

- common assault and battery under s 39 of the Criminal Justice Act 1988
- actual bodily harm under s 47 of the Offences Against the Person Act 1861
- wounding and grievous bodily harm under s 20 of the Offences Against the Person Act 1861
- wounding and grievous bodily harm under s 18 of the Offences Against the Person Act 1861.

Common assault – assault

Assault, sometimes referred to as a 'technical' assault, is a common-law offence. The current definition of assault comes from *Fagan v MPC* (1969) as being 'where the defendant intentionally or recklessly causes the victim to apprehend immediate unlawful personal violence'.

It is a summary offence, and therefore triable only in the Magistrates' Court. It carries a maximum sentence of six months' imprisonment according to s 39 of the Criminal Justice Act 1988.

> **Assault:** where the defendant intentionally or recklessly causes the victim to apprehend immediate unlawful personal violence/force.

> **Typical mistake**
>
> The media use the word 'assault' to mean many things, usually to describe a physical attack. In criminal law, this is incorrect as it describes a threat of force, not the actual infliction of force.

Actus reus of assault

The victim must apprehend immediate unlawful personal violence.

Table 2.4.1 Components of the *actus reus* for assault

Component	Explanation	Key cases
Apprehend	'Apprehend' means the victim need not be put in fear but must be aware that they are about to be subjected to violence. If the victim does not anticipate unlawful personal violence, there is no assault.	*R v Lamb* (1967)
	There does not need to be an actual intended threat.	*Logdon v DPP* (1976)
	The conduct that causes the victim to apprehend can be actions, words or even silence.	*R v Constanza* (1997) and *R v Ireland* (1997)
	Words can also negate an assault.	*Tuberville v Savage* (1669)
Immediate	'Immediate' is satisfied if the victim did not know what the defendant was going to do next.	*Smith v Chief Constable of Woking* (1983)
Unlawful	'Unlawful' relates to the presence of a defence. See Chapter 2.7, as it is possible for an assault to be lawful if it is legally justified, e.g. in self-defence.	
Personal violence	'Personal violence' means the victim needs to apprehend the level of force that amounts to a technical battery, i.e. touching is sufficient.	

Mens rea of assault

This is the intention to cause the victim to apprehend immediate unlawful personal violence or being reckless as to whether such apprehension is caused – see *R v Parmenter* (1991).

Revision activity

Make notes on and explore any issues of the law which you think may be open to criticism – you may be required to write about them

Exam tip

Remember to use the definitions set out in Chapter 2.2 when discussing the *mens rea* of all offences.

Common assault – battery

REVISED

Battery is a common-law offence. The current definition comes from *R v Ireland* (1997) and is where 'the defendant intentionally or recklessly applies unlawful force upon the victim'.

It is a summary offence and therefore triable only in the Magistrates' Court. It carries a maximum sentence of six months' imprisonment according to s 39 of the Criminal Justice Act 1988.

Battery: the intentional or reckless application of unlawful force upon a victim.

Actus reus of battery

This requires the application of unlawful physical force.

Table 2.4.2 Components of the *actus reus* for battery

Component	Explanation	Key cases
Application	'Application' need not be direct.	*DPP v K* (1990)
Unlawful	'Unlawful' relates to the presence of a defence – see Chapter 2.7, as it is possible for an assault to be lawful if it is legally justified, e.g. in self-defence.	*Collins v Wilcock* (1984) stated there could be implied consent where there was jostling in crowded places, handshakes, back slapping, and tapping to gain attention, provided no more force was used than reasonably necessary in the circumstances.
Physical force	Any touching will suffice; it need not necessarily be hostile, rude or aggressive.	*Faulkner v Talbot* (1981)

Mens rea of battery

This is intention to apply unlawful physical force or being reckless as to whether such force is applied – see *R v Parmenter* (1991).

Table 2.4.3 Key cases for assault and battery

Case	Facts	Assault or battery?	Ratio decidendi (where not given above)
R v Lamb (1967)	V did not believe the gun would go off; therefore he did not apprehend immediate unlawful personal violence.	AR assault – 'apprehend'	No assault had been committed.
Logdon v DPP (1976)	D pointed an imitation gun at V in jest. V was terrified. D then told her it was not real.	AR assault – 'apprehend'	There does not need to be an actual threat for an assault to be committed.
Tuberville v Savage (1669)	D put his hand on his sword and stated, 'if it were not assize-time, I would not take such language from you'.	AR assault – 'apprehend'	Words can prevent an apprehension.

Case	Facts	Assault or battery?	Ratio decidendi (where not given above)
Smith v Chief Constable of Woking (1983)	A peeping tom claimed V could not have been frightened of personal violence as he was outside the house and she was inside.	AR assault – 'apprehend'	The basis of her fear was that she did not know what the defendant was going to do next.
R v Parmenter (1991)	D assaulted his baby son.	MR – 'recklessness'	It is necessary to establish that D appreciated the risk. It is not sufficient that he should have foreseen a risk of injury.
DPP v K (1990)	A boy put acid in a hand dryer that caused injury to the next user of the dryer.	AR battery – 'application'	Battery need not be direct.

Assault/battery occasioning ABH

REVISED

Although this offence is set out in s 47 of the Offences Against the Person Act 1861, the common law has had to develop rules around this to give more detail. It is a triable-either-way offence and carries a maximum sentence of five years' imprisonment.

Actus reus of s 47 assault/battery occasioning ABH

This requires an assault or battery which causes actual bodily harm.

Table 2.4.4 Components of the *actus reus* for ABH

Component	Explanation	Key cases
Assault or battery	Either will suffice, but all of the elements of assault or battery must be present.	*R v Chan-Fook* (1994)
Causes	The assault or battery must cause actual bodily harm. The usual rules and cases of causation apply – see Chapter 2.2.	*R v Roberts* (1971)
Actual bodily harm (ABH)	This means hurt or injury calculated to interfere with the health or comfort of the victim. It need not be permanent but should not be so trivial as to be wholly insignificant. ABH can include psychiatric injury and the cutting of hair.	*R v Miller* (1954) *R v Chan-Fook* (1994)

Typical mistake

Do not forget to focus on all three parts of the *actus reus* of ABH: the assault or battery, the causation link and the resulting harm.

Revision activity

Research *R v Chan-Fook* (1994) and find out why Chan-Fook was found not guilty.

Mens rea of s 47 assault/battery occasioning ABH

This is intention or recklessness with regard to the assault or battery. There is no additional *mens rea* for the harm caused – see *R v Roberts* (1971).

Wounding and GBH

REVISED

Wounding and GBH are found under two separate sections of the Offences Against the Person Act 1861.

Section 20 wounding and GBH

'Whosoever shall unlawfully and maliciously wound or inflict any grievous bodily harm on any other person, either with or without a weapon or instrument, shall be guilty of a misdemeanour.'

A conviction under s 20 represents the lesser offence, which is triable either way and carries a maximum penalty of five years' imprisonment. The main difference between the offences relate to the *mens rea*.

Actus reus of s 20 wounding and GBH

This requires the defendant to unlawfully wound or inflict GBH on another person.

Table 2.4.5 Components of the *actus reus* for s 20 wounding and GBH

Component	Explanation	Key cases
Unlawfully	Some wounding or GBH may be classed as lawful. This covers those who are acting in self-defence or prevention of crime, and in limited circumstances where the victim has consented (such as medical procedures and where the injury results from properly conducted games and sports).	
Wound	A wound exists where there is a break in the continuity of the skin causing external bleeding.	*Moriarty v Brookes* (1834) *C v Eisenhower* (1984)
Inflict	'Inflict' simply means 'cause'.	*R v Burstow* (1997)
GBH	'Grievous bodily harm' means really serious harm, such as long-term/permanent injury or injury requiring extensive treatment. It can also include: ● less serious injuries if the victim is vulnerable, e.g. particularly old or young ● multiple ABHs ● psychiatric injury, but it must be a recognisable illness.	*DPP v Smith* (1961) *R v Bollom* (2004) *R v Brown and Stratton* (1997) *R v Burstow* (1997) *R v Dhaliwal* (2006)

Mens rea of s 20 wounding and GBH

This requires the defendant to have the intention to cause, or be reckless as to the causing of, some harm. There is no need to establish that they intended or were reckless as to causing *serious* harm – see *R v Savage* (1991) and *R v Parmenter* (1991).

Section 18 wounding and GBH

'Whosoever shall unlawfully and maliciously by any means whatsoever wound or cause any grievous bodily harm to any person, with intent to do some grievous bodily harm to any person, or with intent to resist or prevent the lawful apprehension or detainer of any person, shall be guilty of felony.'

Section 18 is a more serious offence than s 20. It is indictable and carries a maximum sentence of life imprisonment.

Actus reus of s 18 wounding and GBH

Despite the use of the different verbs – 'inflict' in s 20 and 'cause' in s 18 – there is very little difference between the *actus reus* of s 20 and that of s 18. For the purposes of your course, it is safe to assume they mean the same thing.

Mens rea of s 18 wounding and GBH

This requires either intent to cause GBH, or intent to resist or prevent the lawful detainer (arrest) of any person.

Table 2.4.6 **Key cases for Offences Against the Person Act 1861 (OAPA)**

Case	Facts	Relevant area	*Ratio decidendi* (where not given above)
R v Roberts (1971)	V jumped out of a moving car to escape D's unwanted sexual advances.	Section 47 ABH – 'causation' and MR	Escape from physical danger is not 'daft' and does not break the chain. The MR for the assault or battery is sufficient; no additional MR is required for the harm caused.
Moriarty v Brookes (1834)	V suffered a cut to the skin under his eye in a dispute in a pub.	AR – 'wounding'	If the skin is broken, and there was bleeding, that is a wound.
C v Eisenhower (1984)	Pellets from D's air gun caused bruising and rupturing of internal blood vessels of V's eye, but there was no breaking of the skin.	AR – 'wounding'	There needs to be a break in the continuity of the whole skin.
R v Bollom (2004)	The injuries to a 17-month-old baby consisted of various bruises and abrasions.	AR – 'GBH'	Vulnerable victim of GBH
R v Brown and Stratton (1997)	V sustained a broken nose, lost three teeth, and suffered swelling to her face, lacerations to her eye and concussion.	AR – 'GBH'	Multiple ABHs
R v Burstow (1997)	D engaged in harassment against V. As a result, she suffered a severe depressive illness.	AR – 'GBH'	Psychiatric injury
R v Golding (2014)	D infected V with herpes.	AR – 'GBH'	The fact that there is no effective cure was sufficient for the jury to consider it 'serious'.
R v Savage (1991)	D threw a pint of beer over V in a pub. The glass slipped out of D's hand and cut V's wrist.	MR – s 20	It is sufficient that D intended or could foresee that some harm will result.

Revision activity

Look up *R v Golding* (2014). Why was this relatively minor illness classed as GBH?

Now test yourself

1 What does 'apprehend' mean?
2 Why was the defendant not guilty in *R v Lamb* (1967)?
3 What is the lowest form of *mens rea* possible for assault?
4 Why is tapping someone on the shoulder generally not an offence?
5 In battery, how much harm must be caused by the force used?
6 What case would you use as precedent for throwing a piece of chalk at someone amounting to a battery?
7 What is the highest form of *mens rea* required for battery?
8 A ruptured spleen causing internal bleeding could amount to which offence/s?
9 Can bodily harm be caused by infection? What problems can you foresee with this?
10 What is the difference between s 20 and s 18 wounding and GBH? Why is this so?

Answers online

Exam summary

In the exam, you MAY be asked to:
- respond to a scenario question by advising a defendant, or defendants, whether they are criminally liable for their actions where a victim has:
  - been put in fear that force or violence is to be applied to them
  - had unlawful force applied to them
  - had unlawful force applied and/or a threat or threats of unlawful force, resulting in an injury capable of being charged under ss 47, 20 or 18 of the Offences Against the Person Act 1861
- respond to a scenario question by advising a defendant, or defendants, whether they can raise a defence where a victim has:
  - been put in fear that force or violence is to be applied to them
  - had unlawful force applied to them
  - had unlawful force applied and/or a threat or threats of unlawful force, resulting in an injury capable of being charged under ss 47, 20 or 18 of the Offences Against the Person Act 1861
- discuss common assault in a full-length essay question.

These types of question will each be worth a maximum of 25 marks.

2.5 Offences against property

This chapter looks at three key offences against property:
● theft under s 1 of the Theft Act 1968
● robbery under s 8 of the Theft Act 1968, and
● burglary under s 9(1)(a) and s 9(1)(b) of the Theft Act 1968.

Theft

REVISED

Theft is defined under s 1(1) of the Theft Act 1968:

'A person is guilty of theft if he dishonestly appropriates property belonging to another with the intention of permanently depriving the other of it; and "thief" and "steal" shall be construed accordingly.'

Section 1(1) is the specific charge for theft. Sections 2–6 provide the interpretation and operation of each of the elements stated in s 1.

Theft: the dishonest appropriation of property belonging to another with the intention of permanently depriving the other of it.

Typical mistake

Do not recite every part of each section in your answer unless required. For example, do not state every defence under s 2, or discuss wild flowers or untamed wild creatures under s 4, if this is irrelevant to the specific exam question.

Exam tip

Make sure you have accurate knowledge of ss 1–6 and s 8 of the Theft Act 1968. You need to be able to support any interpretation of these sections with relevant and, where possible, recent case law.

Actus reus of theft

The *actus reus* of theft is established by proving:
● the appropriation
● of property
● belonging to another.

Appropriation (s 3)

Appropriation is defined under s 3(1) as:

'Any assumption by a person of the rights of an owner [which] includes, where he has come by the property (innocently or not) without stealing it, any later assumption of a right to it by keeping or dealing with it as owner.'

The definition is very wide and even includes situations where the owner has consented to the appropriation – see *R v Lawrence* (1972) and *R v Gomez* (1993).

It must be an act which assumes at least one right of the owner.

Appropriation: any assumption by a person of the rights of an owner.

Property (s 4)

Property is defined under s 4(1):

'Property includes money and all other property, real or personal, including things in action and other intangible property.'

The definition under s 4(1) is very wide and includes money and personal property. The rest of s 4 defines, *inter alia*, what cannot be stolen:
● land
● mushrooms, flowers, fruit or foliage growing wild unless picked for financial gain
● wild creatures, unless tamed, in captivity or in the possession of another.

Property: includes money and all other property, real or personal, including things in action and other intangible property.

Revision activity

Make a list of items that you think would be defined as personal property under s 4(1).

Confidential information (held on paper) cannot be stolen – see *Oxford v Moss* (1979) and *R v Akbar* (2002).

Belonging to another (s 5)

Belonging to another is defined under s 5(1):

> 'Property shall be regarded as belonging to any person having possession or control of it, or having in it any proprietary right or interest.'

The wide definition under s 5 includes anyone with possession or control. This covers the situation where the appropriation is not from the owner, but from someone who has the owner's permission to have the property in their possession.

Under s 5(3), property remains belonging to another if there is an obligation to deal with the property in a particular way, and if it is not then this can be theft – see *Davidge v Bunnett* (1984).

Under s 5(4), property received by mistake remains property belonging to another if there is a legal obligation to return the property, and a refusal to return the property will amount to intention to permanently deprive – see *A-G Ref. No. 1 of 1983* (1985).

Revision activity

Using the internet, research the cases of *Oxford v Moss* (1979) and *R v Akbar* (2002) and explain the decisions.

Belonging to another: belonging to any person having possession or control of property or having any proprietary right or interest in it.

Revision activity

Using the internet, research and compare the cases of *Davidge v Bunnett* (1984) and *A-G Ref. No. 1 of 1983* (1985).

Table 2.5.1 **Key cases on the *actus reus* of theft**

Case	Facts	Section of the Theft Act 1968	*Ratio decidendi*
R v Pitham and Hehl (1977)	D sold furniture belonging to another person but did not come into actual possession of the property.	'Appropriation' – s 3	Appropriation – selling was a right of the owner with which D interfered.
R v Morris (1983)	D swapped price labels on two items in a supermarket.	'Appropriation' – s 3	Switching labels and trying to pay the lower price was an appropriation, an interference of the owner's rights.
R v Kelly and Lindsay (1998)	D1 made sculptures, cast from body parts obtained by D2 through his job at the Royal College of Surgeons.	'Property' – s 4	This is an exception to common-law rule that a corpse is not property – acquired body parts can be property.
R (on the application of Ricketts) v Basildon Magistrates' Court (2010)	D took bags containing donated items left outside a charity shop intended for sale in the shop and bags from behind the shop. D claimed they were abandoned.	'Belonging to another' – s 5	The bags, and their contents, outside the shop remained the property of the donor, while those behind the shop were the property of the charity.

Mens rea of theft

The *mens rea* of theft is established by proving:
- dishonesty, and
- the intention to permanently deprive.

Dishonesty (s 2)

The Theft Act does not define 'dishonestly', but instead gives three situations which would not be considered 'dishonest'.

Revision activity

In your own words, what do you think 'dishonest' means?

In effect, s 2 provides three defences to a charge of theft specifically where 'dishonestly' is in question (see below).

When Parliament passed the 1968 Act, it felt that the definition should be left to the common sense of magistrates or a jury, to be decided on a case-by-case basis – see *Brutus v Cozens* (1972). Parliament felt that the changing nature of the public's opinion as to what is meant by 'dishonestly' precluded a specific definition in the Act.

The three appropriations of property belonging to another which are *not* dishonest are:
- if the defendant has in law the right to deprive the other of it, or
- if the defendant would have the other's consent if the other knew of the appropriation and the circumstances of it, or
- if the person to whom the property belongs cannot be discovered by taking reasonable steps.

In *R v Ghosh* (1982), the Court of Appeal set out a two-part test to provide guidance and clarity as to the definition of 'dishonestly' for magistrates and juries, should they require further assistance:
1 Was what the defendant did dishonest according to the ordinary standards of reasonable and honest people?
2 Did the defendant realise that what they did was dishonest by those (rather than their own) standards?

Ghosh did not go without criticism, however, and in *Ivey v Genting Casinos (UK) Ltd t/a Crockfords* (2017), the Supreme Court established a preferred definition for 'dishonestly', distancing itself from the *Ghosh* test.

The court acknowledged serious problems with the second limb of *Ghosh*, in that a defendant could simply say they did not realise they were being dishonest. Here, a jury might assume that the defendant was not dishonest and therefore not guilty. In this 2017 case, the court preferred the civil law's test for dishonesty:
1 Decide what the individual knew about what they were doing and what the surrounding circumstances were, and then
2 Assuming that state of knowledge, decide whether the ordinary decent member of society would say what was done was dishonest, and if so, the behaviour does not become honest simply because the defendant has different or lower standards.

> **Revision activity**
>
> Why do you think the Court of Appeal relented in *R v Ghosh* (1982) and defined 'dishonestly'?

Intention of permanently depriving (s 6)

The meaning is not specifically defined under s 6, but the section clarifies certain situations which would amount to an intention of permanently depriving. The definition is given a very wide interpretation by the courts – see Table 2.5.2 below.

According to s 6(1), intention is found if the person treats the thing as their own to dispose of regardless of the other's rights. A borrowing or lending of the thing may amount to an intention to permanently deprive if it is for a period and in circumstances equivalent to an outright taking or disposal.

Under s 6(2), there is intention to permanently deprive the owner of the thing even if it is returned but some of its value has diminished, such as:
- selling a person's property back to them, pretending to be the true owner
- using some of the charge out of a person's batteries, then giving them back
- eating part of someone's chocolate bar and giving the rest back
- returning a concert, gig or raffle ticket after it has been used.

Table 2.5.2 Key cases on the *mens rea* of theft

Case	Facts	Section of the Theft Act 1968	*Ratio decidendi*
R v Holden (1991)	D took old car tyres from his former employer, believing he had permission or would have had permission if he had asked.	'Dishonestly' under s 2(1)(a)	The question for the jury was whether H had, or might have had, the necessary honest belief, reasonably or not.
R v Lawrence (1972)	D, a taxi driver, took £7 for a £1 fare from an Italian tourist who spoke little English and was unfamiliar with the currency. V had held his wallet open and D took the £7.	'Dishonestly' under s 2(1)(b)	Belief or absence of belief that the owner consented to the appropriation is relevant to the issue of dishonesty.
R v Small (1988)	D took a car which had been left for two weeks with the windows open, keys left in the ignition, a flat battery and no petrol.	'Dishonestly' under s 2(1)(c)	A belief unreasonably held can be an honest belief.
R v Velumyl (1989)	D borrowed over £1,050 from the safe at work, with the intention to pay it back the following Monday. This was against company rules.	'Intention to permanently deprive' – s 6	Held as an intention to permanently deprive as the exact money could not be replaced.
Lavender v DPP (1994)	D removed two doors from a council house to replace two broken doors at his girlfriend's council house.	'Intention to permanently deprive' – s 6	D intended to treat the doors as his own, regardless of the council's rights.
R v Lloyd (1985)	D worked in a cinema and took films so that copies could be made by some associates.	'Intention to permanently deprive' – s 6	This was not theft. The films were returned in their original state and had lost no practical value.
R v Easom (1971)	D rummaged through a handbag in a cinema but took nothing.	'Intention to permanently deprive' – s 6 (conditional intent)	If D decides not to take another's property, then this is not theft under s 1.
Ivey v Genting Casinos (UK) Ltd t/a Crockfords (2017)	D, a professional gambler, had 'won' £7.7m at a casino. The casino owners refused to pay, saying he had cheated.	'Dishonestly' under s 2	The Supreme Court installed the civil test for dishonesty as the preferred test under the criminal law.

Robbery

REVISED

Robbery is defined under s 8 of the Theft Act 1968:

'A person is guilty of robbery if he steals, and immediately before or at the time of doing so, and in order to do so, he uses force on any person or puts or seeks to put any person in fear of being then and there subjected to force.'

> **Robbery:** where someone steals and subjects the person to force or fear of force.

Exam tip

Learn the definition under s 8 accurately. Then learn how the *actus reus* can be broken down into its constituent parts, for example (1) steals, (2) and immediately before or at the time of doing so etc.

As s 8 is so long, it is easy to omit parts of the definition or to apply them incorrectly. For a scenario question, remember the mnemonic ILAC:

- **I**ssues – identify what has happened
- **L**aw – explain the relevant law
- **A**pply the point/case to the facts of the scenario
- **C**onclude – decide whether the defendant is, or is not, guilty.

Actus reus of robbery

Table 2.5.3 Components of the *actus reus* of robbery

Component	Explanation
Steals	A theft must be committed. No theft means no robbery.
Uses force on any person or puts or seeks to put any person in fear of being then and there subjected to force	D must apply force to V or threaten to apply force to V in order to steal.
And in order to do so	The use or threat of force must be in order to steal.
Immediately before or at the time of doing so	The timing of the force or threat of force must be before or at the time of the theft.

Mens rea of robbery

The defendant must have the *mens rea* of theft, i.e. dishonesty and intention to permanently deprive. There must be the intention to use force to steal.

Table 2.5.4 Key cases on robbery

Case	Facts	Element of robbery	*Ratio decidendi*
R v Robinson (1977)	D was owed £7 by V's wife. D argued with V who dropped a £5 note which D picked up and kept.	'Steals'	As D had a genuine belief he had a right in law to the £5, he was not dishonest under s 2(1)(a).
Corcoran v Anderton (1980)	D grabbed V's handbag which was instantly dropped by D, who ran off empty-handed.	'Steals'	D was convicted of robbery, as s 1(1) of the Theft Act 1968 was completed when he grabbed the handbag.
R v Dawson and James (1976)	D1 pushed V so that V lost balance and D2 could take his wallet.	'Force' or threat of 'force'	The Court of Appeal upheld the conviction: force is an ordinary word decided by the jury.
R v Clouden (1987)	D snatched a handbag out of V's hands. It was argued force was not on a person.	'Force' or threat of 'force'	Even though force was only slight, the judge was right to allow the jury to decide.
R v Hale (1979)	D1 and D2 forced their way into a house. D1 tied up V while D2 took items from upstairs.	Timing of force	Theft was seen as a continuing act, even though the force to tie up V was separate to the stealing.
R v Lockley (1995)	D was challenged leaving a shop after he took cans of beer. D pushed the shopkeeper and ran off.	Timing of force	Theft was seen as a continuing act. D appealed arguing the theft was complete when he used force. The Court of Appeal followed *Hale* and upheld conviction.

Burglary

Burglary is defined under s 9 of the Theft Act 1968. Subsection 1 states that a person is guilty of burglary if:

'(a) he enters any building or part of a building as a trespasser and with intent to commit any such offence as is mentioned in subsection (2) below; or

(b) having entered any building or part of a building as a trespasser he steals or attempts to steal anything in the building or that part of it or inflicts or attempts to inflict on any person therein any grievous bodily harm.'

> **Burglary:** where a trespasser enters a building (or part of a building) intending to steal, inflict GBH or do unlawful damage; or having entered a building (or part of a building), a trespasser steals or inflicts GBH, or attempts to do so.

Typical mistake

As s 9 is so long, it is easy to omit parts of the definition or to apply them incorrectly. For a scenario question, remember the mnemonic ILAC:

- **I**ssues – identify what has happened, for example someone has gone into a house 'to find anything to steal'
- **L**aw – explain the relevant law, here ss 9(1)(a) and/or(b)
- **A**pply the point/case to the facts of the scenario, i.e. apply each part of the *actus reus* and *mens rea* to the actual scenario
- **C**onclude – decide whether the defendant is, or is not, guilty, i.e. in your own opinion has the defendant committed the offence of burglary, or if not, why not?

Actus reus of burglary

Table 2.5.5 Components of the *actus reus* of burglary

Component	Explanation
Entry	This is not defined in the Act but has been developed through the common law by judges – see cases below in Table 2.5.6. Actual entry is not required.
A building or part of a building	This is not fully defined in the Act but has been developed through the common law by judges – see cases below in Table 2.5.6. However, s 9(4) includes an inhabited vehicle or vessel, whether or not the person is there at the time.
Trespasser	This is defined under the civil law of tort as a person who enters without permission. The person must know or be reckless as to whether they are trespassing. A person can become a trespasser if they exceed the permission given.

Mens rea of burglary

The *mens rea* of burglary depends on which section the defendant has been charged under:
- For s 9(1)(a), the defendant must have intended to commit one of the three ulterior offences, and conditional intent is sufficient.
- For s 9(1)(b), the defendant must have the *mens rea* for theft or GBH when they commit or attempt to commit the *actus reus* of either of these two offences.
- For both ss 9(1)(a) and 9(1)(b), the defendant must either know they are trespassing or be subjectively reckless as to whether they are doing so.

Table 2.5.6 Key cases on burglary

Case	Facts	Element of burglary	Ratio decidendi
R v Collins (1972)	D climbed a ladder and perched on a window ledge before being invited in through the open window by V.	'Entry'	The Court of Appeal said 'entry' had to be 'effective and substantial'.
R v Brown (1985)	D leaned through an open window while still standing on the ground outside.	'Entry'	The Court of Appeal said 'entry' simply had to be 'effective'.
R v Ryan (1996)	D was found with his head and arm trapped in a window at 2.30 a.m.	'Entry'	The Court of Appeal said that while his entry may not have been 'effective', there was sufficient evidence for a jury to find D had entered.
B and S v Leathley (1979)	A 25-foot freezer container resting on railway sleepers in a farmyard had its own lock and electricity supply.	'Building'	The freezer container was held to be a building.
Norfolk Constabulary v Seekings and Gould (1986)	A lorry trailer used for storage had steps and its own electricity supply.	'Building'	The trailer was held not to be a building because it still had wheels attached.
R v Walkington (1979)	D opened a till housed within a three-sided 'island' on the shop floor of a department store.	'... or part of a building'	D may have had permission to enter the shop (perhaps!), but clearly entered the counter area as a trespasser with the intent to steal.
R v Jones and Smith (1976)	D1 and D2 took two television sets from D2's father's house. The father argued Ds had permission to enter.	'Trespasser'	The Court of Appeal upheld the convictions as both D1 and D2 had exceeded their permission, or 'licence', to enter.
A-G Ref. Nos 1 and 2 of 1979 (1979)	These were two conjoined appeals where burglars had been convicted but both argued they had not been intending to steal a specific item.	Conditional intent – theft	D will satisfy the mens rea if they enter intending to steal anything they can find that is worth taking, rather than a specific item.

> **Exam tip**
>
> Learn: the definition under s 9(1) accurately; the *actus reus* components as shown in Table 2.5.5; the offences required under burglary; and finally the *mens rea* for burglary.

Now test yourself

1 What are the key elements of the *actus reus* of theft?
2 What are the key elements of the *mens rea* of theft?
3 Explain two reasons why the definition of 'dishonestly' may sometimes be difficult to establish.
4 Sections 1–7 of the Theft Act provide a complicated definition for what is in practice a fairly straightforward crime. Discuss.
5 List the essential elements of robbery.
6 Discuss what is meant by 'force' used in robbery.
7 Why was the defendant's appeal in *R v Robinson* (1977) successful, following his conviction for robbery?
8 Section 8 of the Theft Act 1968 provides a complicated definition for what is in practice the fairly straightforward crime of robbery. Discuss.
9 List the essential elements of the *actus reus* of burglary.
10 Explain the differences between s 9(1)(a) and s 9(1)(b) of the Theft Act 1968.

Answers online

Exam summary

In the exam, you MAY be asked to:
- respond to a scenario question by advising a defendant, or defendants, whether they are criminally liable for their actions where one of the following has potentially occurred:
  - theft
  - robbery
  - burglary
- respond to a scenario question by advising a defendant, or defendants, whether they can raise a defence where one of the following has potentially occurred:
  - theft
  - robbery
  - burglary
- discuss in a full-length essay question either the *actus reus* or the *mens rea* of:
  - theft
  - robbery
  - burglary.

These types of question will be worth a maximum of 25 marks.

2.6 Mental capacity defences

In this chapter, we discuss three key mental capacity defences:

- insanity/insane automatism
- automatism/non-insane automatism
- intoxication.

Typical mistake

Do not muddle which case supports which defence, or which exact element of the definition it supports. Also, make sure you match case names accurately to the facts.

Insanity/insane automatism

REVISED

The definition of insanity is contained in the *M'Naghten* rules of 1843:

> 'The defendant must prove that at the time of the offence he was labouring under such a defect of reason, arising from a disease of the mind, that he did not to know the nature and quality of the act he was doing, or, if he did know it, that he did not know that what he was doing was wrong.'

Starting point for the defence

The law here has developed mainly through the common law but also by statute. There are a number of procedural rules:

- The defendant is presumed sane.
- The prosecution, defence or judge can raise the issue of insanity.
- The burden of proof is on the defendant to prove on a balance of probabilities.
- The judge decides whether the defendant is fit to plead.

Due to the social stigma, antiquated definition and the introduction of the diminished responsibility defence, insanity is rarely raised as a defence to crimes.

Revision activity

Why do you think being labelled 'insane' carries a social stigma?

M'Naghten rules

The defendant must satisfy each part of the rules.

Table 2.6.1 The *M'Naghten* rules

Part of the rules	Explanation
'Labouring under a defect of reason' (*mens rea*)	• Being deprived of the power to reason, not just failing to use it • Does not include absentmindedness or being confused – *R v Clarke* (1972)
'Arising from a disease of the mind' (*actus reus*)	• A legal term and not a medical term • Must be supported by medical evidence • Broad definition covering organic or functional, permanent or transient and intermittent • Must be caused by an internal factor existing at the time of the act – *R v Kemp* (1957)
'Did not know the nature and quality of the act' (*actus reus*)	• Means the physical nature and consequences, not the moral quality of the act • May be due to a state of unconsciousness or impaired unconsciousness, or lack of understanding or awareness due to a mental condition while conscious
'Or, if he did know it, that he did not know that what he was doing was wrong'	• Defence will fail if the defendant understood their actions were legally wrong, even if they had a mental illness at the time of the act • Does not mean morally wrong – *R v Windle* (1952) and *R v Johnson* (2007)

Consequences of an insanity verdict

If a defendant is found to have been insane, the jury should return the special verdict 'not guilty by reason of insanity', which amounts to an acquittal.

For murder, the sentence is indefinite hospitalisation under s 24(1)(3) of the Domestic Violence, Crime and Victims Act 2004.

For all other offences, s 5 of the Criminal Procedure (Insanity) Act 1964 (as amended by the 2004 Act) sets out three disposal options:
- hospital order
- supervision order
- absolute discharge.

Revision activity

Using the internet, compare the cases of *R v Windle* (1952) and *R v Johnson* (2007).

Exam tip

Unless the question asks for cases to be explained chronologically, it is not so important to remember case dates. Detailed facts are not needed, but an accurate explanation of the case's legal point is vital.

Table 2.6.2 **Key cases on insanity**

Case	Facts	Element of insanity	Legal point
R v M'Naghten (1843)	D killed an official while suffering from extreme paranoia.	Definition	Judges later formulated the test for insanity after the case.
R v Clarke (1972)	D took items from a shop and forgot to pay for them due to diabetes.	'Defect of reason'	D is required to be deprived of the powers of reasoning.
R v Kemp (1957)	D had hardening of the arteries and attacked his wife with a hammer.	'Disease of the mind'	The defence is concerned with the mind and not the brain.
R v Quick (1973)	D was diabetic. He attacked a patient after taking his insulin but had eaten insufficient food.	'Disease of the mind'	The disease of the mind must originate from an internal source. This was external: the insulin.
R v Hennessy (1989)	D was diabetic and failed to take insulin for three days, during which he took a car without consent.	'Disease of the mind'	The disease of the mind must originate from an internal source. This was internal: the diabetes.
R v Burgess (1991)	D attacked his girlfriend after falling asleep.	'Disease of the mind'	Sleepwalking is an internal factor and therefore insanity.

Reform proposals for insanity defence

In 2013, the Law Commission published a discussion paper, *Criminal Liability: Insanity and Automatism*, outlining their reform proposals:
- To term a person with a disability such as diabetes or epilepsy 'insane' seems arbitrary and outdated. The very name is 'off-putting or even offensive'.
- There is a mismatch between modern psychiatry and the legal definition.
- The decisions in *R v Quick* (1973) and *R v Hennessy* (1989) were described as 'odd'.
- The internal/external requirement made the potential 'scope of the defence ... surprisingly wide'.
- Sleepwalking cases led to inconsistency, with some defendants given the 'special verdict' while others were acquitted.

Automatism/non-insane automatism

Automatism was defined by Lord Denning in *Bratty v A-G for Northern Ireland* (1963) as:

'... an act which is done by the muscles without any control by the mind such as a spasm, a reflex action or a convulsion; or an act done by a person who is not conscious of what he is doing such as an act done whilst suffering from concussion or whilst sleepwalking.'

Automatism: an involuntary act such as a spasm, reflex action or convulsion, or an act performed while a person is unconscious (such as suffering from concussion or sleepwalking).

Typical mistake

Do not confuse the internal/external factor theory and, in particular, the cases that support the theory. Also, do not muddle the specific conditions that give arise to the defences. See the facts of *R v Quick* (1973) and *R v Hennessy* (1989), for example.

Automatism is the situation where the defendant is unable to control their movements because their muscles reacted without any control of the mind. Therefore, there is no *mens rea*.

The evidential burden of proof is on the defence to prove automatism. If successful, it results in a complete acquittal – see *Hill v Baxter* (1958) and *R v C* (2007).

The legal burden of proof is on the prosecution.

There must be an external factor – this is essential in proving automatism. Examples include being struck on the head by an object, slipping on ice, being overcome by a sudden illness, hiccups, a coughing fit, or a temporary loss of control due to a radical event such as being attacked by a swarm of bees.

There must be a total loss of control – any impaired, reduced or partial control will invalidate the defence.

Revision activity

Using decided cases, make a list of external factors that can satisfy the defence of automatism.

Self-induced automatism

Automatism will not be successful as a defence if a defendant knows their conduct will bring about an automatic state, for example through intoxication. In such situations, the defendant will have a defence to specific intent crimes. However, the defendant will not have a defence to basic intent crimes if it is their fault.

There is an exception, where the defendant does not realise that their self-induced (voluntary) actions would cause automatism and they were not reckless – see *R v Hardy* (1984).

Revision activity

Using the internet, research the three rules of self-induced automatism that were decided in *R v Bailey* (1983).

Table 2.6.3 Key cases on automatism

Case	Facts	Element of automatism	Legal point
Bratty v A-G for Northern Ireland (1963)	D strangled and killed his girlfriend during a 'blackout'.	Definition	Legal test of automatism created by Lord Denning
Hill v Baxter (1958)	D hit a car at a junction and said he remembered nothing.	Must be an external factor	The burden of proof for automatism is on the defence.
R v Quick (1973)	See Table 2.6.2.		
R v Hennessy (1989)	See Table 2.6.2.		

Case	Facts	Element of automatism	Legal point
R v T (1990)	D took part in a robbery, using a pen-knife, three days after being raped. She argued she was in a dream-like state and suffered PTSD.	Must be an external factor	External stress can give rise to automatism if severe enough. The prosecution argued that opening the pen-knife was a 'controlled and positive action'; the judge disagreed, saying D was 'acting as though in a dream'.
R v Narborough (2004)	D was charged with a s 18 offence after he stabbed V. D argued on appeal that he was sexually abused as a young child and, as a consequence, he suffered PTSD which caused flashbacks. D said he had suffered a flashback at the time when he stabbed V.	Must be an external factor	In contradiction with *R v T*, the Court of Appeal rejected D's argument saying that the defence psychiatrist had not referred to any authority to support the notion that PTSD 'affects a person's mental processes that his mind is no longer in control of his actions'.
A-G Ref. No. 2 of 1992 (1993)	D drove in a trance-like state along the motorway's hard shoulder and hit and killed two people.	Must be a loss of total control	As there was some control, the Court of Appeal dismissed automatism.
R v Coley, McGhee and Harris (2013)	D pleaded automatism against a charge of ABH and s 18, having drunk himself into an involuntary state.	Self-induced automatism	The defence was rejected. Even if he was in an involuntary state, this was because of his voluntary fault.

Reform proposals for automatism defence

In 2013, the Law Commission published a discussion paper, *Criminal Liability: Insanity and Automatism*, which proposed:

- abolishing the existing common-law defence of automatism and replacing it with a new defence of automatism triggered 'only where there is a total loss of capacity to control one's actions which is not caused by a recognised medical condition and for which the accused was not culpably responsible'
- defendants who raised the defence due to a recognised medical condition which caused a lack of capacity (such as diabetes or epilepsy) would be required to plead the new 'recognised medical condition defence'
- a successful outcome in raising the new defence would lead to a complete acquittal
- the defence would continue to have the evidential burden, while the legal burden would remain with the prosecution.

Revision activity

Using the internet, compare the cases of *R v Bailey* (1983) and *R v Hardy* (1984).

Intoxication

REVISED

Typical mistake

In essay questions, always use the best cases to illustrate the points being made. For your evaluation, do not ignore the basic evaluative points, such as why intoxication is a defence.

Why is intoxication a defence?

'Intoxication' covers the effects of alcohol, drugs and other substances such as solvents. It is not a defence *per se*, but it can throw doubt on the defendant's ability to form the required *mens rea* for an offence.

The 'defence' is based strongly on public policy. On the one hand, we cannot usually punish someone who cannot form the *mens rea*, but this must be balanced with punishing people who commit crimes after having become intoxicated.

There are two main ways of identifying intoxication in law:
● voluntary, or
● involuntary.

Voluntary intoxication

This is where the defendant chooses to take a substance that they know can cause intoxication. This can be a complete defence to specific intent crimes but will usually not be a defence to crimes of basic intent.

Revision activity

Using the Institute of Alcohol Studies website (www.ias.org.uk), find out the number of alcohol-related criminal offences between 2006 and 2015.

Exam tip

Learn the definitions of intoxication clearly, and make sure you have the correct category of intoxication along with accurate and stimulating evaluation of the defence.

Table 2.6.4 Intoxication and specific intent/basic intent crimes

Specific intent crimes and intoxication	● If the defendant is so intoxicated as to be incapable of forming the *mens rea*, they have a complete defence. ● If the defendant is intoxicated but still has the intent to form the *mens rea* of the offence, they can be guilty of the offence. A drunken intent is still an intent.
Basic intent crimes and intoxication	● Where recklessness is sufficient to prove *mens rea*, the defence will fail if the defendant is voluntarily intoxicated. ● Becoming intoxicated is a reckless course of action and sufficient evidence of *mens rea* for basic intent (recklessly committed) crimes such as ABH or common assault.

Involuntary intoxication

This is when the defendant was unaware they were taking an intoxicating substance. Substances such as prescription drugs may have unexpected or unforeseen effects on the defendant.
● If the defendant while involuntarily intoxicated did not form the *mens rea*, then they are not guilty of the crime.
● If the defendant while involuntarily intoxicated did form the *mens rea*, then they can be guilty of the crime.

Revision activity

Research the case of *R v Lipman* (1970) and explain the difference between specific and basic intent crimes.

Reform proposals for intoxication

In 2009, the Law Commission published a report *Intoxication and Criminal Liability*. The report made a number of recommendations, including the following:
● References to basic and specific intent should be abolished.
● The distinction between voluntary and involuntary intoxication should be retained.
● There should be a primary presumption that the defendant was not intoxicated, and it should be up to the defendant to prove that they were.
● A secondary presumption would be that the defendant was voluntarily intoxicated.
● If the defendant states that they were involuntarily intoxicated, then they would have to prove that they were.

Table 2.6.5 Key cases on intoxication

Case	Facts	Element of intoxication	Legal point
DPP v Beard (1920)	D argued intoxication as a defence to murder.	Definition	D must be completely incapable of forming the *mens rea* for the defence to apply.
A-G for Northern Ireland v Gallagher (1963)	D decided to kill his wife and bought some whiskey and a knife. He drank some of the whiskey before he killed her.	Definition	*Mens rea* was formed to kill his wife before the intoxication. 'Dutch courage' is no defence – a drunken intent is still an intent.
DPP v Majewski (1977)	D drank excessive amounts of alcohol and took drugs. He got into a fight.	Voluntary intoxication and basic intent crimes	His conviction for ABH was upheld due to his recklessness in getting intoxicated.
R v Kingston (1994)	D, a known paedophile, drank a drugged coffee and went on to abuse a young boy as part of an attempt by others to blackmail D.	Involuntary intoxication	Despite the involuntary intoxication, D still knew what he was doing; he just could not stop himself.

Now test yourself

TESTED ☐

1 Explain the *M'Naghten* rules and why they have proved to be controversial.
2 Explain the difference between the decisions in *R v Quick* (1973) and *R v Hennessy* (1989).
3 Explain the importance of the following cases:
   - *Hill v Baxter* (1958)
   - *R v T* (1990)
   - *A-G Ref. No. 2 of 1992* (1993).
4 Explain what is meant by self-induced automatism.
5 Why is intoxication not a 'true' defence?
6 Explain the suggestion that the 'defence' of intoxication is a balance between a defect in the defendant's *mens rea* and the need to protect the public.

Answers online

Exam summary

In the exam, you MAY be asked to:
- respond to a scenario question by advising a defendant, or defendants, whether they can raise a defence where their mental capacity is brought into question
- discuss insanity, automatism, voluntary intoxication or involuntary intoxication in a full-length essay question.

These types of question will each be worth a maximum of 25 marks.

2.7 General defences

The information in this chapter relates to four key 'general' defences:
- self-defence and the prevention of crime
- duress by threats
- duress of circumstances and necessity
- consent.

Self-defence

The most basic form of **self-defence**, defending yourself, comes under the common law. It must be necessary to use force and reasonable to do so.

> **Self-defence:** using reasonable force in order to defend oneself.

Coverage of the defence

The law was clarified in s 76 of the Criminal Justice and Immigration Act 2008 as to the test of reasonableness. It is a complete defence, including to murder, as the defendant's use of force is justified in the circumstances.

The defence is mainly common law and covers:
- actions needed to defend oneself from attack
- actions taken to defend another person
- under s 3 of the Criminal Law Act 1967, actions taken to prevent a crime or arrest an offender, suspected offender or person at large.

> **Exam tip**
>
> Learn the definitions of each necessity defence. Some are easier than others but can appear confusing. To understand each case, apply the facts to your definition and see if you agree with each judge's decision.

Main rules or elements of the defence

Must be necessary to use some force

This is a subjective test, based on the defendant's genuine belief. The defendant can be mistaken but still plead the defence.

Pre-emptive strike is possible and allowable. The defendant can prepare for an attack and there is no duty to retreat.

> **Revision activity**
>
> Research the case of *R v Bird* (1985). Explain whether you think it was necessary to use self-defence.

Degree of force must be reasonable

Following several 'home invasions' before 2007, the 2008 Act's definition acknowledges that in a pressurised situation it might be difficult to weigh up the exact degree of force needed.

The 2008 Act states that such a situation must be assessed by what the defendant honestly and instinctively thought was reasonable. This is an objective test for the jury but based on the defendant's genuine perception of events, and there is no duty to retreat.

However, the force must be used when the danger of the situation is still ongoing and must not be excessive or 'disproportionate'.

> **Revision activity**
>
> Research s 76(4)–(6) of the Criminal Justice and Immigration Act 2008. Explain whether 'householders' are given any special consideration in self-defence cases.

> **Typical mistake**
>
> It is easy to get confused with the elements of self-defence, especially as they can overlap with other defences, so make sure you have a clear and accurate definition.
>
> Some of the cases are also confusing, especially around mistaken self-defence. Make sure you fully understand the judges' rationales behind them.

70   OCR A Level Law

Table 2.7.1 Key cases for self-defence

Case	Facts	Element of self-defence	Legal point
R v Bird (1985)	D gouged out V's eye during a major row after V hit D.	Duty to retreat	B's conviction was quashed. Evidence of a retreat is helpful but not essential.
R v Williams (1987)	D grabbed V, an off-duty police officer, whom he mistakenly thought was attacking a youth.	Mistaken use of self-defence/ prevention of crime	An honest but mistaken belief will allow the defence to operate. The conviction was quashed.
A-G Ref. No. 2 of 1983 (1984)	D kept petrol bombs for protection after his shop had been attacked several times during riots.	Pre-emptive strike	A person is entitled to make preparations in self-defence for a future attack against them.
R v Clegg (1995)	D, a soldier, shot and killed a joyrider whom he thought was a terrorist.	Excessive force	C was not acting in self-defence, as the last shot was excessive force as the 'threat' had passed.
R v Martin (Anthony) (2002)	D shot and killed a burglar.	Excessive force	It was not self-defence, as M shot when V was making his escape.
R v Hussain (2010)	D chased and caught a burglar that he found in his house. H beat the burglar with a cricket bat.	Excessive force	It was not self-defence; violence was just used as retribution. The burglary was over and no one was in danger.
R v Oye (2013)	D was arrested after behaving oddly in a café. He threw plates at police officers and fought with them when arrested.	Psychological characteristics are not relevant	Self-defence was rejected, but an insanity plea was allowed.

Duress by threats

REVISED

Duress by threats is a common-law defence, and therefore its entire definition is based on the decisions of judges rather than statute.

Purpose of the defence

The defence operates where the defendant is forced to commit a crime due to a direct threat. It is common-law based and 'founded on a concession to human frailty', where a person's will is overcome by threats. If the defendant had not been threatened, they would never have committed the offence.

It is available to all crimes committed by a defendant under duress, other than murder, attempted murder and probably treason.

Exam tip

Ensure you learn each of the elements of this defence and can discuss the need for each. Being able to justify or criticise each element will create a more accurate response in an essay.

Definition and rules

The definition has evolved over time and its fundamentals are:

- There must be a threat of death or serious injury (and probably a threat of rape).
- There can be a combination of threats, but a threat of death or serious injury must be present and play a major part.

Revision activity

Using the case of *R v Martin (Anthony)* (2002), explain whether you think the force used was reasonable or not.

Duress by threats: a common-law defence whereby someone committed a crime because they were subject to a threat of death or serious injury.

Revision activity

Is there ever, really, any justification to committing a crime if someone threatens you unless you carry it out?

- The threat can be towards the defendant, a close family member or people for whom the defendant is responsible.
- The two-part *Graham* (1982) test must be satisfied:
  1 Was the defendant compelled to act because they reasonably believed they had a good reason to fear death or serious injury?
  2 Would a sober person of reasonable firmness, sharing the same characteristics as the defendant, have acted in the same way?
- If there is a safe avenue of escape, then this must be pursued, although there may be exceptions to this rule – see *R v Gill* (1963) and *R v Hudson and Taylor* (1971).
- The threat must be effective and be operational when the defendant carries out the crime. The threat of death or serious harm must be immediate or almost immediate.
- There must be a nexus between the crime nominated and the crime committed.
- The defence will usually fail if the defendant associates with people who are known to make threats, for example criminal gangs or terrorists – see *R v Sharp* (1987) and *R v Shepherd* (1987).

Revision activity

Using the internet, compare the cases of:
- *R v Gill* (1963) and *R v Hudson and Taylor* (1971), and
- *R v Sharp* (1987) and *R v Shepherd* (1987).

Typical mistake

Do not forget to mention certain key elements of this defence, such as the requirement of a nexus between the crime and the threat.

Table 2.7.2 **Key cases on duress by threats**

Case	Facts	Element of duress by threats	Legal point
R v Howe (1987)	D was party to the torture and killing of a man. He later did the same while on his own. D said he had been threatened to do so.	Availability	The defence to murder was refused, as one person's life is not worth more than another's.
R v Gotts (1992)	D, 16, was threatened by his father into stabbing his mother to death.	Availability	There was no defence to attempted murder.
R v A (2012)	D stated she had been threatened with rape in order to commit a crime.	Availability	The Court of Appeal stated that rape is acceptable as a threat, but evidence for the threat was rejected. This contention remains *obiter*.
R v Valderrama-Vega (1985)	D imported cocaine, threatened with the exposure of his homosexuality, death and financial ruin.	Type of threat	All threats can be considered but must contain a threat of death. Other kinds of threat are insufficient.
R v Wright (2000)	D was arrested with cocaine but said she had it because her boyfriend had been threatened.	Personal responsibility for another	Persons to whom the threat is made includes those outside the immediate family.
R v Graham (1982)	D lived with his wife and his homosexual lover, K. D helped K kill his wife. D said he was frightened of K.	'Graham' suitability of defence test	A test of general suitability was created.

Case	Facts	Element of duress by threats	Legal point
R v Hasan (2005)	D associated with a violent drug dealer and was threatened into carrying out a burglary/robbery.	Imminence	The threat must be, or be believed to be, immediate or almost immediate.
R v Cole (1994)	D robbed a building society to repay a debt after he and his family were threatened.	Nexus	D chose this course of action to repay debt; there was no threat or duress.

Duress of circumstances and necessity

REVISED ☐

Duress of circumstances and **necessity** are common-law defences. Most of their definitions are based on the decisions of judges rather than statute.

> **Typical mistake**
>
> The reason behind the defences of duress of circumstances and necessity can be difficult to understand. It is not a direct threat of death or violence, but a perceived danger of death or serious injury in the circumstances.

Scope of the defence – duress of circumstances

For this defence, the defendant was forced to react due to the circumstances in which they found themselves, rather than from a direct threat of death or serious injury. This defence has evolved to compensate for the restrictive nature of duress by threats.

The two-part *Martin* test must be satisfied:

1 From an objective point of view, the accused acted reasonably and proportionately to avoid a threat of death or serious harm, and
2 The same two-part *Graham* test applies.

> **Exam tip**
>
> Learn the cases for the two duress defences to identify the differences between them. The *Graham* test applies to threats and the *Martin* test applies to circumstances.

Originally, the defence was raised against driving offences, but this has been extended on a case-by-case basis.

Scope of the defence – necessity

For this defence, the defendant acted to prevent a greater evil from happening. The defence has faced much criticism, and its actual existence was questioned until 1990. While it is currently recognised by the courts, it is limited in scope with very restricted guidelines.

The Court of Appeal in *Re A* (2000) acknowledged the existence of necessity and its parallels with duress of circumstances. In order to successfully plead necessity:

1 the act done must be done only to prevent an act of greater evil from occurring, and
2 the evil must be directed towards the defendant or a person or persons for whom they have responsibility, and
3 the act must be reasonable and proportionate to the evil.

> **Duress of circumstances:** a common-law defence whereby someone committed a crime because of the circumstances in which they found themselves.
>
> **Necessity:** a common-law defence whereby someone committed a crime because it was necessary to avoid a greater evil.

> **Exam tip**
>
> Learn the different circumstances to which the defences of duress by threats, duress of circumstances and necessity apply and the consequent respective tests from *Howe/Gotts*, *Martin* and *Re A*.

Table 2.7.3 Key cases on duress of circumstances/necessity

Case	Facts	Element of duress of circumstances/ necessity	Legal point
R v Willer (1986)	D drove on a pavement to avoid being attacked by youths. There was no threat to carry out a crime.	Origins	The jury should be allowed to consider some type of duress in such circumstances.
R v Conway (1988)	D drove fast after he thought he had been shot at.	Origins	Duress was available if from an objective point of view D was acting to avoid a threat.
R v Martin (1989)	D drove while disqualified because his wife threatened suicide if he did not take their son to work.	Test	The Court of Appeal adapted the two-part *Graham* test.
R v Pommell (1995)	D was found with a gun at his house, saying he had taken it from a man and intended to hand it in.	Extent and availability	The Court of Appeal said whether duress of circumstance applied was a matter for the jury.
DPP v Davis (1994)	D drove while intoxicated to avoid being attacked.	Extent and availability	The convictions were quashed. Duress of circumstances was available.
R v Cairns (1999)	V threw himself on the bonnet of D's car. D warned V to get off. D drove and braked. V fell off and was seriously injured.	Extent and availability	There was a reasonable perceived threat of death or serious injury and the defence was allowed.
R v Dudley and Stephens (1884)	Two sailors cast adrift ate the cabin boy to stay alive.	Existence of necessity as a defence	The defence was refused – no life is worth more than another.
Re F (1990)	A health authority applied to have a severely mentally disabled patient sterilised due to high risk of pregnancy.	Existence of necessity as a defence	Sterilisation was allowed by the House of Lords on grounds of necessity.
Re A (2000)	A health authority applied to have conjoined twins separated, which would result in one twin's death.	Limitation of necessity as a defence	Lord Brook stated and applied a three-part test of necessity, allowing the surgeons the defence if charged with murder.
R v Shayler (2001)	D, a former member of MI5, was charged with breaching the Official Secrets Act 1989.	Limitation of necessity as a defence	There was no defence, and the test in *Re A* applied.

Consent

REVISED

Consent is a defence specific to non-fatal offences and, perhaps, homicide. There have been some unusually decided cases under this defence. Indeed, in *R v Brown and others* (1993) the majority of Law Lords felt that all physical contact is assault, unless the defence of consent applies.

Coverage of the defence

The defence of consent has been essentially developed through the common law. The burden of proof is on the prosecution to prove a lack of consent.

Revision activity

Using the internet, explain the decision in *R v Pommell* (1995).

Consent: express or implied permission from the 'victim' for the defendant to carry out the injury.

There are several constituent parts that must be proved in order for the defendant to raise the defence successfully:

- There must be real consent.
- Consent must be obtained without fraud.
- Force applied must be for socially acceptable reasons.

Main rules or elements of the defence

There must be real consent

The person consenting must be able to understand to what they are consenting.

A child or a person with learning difficulties may give consent, but this does not mean the law will recognise the consent as real, since such a person may not fully comprehend what it is they are consenting to – see *Burrell v Harmer* (1967).

Consent must be obtained without fraud

Fraudulent activity may negate the victim's apparent consent to injury, only if the victim is deceived as to the:

- defendant's identity, see *R v Richardson* (1998), or
- 'nature and quality' of the defendant's actions, see *R v Tabassum* (2000).

Force applied must be for socially acceptable reasons

The defence is a balance between allowing force for socially acceptable reasons through an individual's autonomy balanced against the need for public protection. Such a balance should change as public opinion changes.

Table 2.7.4 Key cases for consent

Case	Facts	Element of consent	Legal point
R v Donovan (1934)	D caned a girl for sexual gratification, causing her some discomfort and bruising.	Definition	An act is not simply lawful just because the person to whose detriment it is done consents to it.
A-G Ref. No. 6 of 1980 (1981)	There was a street fight between two consenting adults.	Coverage of defence	There was no consent, based on public policy considerations.
R v Slingsby (1995)	D fisted V's vagina with her consent. His signet ring caused internal injuries and V died.	Coverage of defence	Consent can be a defence to manslaughter but not to murder.
Burrell v Harmer (1967)	D caused injury to two boys of 12 and 13 by tattooing them.	Real consent	Where V consents but is unable to appreciate the nature of the act, this is not real consent.
R v Clarence (1888)	D infected his wife with an STD during unprotected consensual sex.	Real consent	There was no offence as the wife consented to sex with her husband.
R v Dica (2004)	D infected Vs with HIV during unprotected consensual sex.	Real consent	While the Vs consented to sex, they did not consent to HIV, overruling *Clarence*.
R v Billinghurst (1978)	D punched another player during a rugby match, fracturing his jaw.	Consent in sport	Rugby players consent to a degree of force during a match, but they do not consent to being punched.

Case	Facts	Element of consent	Legal point
R v Jones (1986)	Ds gave another boy the 'birthday bumps' and tossed him in the air, injuring him.	Consent in 'horse-play'	Ds' belief in V's consent in rough horseplay was sufficient for a defence against a charge of GBH.
R v Aitkin (1992)	During an RAF initiation ceremony, V's flame-proof overalls were set on fire.	Consent in 'horse-play'	V can give consent to the risk of accidental injury in the course of rough, undisciplined play.
R v Coney (1882)	Spectators at a prize fight were charged with aiding and abetting.	Consent and fighting	Ds were convicted since prize-fighting is illegal and the fighters' consent to injury provided no excuse.
R v Brown and others (1993)	Homosexual sadomasochists were charged and convicted with ss 47 and 20, despite consent of the 'victims'.	Consent and sexual activity	The acts were simply violence masked as sexual activity and against public policy.
R v Richardson (1998)	A suspended dentist continued to practice.	Consent and fraud	D's identity was as a dentist, albeit a suspended dentist, and therefore there was no fraud as to identity.
R v Tabassum (2000)	Several women's breasts were examined by D who claimed to be carrying out cancer research.	Consent and fraud	The consent was obtained through fraud as D had no medical training – the Vs consented to the act, but not as to its quality.
R v BM (2018)	A tattooist added 'body modifications' to his list of services and was charged with three offences under s 18, having removed one customer's ear and another's nipple, and carried out the division of a customer's tongue to replicate that of a reptile.	Consent and body modification	While the customers had consented, the Court of Appeal stated that personal autonomy provided no justification in the three cases and that such body modification should not be placed in the special category. This allowed consent as a defence where D inflicts an injury of ABH or above.

Now test yourself

TESTED

1 What are the three situations in which self-defence can be used?
2 Explain how the courts decide whether it was necessary to use force in self-defence and whether it was reasonable to do so.
3 Explain why there is a defence of duress by threats.
4 What is the *Graham* test, and why it was introduced?
5 Explain the differences between the defences of duress by threats, duress of circumstances and necessity.
6 Explain how the defence of duress of circumstances was extended in *R v Martin* (1989).
7 Explain the defence of consent in relation to fraud.

Answers online

Exam summary

In the exam, you MAY be asked to:
● respond to a scenario question by advising a defendant, or defendants, whether they can raise a general defence where an offence has potentially occurred
● discuss self-defence, duress by threats, duress of circumstances, necessity or consent in a full-length essay question.

These types of question will each be worth a maximum of 25 marks.

2.8 Preliminary offences

This chapter outlines three key areas of attempted crimes:
- *actus reus* of **attempt**
- *mens rea* of attempt
- attempting the 'impossible'.

Definition and components

Criminal law can punish a defendant who tries but fails to carry out a crime. Attempted crime is defined under s 1(1) of the Criminal Attempts Act 1981:

> 'If, with intent to commit an offence to which this section applies, a person does an act which is more than merely preparatory to the commission of the offence, he is guilty of attempting to commit the offence.'

Before 1981, an attempted crime was decided by any one of a number of common-law tests, for example last act, Rubicon or series of acts test. The common-law tests could produce different results for the same defendant and were used unscrupulously by defence lawyers, so the Criminal Attempts Act 1981 was passed in order to clarify the law.

> **Attempt:** if, with intent to commit an offence under s 1(1) of the Criminal Attempts Act 1981, a person does an act which is more than merely preparatory to the commission of the offence, they are guilty of attempting to commit the offence.

Typical mistake

While pre-1981 Act common-law cases provide some guidance, cases after 1981 give a more accurate interpretation of what is, or is not, an attempted crime. Do not unnecessarily discuss the pre-1981 common-law tests.

Actus reus of attempt

An attempt must be:
- a positive act, not an omission
- an act that is 'more than merely preparatory to the commission of the offence' (MTMP).

Therefore, an act which is 'merely preparatory' (MP) is not an attempt, but could be another offence, such as conspiracy, going equipped etc.

Exam tip

Learn the statutory definitions and the relevant MP and MTMP cases to support your answers. Use cases confidently and accurately. Many scenario questions will have their basis in an actual case, for example *R v Campbell* (1990), which should give you a clear, if meandering, steer to the answer.

Revision activity

What is meant by an omission in criminal law? Refer back to Chapter 2.2 to check your answer.

Table 2.8.1 Cases of 'merely preparatory' (MP)

Case	Facts	Offence attempted	Ratio decidendi
R v Gullefer (1987)	D tried to stop a greyhound race to recover his stake, as his dog was losing.	Theft	Court of Appeal: MP – D had to go and ask for his money back first.
R v Campbell (1990)	D approached a post office wearing a crash helmet and carrying a knife and threatening note. He was arrested outside by police.	Robbery	Court of Appeal: MP – D did not enter the post office and threaten staff.
R v Geddes (1996)	D was seen in the boys' toilets and ran off when challenged. Later, his rucksack was found nearby containing rope, a large knife and masking tape.	False imprisonment	Court of Appeal: MP – D had not tried to commit the crime itself.
R v Nash (1999)	Two letters in the street were addressed to 'Paper Boy', inviting V to engage in acts of gross indecency. A third letter offered employment. Police set up a 'sting' in the local park using a volunteer to meet D as per letter 3.	Procure an act of gross indecency	Court of Appeal: letter 3 was MP; as it did not involve a request for an act of gross indecency, it could not be an attempt of such.

Table 2.8.2 Cases of 'more than merely preparatory' (MTMP)

Case	Facts	Offence attempted	Ratio decidendi
R v Boyle and Boyle (1987)	D1 and D2 were found standing next to a door with a broken lock and hinge.	Burglary	MTMP – all Ds had to do was enter the building to commit the full crime.
R v Jones (1990)	D got into V's car and pointed a shotgun at him.	Murder	MTMP – all D had to do was pull the trigger to commit the full crime.
A-G Ref. No. 1 of 1992 (1993)	D dragged V into a shed to have sex with her but could not maintain an erection.	Rape	MTMP – all D had to do was penetrate V to commit the full crime.

Mens rea of attempt

This is normally an intent to commit the full crime and recklessness will not suffice – see *A-G Ref. No. 3 of 1992* (1994) and *R v Khan* (1990) below.

> **Revision activity**
>
> Using the internet, research the case of *R v Khan* (1990). How did this case extend the law on attempt?

Table 2.8.3 Key cases on the mens rea of attempt

Case	Facts	Offence attempted	Ratio decidendi
R v Whybrow (1951)	D wired a soap dish next to the bath to electrocute V.	Murder	Court of Appeal: *mens rea* is an intent to kill for attempted murder.
R v Easom (1971)	See Table 2.5.2.		
R v Millard (1987)	D was arrested after pushing against a wooden fence at a football match.	Criminal damage	There was no attempt, no intent and recklessness will not suffice.
A-G Ref. No. 3 of 1992 (1994)	D threw a petrol bomb at a car containing four men.	Arson with intent to endanger life	Need intent to damage property but could be reckless as to endangering life.

Case	Facts	Offence attempted	*Ratio decidendi*
R v Khan (1990)	D was convicted of attempted rape, being unsuccessful in trying to have sex with the victim.	Rape	The conviction was upheld, despite the trial judge's direction that the Crown only had to prove an intent to have sex knowing V was not consenting or not caring.
R v Pace and Rogers (2014)	D1 and D2 bought what they suspected as being stolen scrap metal. The metal was not stolen but sold to them by the police as test purchases (*R v Khan* distinguished)	Conversion of criminal property	The Court of Appeal stated D must have an intent to commit all the elements of the offence, not just some of them. A suspicion was insufficient.

Attempting an 'impossible' crime

REVISED

The Criminal Attempts Act 1981 introduced two new offences in relation to attempting the impossible.

Factual impossibility

Section 1(2):

'A person may be guilty of attempting to commit an offence to which this section applies even though the facts are such that the commission of the offence is impossible.'

Legal impossibility

Section 1(3):

'In any case where –

(a) apart from this subsection a person's intention would not be regarded as having amounted to an intent to commit an offence; but

(b) if the facts of the case had been as he believed them to be, his intention would be so regarded,

then, for the purposes of subsection (1) above, he shall be regarded as having had an intent to commit that offence.'

Table 2.8.4 Cases of attempting the 'impossible'

Case	Facts	Offence attempted	*Ratio decidendi*
Anderton v Ryan (1985)	D admitted to the police that she bought a video recorder which she thought was stolen.	Handling stolen goods	House of Lords quashed the conviction, ignoring the 1981 Act. D could not be convicted for something she believed but turned out to be wrong.
R v Shivpuri (1986)	D, a drugs courier, was arrested with what he thought was heroin but was actually a harmless vegetable-type substance.	Knowingly concerned in dealing with a controlled drug	Overruling *Anderton* above, D was convicted of attempting the impossible.
R v Jones (2007)	D tried to solicit young girls for sex, including 'Amy' who he thought was 12, but was, in fact, an undercover policewoman.	Inciting a child under 13 to engage in sexual activity	Even although 'Amy' was not a real 12-year-old girl, D was still convicted for attempting the impossible.

1. Explain why there is a law on attempted crimes.
2. Discuss why the decisions in *R v Geddes* (1996) and *R v Campbell* (1990) are controversial.
3. Discuss why the decisions in *R v Easom* (1971) and *R v Millard* (1987) are controversial.
4. Explain the purpose behind the law on attempting the impossible.
5. The Criminal Attempts Act 1981 has provided clarity to the law on attempted crimes. Discuss.

Answers online

Revision activity

Would the defendant in *R v Jones* (2007) have been convicted of such an offence before the passing of the 1981 Act?

Exam summary

In the exam, you MAY be asked to:
- respond to a scenario question by advising a defendant, or defendants, whether they can be convicted of an attempted crime
- discuss attempted crimes in a full-length essay question relevant to the criminal law.

These types of question will each be worth a maximum of 25 marks.

2.9 Evaluation

In this chapter, we critically evaluate:
- fatal offences against the person
- non-fatal offences against the person
- offences against property
- defences
- reform of all the above.

Fatal offences against the person

Critical evaluation

Table 2.9.1 **Critical evaluation of fatal offences against the person**

Area of criticism	Criticism	Justified?	Unjustified?
Definition of murder	It is described as a 'rickety structure set upon shaky foundations'.	There has been piecemeal development through common law with little involvement by Parliament.	The definition is sound and developed by eminent judges where rare idiosyncrasies are challenged.
Intent to cause GBH (implied malice aforethought)	If D intends to cause GBH and death occurs, then D is guilty of murder.	If D intends to cause a level of serious harm which results in the death of V, then they must take that responsibility with their actions.	This makes murder too broad an offence, especially as D may not realise/want death to occur.
Mens rea for murder – direct intent	There is no statutory guidance or definition.	A person's intent is a person's intent. Juries can make up their own minds based on common sense.	An intent is not such a straightforward concept, and the common law has had to provide definitions should a jury require such.
Mens rea for murder – oblique intent	D may not have had the true desire or set out to bring about death, but death was a virtual certainty.	If D realised subjectively (s 8 CJA 1967) that it is almost inevitable or virtually certain that their actions would lead to death, then this must be intent.	An intent should be an absolute intent, and not something that might have been likely to have happened, since it may not have happened, but instead it just, by chance, did happen. A chance surely cannot be seen as a true desire to bring about a consequence.
Self-defence and murder	Self-defence is a defence to murder.	D must respond to a threat with reasonable force, even if it is an honest but unreasonable belief.	A D who uses unreasonable force against a threat will be treated in the same way as a calculated killer.
Defence of duress and murder	There is no defence even if D finds themselves in an extreme situation.	The law should not allow a coward to act in killing another simply because they themselves are threatened with death.	There may be some situations where certain types of people may be more susceptible to threats and are genuinely unable to resist a threat.
Mandatory life sentence for murder	If convicted with murder, D is given a life sentence.	If D intentionally takes the life of another, then they should bear the responsibility for the duration of their own life.	A judge can set minimum sentences, so that D does not have to spend the rest of their life in jail.

Area of criticism	Criticism	Justified?	Unjustified?
Euthanasia	Consent is no defence to an intentional killing.	No one should be allowed to consent to their own murder.	If life is so unbearable, then a person who is unable to take their own life should be allowed to use another person for that purpose.
Voluntary manslaughter	The definitions are complicated and out of date.	Sections 52, 54 and 55 of the Coroners and Justice Act 2009 replaced previous involuntary manslaughter defences to murder.	Definitions under the Coroners and Justice Act 2009 are complicated and unnecessarily lengthy and overcompensate previous criticisms, e.g. misogyny.
Involuntary manslaughter	There are two, possibly three, types of involuntary manslaughter, with piecemeal common-law-driven definitions.	Definitions, including the potential reckless manslaughter, cover different situations and are adaptable under the common law.	Definitions are unclear and complicated, particularly the level of negligence required in gross negligence manslaughter. Parliament must redefine and simplify the definitions.

Ideas for reform

The 2006 Law Commission report *Murder, Manslaughter and Infanticide* (Law Com No. 304) proposed the following.

For murder

First-degree murder would carry a mandatory life sentence where the defendant intended either:

● to kill, or
● to cause serious bodily harm being aware their actions posed a serious risk of death.

Second-degree murder would carry a maximum life sentence where the defendant:

● had intent for first-degree murder but pleads one of the partial defences, or
● intends to do serious injury but was not aware of a serious risk of death, or
● was aware of the serious risk of death and had intent to cause some injury, a fear of injury or a risk of injury – thus upgrading 'reckless manslaughter' to murder.

Manslaughter – voluntary manslaughter was reformed by the Coroners and Justice Act 2009 and, in consequence, there would be no need to refer to 'involuntary' manslaughter, simply manslaughter.

However, in its 2008 consultation paper *Murder, Manslaughter and Infanticide: Proposals for Reform of the Law*, the Ministry of Justice was dismissive of the proposals and felt that such reforms 'may be considered at a later stage'.

For manslaughter

Unlawful act (constructive) manslaughter would occur when death is caused by a criminal act where the defendant:

● intended to cause injury, or
● had an awareness that the act would involve a serious risk of causing injury.

Gross negligence manslaughter would occur where:

- death occurred as a result of the defendant's conduct falling far below what could reasonably be expected in the circumstances, and
- there was a risk that their conduct would cause death, and
- the risk would be obvious to a reasonable person and the defendant had the capacity to appreciate this risk.

Non-fatal offences against the person

REVISED

Critical evaluation

Table 2.9.2 Critical evaluation of non-fatal offences against the person

Area of criticism	Criticism	Justified?	Unjustified?
Offences Against the Person Act 1861	The Act consolidated, but did not rationalise, the definitions of non-fatal offences.	There was no attempt to set out a new and coherent set of offences, leaving ambiguities in the definitions.	Most alleged ambiguities have their genesis from Ds trying to avoid conviction by aggravating the existing definitions' brevity.
Offences Against the Person Act 1861	The hierarchical order of seriousness of offence according to injury does not run in chronological order.	The least serious offence of ABH is charged under s 47, the next serious offence is charged under s 20, while the most serious is charged under s 18.	While unusual, perhaps the reverse chronological order does not have an impact on, for example, conviction rates etc.
Criminal Justice Act 1988	The Act does not provide a statutory definition of common assault.	Common assault is defined under the common law in various but nuanced ways.	Judges have defined common assault in far greater clarity than the other non-fatal offences.
Common assault	There is confusion to the lay person over the word 'assault'.	The public perception of an 'assault' is a physical attack and not, as it is under law, a threat.	The media use the word 'assault' as a generic term to simplify the news, and this creates a common misconception that some sort of violence, or at least contact, is required.
Technical assault	(a) Words alone can constitute a technical assault, e.g. a letter or an email can be sufficient. (b) A silent telephone call can be a technical assault.	Despite no threat of force then and there, the courts have allowed a fear of violence at some time, not excluding the immediate future.	The courts have stretched the definition of 'immediate' to such a degree that it is not synonymous with 'instantaneous' which may be confusing.
Battery	There are conflicting cases over whether there must be hostility by D to satisfy a battery.	The normal jostling or brushing past in everyday life must be forgiven, but to move physical contact up to a criminal offence must require a degree of hostility.	Potentially, low-level incidents are seen as lawful when the D's intention or recklessness was to act unlawfully.

Area of criticism	Criticism	Justified?	Unjustified?
Common assault – *mens rea*	Common assault is a basic intent crime and so can be committed recklessly where D can be intoxicated and not recall the events surrounding the infliction or threat of force.	For public policy reasons, the courts have allowed excessive drinking or drug-taking as evidence of a reckless course of action justifying the formation of *mens rea*.	Even if excessive drinking or drug-taking is a reckless course of action, this could be hours before the point at which the *actus reus* is carried out.
Section 47 assault occasioning actual bodily harm	The Act does not provide a statutory definition under s 47 and the language used is antiquated.	The offence is historic and the literal definition is more than the physical touching of a battery as there must be actual harm to the body but which falls short of grievous.	The lack of a specific definition has led to confusion and the necessary introduction of common-law and CPS guidelines, neither of which have legislative backing.
Section 20 malicious wounding or inflicting grievous bodily harm	The Act does not provide a statutory definition under s 20 and the language used is antiquated.	The offence is historic and the literal definition of a wound and grievous bodily harm is sufficient.	The lack of a specific definition has led to confusion and the necessary introduction of common-law and CPS guidelines, neither of which have legislative backing.
Section18 wounding with intent or causing grievous bodily harm	The Act does not provide a statutory definition under s 18 and the language used is antiquated.	The offence is historic and the literal definition of a wound and grievous bodily harm is sufficient.	The lack of a definition has led to confusion and the necessary introduction of common-law and CPS guidelines, neither of which have legislative backing.
Section 20 'inflict' and s 18 'cause'	The Act appears to differentiate the method of carrying out the offences under each section.	Lord Hope stated in *Burstow* that for all practical purposes there is no difference between the two words.	If the words are synonymous, why did the legislators in 1861 not use the same word? Lord Hope did qualify his opinion in *Burstow* by saying 'inflict' suggests something unpleasant, while 'cause' may not do so.
Maximum sentences for common assault under s 39	There is a huge jump from a maximum of six months' imprisonment for common assault to five years' imprisonment for the next serious offence under s 47.	This creates a problem as to where the court draws the line between a s 39 injury and a s 47 injury?	The sentence reflects the difference in severity of injury between s 39 and s 47.
Maximum sentences for ss 47, 20 and 18	Sections 47 and 20 carry the same maximum sentence of five years' imprisonment, while ss 20 and 18 carry different sentences for the same level of injury – wounding/GBH: five years' and life imprisonment respectively.	These maximum sentences reflect the level/severity of the *mens rea* and injury.	The *mens rea* and severity of injury are not sufficiently differentiated between these offences.

Ideas for reform

There has been much suggestion for reform in this area, notably in recent years:

- In 1980, the Criminal Law Revision Committee made recommendations in its 14th report, *Offences Against the Person*.
- The Law Commission's Draft Criminal Code of 1989 adopted the 1980 proposals.
- The 1993 Law Commission report *Legislating the Criminal Code: Offences Against the Person and General Principles* again adopted the 1980 proposals.
- In 1998, the Home Office published a consultation document *Violence: Reforming the Offences Against the Person Act 1861*.
- The 2015 Law Commission report *Offences Against the Person – Modernising the Law on Violence* aimed at modifying the previous recommendations already suggested by the Home Office's Draft Bill in 1998 (based on previous Law Commission recommendations) to bring *inter alia* the main non-fatal offences into a scheme of offences that:
  - is structured in a more logical manner
  - provides greater clarity in the offences' interpretations, and
  - ensures cases are tried in the most appropriate level of court given the gravity and complexity of the circumstances.

Law Commission proposals 2015

Assault and battery

The Law Commission has recommended that reform to assault and battery would provide the following two offences:

1 Physical assault: where a person intentionally or recklessly applies force to or causes an impact on the body of another, without the consent of that other.

2 Threatened assault: where a person intentionally or recklessly causes another to think that any such force or impact is or may be imminent, and that other does not consent to the conduct in question.

Offences Against the Person Act 1861

The Law Commission referred to the old ss 18, 20 and 47 as 'the injury offences', and the draft Bill organises the three offences from most serious to least serious:

- Clause 1: intentionally causing serious injury; maximum sentence of life imprisonment (in effect replacing s 18).
- Clause 2: recklessly causing serious injury; maximum sentence of seven years' imprisonment (in effect replacing s 20).
- Clause 3: intentionally or recklessly causing injury; maximum sentence of five years' imprisonment (in effect replacing s 47).

In summary, the proposed new offences are different from the current law in three ways:

1 The mention of wounding is specifically removed from ss 20 and 18 and categorised under 'serious injury', if it is such a 'serious injury'. Alternatively, it will be charged under Clause 3 if it is not 'serious' but still an 'injury'. Therefore, under the three new offences a wound can be either a 'serious injury' or simply an 'injury', which will remain a matter of fact. GBH is clearly replaced by the more definable 'serious injury' and again is a matter for the jury to decide.

2 The Law Commission was specific that to satisfy 'recklessly' under Clause 2's 'recklessly causing serious injury', the defendant must foresee 'a risk of serious injury' during their act that led to the 'serious injury'.

3 Under Clause 3, the replacement for s 47, the offence does not need an assault or battery to occur; simply any means of causing an injury would be acceptable.

Short, snappy, understandable and specific. Too good to be true? At the time of writing, the proposals remain as such and given the current political turmoil in the UK, such reform on non-fatal offences may appear a low priority.

Offences against property

REVISED

Critical evaluation

Table 2.9.3 Critical evaluation of theft, robbery and burglary

Area of criticism	Criticism	Justified?	Unjustified?
Section 3 appropriation	The definition is broad.	Appropriation can occur in many ways and while appearing theoretic are perfectly acceptable as a means of assuming the rights of others.	This is not what Parliament intended and it puts strain on other parts of the definition of theft, especially dishonesty.
Section 3 appropriation	Section 3 does not cover continuing acts.	Certain judgments in robbery have allowed for pragmatic reasons that appropriation can be a continuing act.	This is inconsistent with robbery, where continuing acts have been successfully prosecuted.
Section 4 property	The definition is broad.	The definition must cover items that can be appropriated, and further guidance is given for more unusual items.	In effect, anything can be stolen. This covers too much ground and is complicated by reference to flowers and animals.
Section 5 belonging to another	The definition is broad.	The definition covers not only the owner but also theft from a person who is in control of the property but not the true owner.	This is unhelpful, since D can steal their own property, which seems ridiculous.
Section 2 dishonesty	There is no definition in the Act.	Juries are left to decide, using their common sense, whether D was dishonest, which will evolve as society changes.	Differences in opinion as to what is dishonest can lead to different outcomes for Ds, and an uncomfortable civil-law test defined in *Ivey* (2017) is to be used.
Section 6 intent to permanently deprive	Is this unnecessary?	There must be some degree of permanency of the deprivation, or else it would just seem D was 'messing about' or not seriously contemplating theft at all.	The idea that D must absolutely intend to prevent V from getting their property back seems too high a standard. Simply hiding the item should be enough.
Sections 8 and 9	Theft must be committed for robbery, but an intent to steal or attempted theft is allowed for burglary.	Burglary must be a broader offence in order to cover all permutations on D's mind.	There should be parity between the offences to avoid confusion by juries.

Area of criticism	Criticism	Justified?	Unjustified?
Section 8	There is no definition of force.	The level of force can be low, which covers nudges and pushes.	The level of force should be high to differentiate between a simple theft, e.g. pickpocketing, and the more serious robbery carrying a potential life sentence.
Section 9	There are no definitions of entry, building or trespasser.	This allows a wide interpretation to convict a D who clearly intends or attempts to steal etc. from inside somewhere.	The definition could lead to strange results where D was not physically inside somewhere but could be guilty of burglary.

Ideas for reform

In its 2002 report *Fraud*, the Law Commission stated that a legal definition of dishonesty was 'elusive' and that it was 'unaware of any proposed definitions which the law could adopt'.

Mental capacity defences

Critical evaluation

Table 2.9.4 **Critical evaluation of mental capacity defences**

Area of criticism	Criticism	Justified?	Unjustified?
Definition of insanity	It dates from 1843 and has failed to keep up with modern medical definitions.	The test is robust and as such Parliament, despite various suggestions for reform, has not intervened.	This explains why the defence is underused and medical professionals are at odds and do not apply the correct test.
Definition of insanity	The label of 'insane' is outdated.	No matter what term is used, society will find ways to stigmatise the condition.	The term is discriminatory and offensive and stigmatises mental illnesses such as epilepsy, diabetes etc.
Case law on insanity	Case law is inconsistent.	Ds with the same condition, e.g. diabetes, can be deemed insane or not insane, but this is due to the source of the 'trigger' in committing an offence, which may, or may not be the illness itself. See *R v Quick* (1973) and *R v Hennessey* (1989).	It produces results that are inconsistent and contrary to common sense, e.g. someone with diabetes or epilepsy can be deemed insane.
Definition of automatism	It is too easy to plead.	D might lie and say they were having a sneezing fit or a spasm.	Common law establishes strict guidelines for the defence.
Definition of automatism	Case law is inconsistent in relation to PTSD.	There is a conflict between the decisions in *R v Narborough* (2004) and *R v T* (1990).	Differences in facts allow 'stress' in some cases but not others, depending on the severity.
Definition of intoxication	There is a distinction between crimes of specific and basic intent.	It seems reasonable to argue that getting drunk is a reckless course of action and therefore such *mens rea* is proved.	*Mens rea* is formed, potentially, hours before the unplanned criminal conduct satisfying the *actus reus*.
Definition of intoxication	There is requirement of foresight of a particular risk.	*Majewski* recklessness does not require foresight of a particular risk for public policy reasons, or else any intoxicated D could plead the defence having not seen the risk while getting intoxicated.	*Majewski* recklessness does not require foresight of a particular risk, which is at odds with *Cunningham* recklessness.

Ideas for reform

See Chapter 2.6 for reform of insanity, automatism and intoxication defences.

General defences

REVISED

Critical evaluation

Table 2.9.5 Critical evaluation of general defences

Area of criticism	Criticism	Justified?	Unjustified?
Definition of self-defence	The defence is restrictive as to the force allowed.	A restrictive defence prevents unwarranted violence.	Juries have to place themselves in D's position to be empathetic in an imaginary situation that D actually experienced.
Mistaken use of self-defence	Mistaken use of self-defence is allowed.	Placed in a unique situation, D can make an honest mistake as to the use of self-defence.	An unscrupulous D could argue their extreme reaction in the use of force was an honest belief.
D's characteristics in self-defence	Characteristics are not relevant to whether D used reasonable force.	This would require so much evidence and nuanced medical opinion even among similar Ds in different cases.	Arguably they are relevant under s 76 CJIA 2008 and CJA 2009 in relation to self-control.
Successful plea of defence by threats	Duress by threat is a complete defence.	D was forced to act through a threat of death or serious injury.	D is given an excuse after committing a crime rather than standing up to the person making the threat.
Duress and s 18 OAPA 1861	Duress is available for s 18.	The law is clear – duress is not available for murder but is available for lesser offences, despite the idiosyncrasy under homicide law.	Intentional GBH leading to a death is not allowed, but intentional GBH where V survives a serious injury is allowed under the defence.
D's characteristics for duress by threats	A potential objective test for duress by threats is include in *Graham*.	There must be a standard of composure incorporated into the reasonable person, or else any characteristic, however small, would need to be considered.	Low IQ is unlikely to be taken into consideration when looking at the reasonable person, despite making such a D more susceptible to threats.
Definitions of duress of circumstances and necessity	There is overlap between duress of circumstances and necessity.	As the necessity defence had been stifled and dismissed at the common law, it was important to develop an alternative broader defence to duress by threats.	Development of duress of circumstances and the resurrection of necessity has led to confusion and overlap in the law.
Consent – boundaries of defence	Autonomy allows serious injury to be caused, e.g. tattooing, boxing, martial arts etc.	The public should be able to consent to a degree of injury, even in non-therapeutic situations.	It is difficult to reconcile criminalising serious and deliberate sports injuries in football but not those in boxing and martial arts.
Sexual activities and consent	Consent law condones violent behaviour during alleged sexual activity.	Autonomy, short of intentional serious injury, should be allowed in sexual activity if it provides pleasure for the participants, even where they may be considered by some to be extreme acts.	Current opinion seems to allow a level of violence that was previously outlawed, e.g. S&M activities.
Consent and euthanasia	Consent is no defence to an intentional killing.	No one should be allowed to consent to their own murder.	If life is so unbearable, then a person who is unable to take their own life should be allowed to use another person for that purpose.

Ideas for reform

Self-defence

Section 43 of the Crime and Courts Act 2013 amended s 76 of the Criminal Justice and Immigration Act 2008, allowing a 'householder' to use 'disproportionate' force against an intruder and still be able to raise self-defence.

Duress

- The 1993 Law Commission report *Legislating the Criminal Code: Offences Against the Person and General Principles* recommended that duress should be available to all crimes.
- The 2005 Law Commission consultation paper *A New Homicide Act* recommended that duress should be a partial defence to murder.
- The 2006 Law Commission report *Murder, Manslaughter and Infanticide* recommended that duress should be a defence to murder.

Exam practice

Questions 1 and 2 could appear on the AS exam paper. Questions 3–5 could appear on the A Level exam paper only.

1 Explain what is meant by *mens rea* in criminal law. [10 marks]
2 Rival supporters Sue and Tara are going to a football match. Sue decides to trip Tara up, as she is annoyed by Tara's loud singing and chanting. Sue sticks out her foot and Tara does trip, but she falls headlong into some bushes to which she suffers an allergic reaction which lasts several days. Advise how the law relating to non-fatal offences against the person will apply to Sue. [10 marks]
3 Angela's brother Bob and his friend Charlie were sailing. Bob fell in the water and died. Angela believes Charlie could have saved Bob. Angela is depressed and her doctor has prescribed medication. The instructions state she must take one pill a day and not drink alcohol. At Bob's funeral, Angela is wearing a brooch he gave to her. She hears Charlie say that Bob was a dangerous sailor who 'had it coming'. Angela is upset and takes one of her prescribed pills, washed down with a glass of sherry. An hour later, Charlie comes and hugs her. She runs off and falls, breaking her brooch. Angela sees Charlie laugh. She grabs a sharp knife from the lunch table and stabs Charlie several times, killing him. Advise whether Angela can avoid liability for murder by using the defences of loss of control or diminished responsibility. [25 marks]
4 Dave and his friend Ernie approach Farah, who is using a mobile phone to show directions. Dave puts his fingers in his pocket to look like a gun and Ernie pulls the phone from Farah. Farah tries to hold on but Ernie knocks her to the ground and runs off with the phone. Dave has a key to his neighbour's flat and the next day he decides to sell his neighbour's television. Dave and Ernie go to the flat but once inside they discover that the television is missing. Ernie is angry and drinks a bottle of vodka belonging to Dave's neighbour. Advise whether Dave and Ernie are guilty of robbery and burglary, including any defences they may raise. [25 marks]
5 'Reform for non-fatal offences is long overdue.' Discuss the extent to which this statement is accurate. [25 marks]

ONLINE

3 Law making

The English legal system and the nature of law are divided into three sections on the OCR A Level Law H415 specification. The second section, *Law making*, is compulsory and is assessed in Section A of the Component 2 exam paper.

This chapter explores your ability to explain, describe or discuss:
- parliamentary law making
- delegated legislation
- statutory interpretation
- judicial precedent
- law reform
- European Union law.

Do not view this chapter in isolation: it complements two other chapters – *The legal system* and *The nature of law* – as well as the substantive law chapters. Use the information where necessary to appreciate how the English legal system operates, and also the impact of sources of law on substantive areas of law such as criminal law and tort law.

3.1 Parliamentary law making

Influences on Parliament

REVISED

Where do the ideas come from for new laws? This is often government policy, but who influences this?

Table 3.1.1 Influences on Parliament with evaluation

Type of influence	Example	Advantages	Disadvantages
Political When a general election is called, the political parties publish a manifesto, which amounts to a promise of what new laws they will introduce.	The Hunting Act 2004 followed the promise by the Labour Party to outlaw fox hunting if elected (also a great example of using the Parliament Acts 1911 and 1949).	Each political party has its proposals ready. A government majority means that most of the Bills it introduces will be passed.	While it is easy to make a promise, it is much more difficult when in power to fulfil that promise, particularly without an overall majority (as the Conservative/Liberal Democrat coalition found in 2010–15).
Public opinion These are the views of members of the general public in the UK. This is a strong influence upon Parliament, as those aged over 18 are entitled to vote in general elections.	Public opinion was mixed as to whether or not the UK should leave the EU. In a national referendum in 2016, the majority of those who voted chose to leave the EU. This allowed Parliament to legislate in 2017, to allow this to happen.	Where the majority of the public has certain beliefs or demands, then Parliament can safely pass legislation on that issue.	Gauging public opinion can be notoriously difficult. Realistically, no one can definitively say that the majority of the public believe one way or another in a specific issue.

Type of influence	Example	Advantages	Disadvantages
Media When there is strong public opinion about an issue, the government may bow to it. Where an issue is given a high profile in the media, it may add to the weight of public opinion.	Following the Dunblane massacre in 1996, private ownership of handguns was banned.	The UK's free press is able to criticise government policy or bring any other issue to the attention of the government using public opinion.	Responding too quickly to high-profile incidents leads to poorly drafted law, e.g. the Dangerous Dogs Act 1991. Media companies can manipulate the news to create public opinion.
Pressure groups Sectional: represent the interests of a particular group of people Causal: promote a particular cause	In 2007, laws against smoking in public places were introduced because of public and medical opinion.	Pressure groups often bring important scientific discoveries to the government's attention, e.g. the damage being done by greenhouse gases and other pollutants.	There are occasions when two pressure groups have conflicting interests, e.g. the League Against Cruel Sports wanted to ban fox hunting but the Countryside Alliance wanted it to continue.
Lobbyists/lobbying firms These are usually professionals or organisations who try to persuade or influence governments to enact, amend or repeal legislation that affects their or their representatives' interests.	Most multi-national companies have or use lobbyists, e.g. Bell Pottiger Private.	Like any service industry, citizens or organisations can approach a lobbyist to represent and present their interests direct to government ministers or their departments, where lobbyists have political contacts.	Lobbyists are expensive and, in consequence, may only represent those citizens or groups who can afford to pay for their services. Accusations of dubious and corrupt methods, e.g. 'cash for questions', have been made against lobbyists.

The Law Commission is the law reform body (see Chapter 3.5 for how it influences changes to the law).

Revision activity

Research the case of former MP Stephen Byers, who was filmed by an undercover reporter in 2010 saying he was like a 'cab for hire' and would work for up to £5,000 per day after the media alleged he was willing to help a lobbying firm.

Green Paper: a consultative document issued by the government putting forward proposals for reform of the law and often inviting suggestions.

Legislative process

REVISED

Green and White Papers

Each government department (sometimes known as a 'ministry', such as the Ministry of Defence, or a 'department', such as the Department for Education) is responsible for an area of government.

If a change in the law is being considered, it will draft ideas for change. These draft documents are known as Green and White Papers:
- **Green Paper** – a consultative document issued by the government putting forward proposals for reform of the law and often inviting suggestions
- **White Paper** – a document issued by the government stating its decisions as to how it is going to reform the law; this is for information, not consultation.

White Paper: a document issued by the government stating its decisions as to how it is going to reform the law; this is for information, not consultation.

Different types of Bill

While a new law is making its way through the formal stages of becoming an Act of Parliament, it is known as a Bill. There are three types of Bill, outlined in the table below.

Table 3.1.2 Types of Bill

Public Bills	These involve matters of public policy affecting the whole country or a large section of it. Most government Bills are in this category, e.g. the Legal Aid, Sentencing and Punishment of Offenders Act 2012.
Private Members' Bills	Individual (private) MPs introduce a Bill. They can be from any political party and are known as 'backbenchers' because they do not sit in the front row in the House of Commons with the government. There are two ways a private MP can introduce a Bill: ● by ballot ● through the 'ten-minute' rule.
Private Bills	These are designed to create a law which will affect only individual people or corporations. They do not affect the whole community.
Hybrid Bills	These are a cross between Public Bills and Private Bills. They are introduced by the government, but if they become law they will affect a particular person, organisation or place.

Revision activity

Research how private MPs can introduce Bills. Find some Acts that started as Private Members' Bills.

Legislative stages

As discussed in Chapter 5.1, there have to be checks and balances built into the process of a Bill becoming an Act, to prevent any abuses of power.

Bill is drafted
↓
First reading in the House of Commons
↓
Second reading in the House of Commons
↓
Committee stage
↓
Report stage
↓
Third reading in the House of Commons
↓
Same procedures in the House of Lords
↓
Royal Assent

Revision activity

Write a sentence explaining each stage of the legislative process.

Role of the Crown

The UK is a constitutional monarchy. This means the queen (or king) is bound to exercise powers and authority only within the limits prescribed by the law.

Rules are not in a written constitution in the UK as they are in some other countries, but originate in the conventions, practices and precedents of Parliament, which form what is known as the Constitution of the United Kingdom.

The monarch is a ceremonial figurehead – a theoretical source of executive power who does not actually exercise executive powers. Executive powers may be exercised in the monarch's name by Parliament and the government.

No person may accept significant public office without swearing an oath of allegiance to the Queen. However, she is bound by constitutional convention to act on the advice of the government in making these appointments.

Political theorist Walter Bagehot identified three main political rights which a constitutional monarch may freely exercise, namely the right to be consulted, to encourage and to warn.

> **Typical mistake**
>
> In exam questions, do not discuss the role of the Crown in great detail unless you are specifically asked to do so.

Evaluation of the legislative process

Sir Henry William Rawson Wade QC FBA, Professor of English Law at both the University of Oxford and the University of Cambridge, referred to the parliamentary system as being 'in a state of acute malfunction, producing laws which are excessive in quantity and deficient in quality'.

Table 3.1.3 Evaluation of the legislative process

Advantages	Disadvantages
Parliament makes law in a democratic way through its elected members.	It is not true democracy, which would be impossible as we would all have to vote on every law. Even as a representative democracy, it is only partial due to the unelected nature of the House of Lords.
Law-making powers may be delegated to other bodies, meaning complex law can be made by the relevant experts in the field.	• Governments undertake too much legislation – 215 Acts of Parliament were passed between 2007 and 2012 (creating 20,000 pages of new laws). • Changes in the law are not well known, e.g. in *R v Chambers* (2008) it was discovered that the law on tobacco smuggling had been changed seven years before, but there had been 1,000 prosecutions in the meantime.
Suggestions for new, simpler and clear legislation often come from the Law Commission – highly specialised lawyers who take detailed consultation.	Parliament is not bound to follow the advice of the Law Commission; this is evident in relation to loss of control in the Coroners and Justice Act 2009.

Bills are subjected to high levels of scrutiny and detailed consideration from:
• the consultation papers where all interested parties can become involved in the drafting
• the stages of the parliamentary process where MPs and Lords from opposing political persuasions will examine and vote on the Bill.
 	
This means the scrutiny is balanced, objective and thorough.
	• Due to the restrictive parliamentary timetable, governments often force legislation through Parliament, e.g. the Dangerous Dogs Act 1991.
	• There is a tendency for Portmanteau bills, which combine several distinct areas of law into one long Bill. This means less scrutiny by experts. Examples include:
	  – the Justice and Immigration Act 2008 contains law relating to self-defence (s 76)
	  – the Coroners and Justice Act 2009 contains controversial laws relating to manslaughter (ss 52–6).
	• In the committee stage: the membership of the committee is often not specialised; the committees divide on party lines; and there is too little time to cover the whole Bill.

Since 1997, all Acts are accompanied by explanatory notes. This is a great help to all trying to access the law.	The language used in many Acts is too complex, because draftsmen try to provide for every eventuality.

Now test yourself

1 Which is the most effective influence on Parliament?
2 What is the difference between a Green Paper and a White Paper?
3 How many bodies make up Parliament?
4 What is a constitutional monarchy?
5 Is Parliament actually supreme?
6 Why are Portmanteau Bills an advantage, and why are they a problem?

Answers online

Exam summary

In the exam, you MAY be asked to:
- explain the influences on Parliament
- describe the stages of the legislative process
- discuss the advantages and disadvantages of:
  - the influences on Parliament, or
  - using the legislative process to pass laws, such as using Acts of Parliament.

These types of question will generally require mid-length answers and be worth 10 or 15 marks.

3.2 Delegated legislation

Reasons for delegated legislation

REVISED

Parliament is incredibly busy and does not always have the time or expertise to deal with every new law that is required. Therefore, it delegates some of its law-making powers to secondary bodies, allowing them to make new laws on Parliament's behalf. These new laws are sometimes known as secondary legislation.

In order to delegate its power to a secondary body, an Act of Parliament is passed giving the secondary body the power to carry out tasks. These Acts are known as parent Acts or enabling Acts and are regarded as primary legislation.

People must obey these new laws: they have the same effect as if Parliament itself had written them.

> **Delegated legislation:** secondary legislation, i.e. laws passed in a specific area by a secondary body to which Parliament has passed its power.

> **Typical mistake**
>
> Do not forget to refer to the parent Act that gives the secondary body its power.

Types of delegated legislation

Types of delegated legislation

REVISED

Table 3.2.1 Types of delegated legislation

Type	Secondary body	Reason used	Example
Orders in Council	Privy Council	• They save Parliament time. • There can be a quick response in emergency situations.	• The Constitutional Reform Act 2005 allows the Privy Council to alter the number of judges in the Supreme Court. • The Civil Contingencies Act 2004 gives the Privy Council power to make law in times of emergency when Parliament is not sitting.
Statutory instruments (SIs)	Government ministers	Over 3,000 SIs are made each year. Parliament could not cope with this volume or complexity, which is best left to the departments with expertise and responsibility in specific areas.	• The Building Regulations 2010 are incredibly complex, made by the Department for Communities and Local Government under the Building Act 1984. • Police powers are made by the Ministry for Justice under the Police and Criminal Evidence Act 1984.
By-laws	Local authorities and public corporations for matters within their jurisdiction, e.g. the British Airports Authority	Parliament has neither the time nor the local knowledge to deal with these types of matter.	• The drinking ban zone is a Designated Public Place Order. It was put in place by local councils under the Criminal Justice and Police Act 2001. Within the designated area, alcohol consumption is restricted in any open space, other than licensed premises. • Others examples include 'no ball games', 'no parking' etc.

> **Revision activity**
>
> What by-laws can you think of in your local community?

Controls on delegated legislation

Controls by Parliament

Table 3.2.2 Controls on delegated legislation by Parliament

Parent Act	Parliament's first attempt to control delegated legislation made in its name comes with the drafting of the parent Act. This should be clear, unambiguous and give 'what' and 'how' instructions that are open to very little interpretation.
Affirmation Resolution Order (ARO)	In controversial areas, such as human embryology, Parliament can also insist that the draft delegated legislation is subject to parliamentary scrutiny and vote before coming into force, by including a requirement for an Affirmative Resolution Order (ARO) in the parent Act.
Negative Resolution Order (NRO)	Delegated legislation is designed to save parliamentary time, but AROs can defeat this object and could not possibly be used for all 3,000 SIs each year. In the absence of an ARO, Parliament has 40 days to pass a Negative Resolution Order (NRO) to prevent a SI coming into force. If Parliament misses this deadline, only primary legislation or repealing the parent Act can remove the delegated legislation.
Delegated Powers Scrutiny Committee in the House of Lords	This considers whether the provisions of any Bills going through Parliament delegate legislative power inappropriately. It reports its findings to the House of Lords before the committee stage of the Bill, but it has no power to amend Bills.
Joint Scrutiny Committee	Its role is simply to scrutinise SIs. It is looking for SIs that are retrospective in effect, badly worded or attempting to impose taxation.

Controls by the courts

These controls require a party affected by the delegated legislation to apply to the Queen's Bench Division of the High Court for a judicial review. This review could find the delegated legislation to be *ultra vires* (UV) and therefore void, i.e. without legal effect. There are two types of UV, outlined in the table below.

Table 3.2.3 Types of *ultra vires* (UV)

Type	Description	Key case
Procedural UV	The secondary body has exceeded its powers and failed to follow the procedural instructions in the parent Act.	*Agricultural Training Board v Aylesbury Mushrooms Ltd* (1972) (see Table 3.2.4)
Substantive UV	The secondary body has gone beyond the powers granted to it and made more regulations than permitted.	*R v Secretary of State for Health ex parte Pfizer Ltd* (1999) (see Table 3.2.4)

Furthermore, the judicial review can conclude that a piece of delegated legislation is without legal effect because it is 'outrageous in its defiance of logic' – see *Associated Provincial Picture Houses Ltd v Wednesbury Corporation* (1948).

> **Revision activity**
>
> Find out about the Legislative and Regulatory Reform Act 2006. How does this change the controls on delegated legislation?

> ***Ultra vires***: a Latin term meaning 'beyond the powers', i.e. the secondary body has exceeded the powers given to it by the parent Act.

> **Revision activity**
>
> Look up the facts of *Associated Provincial Picture Houses Ltd v Wednesbury Corporation* (1948). Do you agree that the corporation's behaviour was unreasonable?

Table 3.2.4 Summary of parliamentary and court controls on delegated legislation

Type of control	Example	Effectiveness
Parent Act	The Police and Criminal Evidence Act 1984 gives the Ministry of Justice powers to alter police powers.	This is usually very effective, but Parliament is not fool-proof when it comes to making new Acts.
Affirmative Resolution Order	An affirmative resolution is required before new or revised police Codes of Practice under the Police and Criminal Evidence Act 1984 can come into force.	This could not be used 3,000 times a year, and so is very restricted to highly controversial areas.
Negative Resolution Order	Paraffin (Maximum Retail Prices) (Revocation) Order 1979	It is difficult to spot the problem within the 40 days, given the huge volume of SIs (3,000 per year). Also, even if spotted, it means bad law has been in place for 40 days and so still applies to those 40 days.
Joint Scrutiny Committee	The Code of Practice (Picketing) Order 2017 reportedly failed to comply with proper legislative practice.	It cannot possibly scrutinise all 3,000 SIs each year, so problematic ones must slip through the net.
Procedural *ultra vires*	*Agricultural Training Board v Aylesbury Mushrooms Ltd* (1972): the Horticultural Society was obliged to 'consult' all interested parties before bringing in new regulations, but did not consult the mushroom growers.	While these controls are effective, they are only available once the piece of delegated legislation has come into effect, and only then if an affected party seeks (and funds!) a judicial review.
Substantive *ultra vires*	*R v Secretary of State for Health ex parte Pfizer Ltd* (1999): the government lacked the power to ban the prescription of Viagra on the NHS for cost reasons – the ban was void.	This can be a very expensive process, e.g. the recent case regarding Jon Warboy's parole – see *R (DSD And Ors) v The Parole Board And Ors* (2018).
Wednesbury unreasonableness	*Associated Provincial Picture Houses Ltd v Wednesbury Corporation* (1948)	

Revision activity

Create a spidergram which explains each different type of control shown in Table 3.2.4.

Evaluation of delegated legislation

Table 3.2.5 Evaluation of delegated legislation

Advantages	• Granting law-making powers to others saves much parliamentary time. Parliament could not possibly make all of these laws itself.
	• Laws can be made quickly to respond to emergency situations.
	• Parliament can concentrate on producing parent Acts, giving a broad outline and leaving the detail to others.
	• Local people are experts in local issues and so can produce detailed local laws once given the framework.
	• Delegated legislation is often used as a fast way of implementing directives from the EU.
	• Ministers making laws is considered a contradiction of the doctrine of the separation of powers, i.e. the executive doing the legislature's job.

Disadvantages	• Delegated legislation lacks publicity. Over 3,000 SIs are made each year. It is impossible for the public to keep up with this, but ignorance of the law is no defence.
	• Parliamentary controls on delegated legislation are not always very effective. The Scrutiny Committee cannot possibly scrutinise all of them.
	• There is danger of the delegated bodies sub-delegating, i.e. passing the work onto someone else to do.
	• The doctrine of parliamentary sovereignty is eroded, as judges are able to void delegated legislation by using *ultra vires*.
	• Delegated legislation is not a democratic source of law, as it is often made by people who are not democratically elected.
	• Judges cannot exercise their control over delegated legislation without a member of the public taking legal action, which is time consuming and expensive.

Now test yourself

TESTED ☐

1 What is the difference between primary and secondary legislation?
2 Why does Parliament need to delegate some of its powers?
3 What type of delegated legislation is sometimes called ministerial regulations? Why?
4 What does *ultra vires* mean?
5 How does delegated legislation undermine parliamentary supremacy?

Answers online

Exam summary

In the exam, you MAY be asked to:
• explain one or more of the different types of delegated legislation
• describe the controls on delegated legislation, such as control by Parliament
• discuss the advantages and disadvantages of:
  – one or more of the different types of delegated legislation
  – controls on delegated legislation, such as control by Parliament and/or the courts.

These types of question will generally require mid-length answers and be worth 10 or 15 marks.

Revision activity

Use these points to write model answers on advantages and disadvantages of delegated legislation, then try a combination essay – 'Write a critical evaluation of delegated legislation'. Remember to include examples that you have researched.

Exam tip

Look out for 'advantages' questions in disguise, such as 'why is delegated legislation necessary?'

3.3 Statutory interpretation

This chapter looks at how judges interpret the language used in Acts of Parliament. This is necessary because sometimes:

- an act contains ambiguous words – see *Fisher v Bell* (1961)
- words used are too broad – see *R (Miranda) v Home Secretary* (2016)
- the progress of technology means the words may need to be considered in light of new advances – see *Royal College of Nursing v DHSS* (1981)
- there has been an error in drafting – see *R v Burstow* (1997).

> **Typical mistake**
>
> An evaluation without cases to boost your answer will not score highly. Make sure you illustrate each rule with relevant cases and explain why the word needed to be interpreted.

Rules of statutory interpretation

REVISED

In order to interpret words, over time judges have come up with rules to guide them. No rule is obligatory and judges can use which they prefer. Often, bodies such as the Judicial Studies Board issue guidelines as to the preferred approach.

The table below explains the difference between the:

- **literal rule**
- **golden rule**
- **mischief rule**
- **purposive approach**.

> **Literal rule:** where judges use the exact meaning of words when interpreting statute, no matter how absurd the outcome.
>
> **Golden rule:** where judges decide that the literal rule produces absurd results when interpreting statute.
>
> **Mischief rule:** a rule of statutory interpretation used to prevent the mischief an Act is aimed at.
>
> **Purposive approach:** where judges look to see what the purpose of the law is when interpreting statute.

Table 3.3.1 Rules of statutory interpretation

Rule	Explanation	Cases
Literal rule	• Popular in the late nineteenth and early twentieth centuries, this gives the literal and grammatically correct meaning to the section, regardless of how absurd the result. • Lord Reid: 'We are seeking not what Parliament meant, but the true meaning of the words they used.'	• *Whiteley v Chappell* (1868) • *London and North Eastern Railway Co. v Berriman* (1946) • Also see *R v Judge of the City of London Court* (1892) for a quote from Lord Esher
Golden rule	• An extension of the literal rule, where words will be given their literal meaning unless the result would be absurd. • Lord Wensleydale in *Grey v Pearson* (1857): 'The ordinary sense of the words is to be adhered to, unless it would lead to absurdity, when the ordinary sense may be modified to avoid the absurdity but no further.' • Narrow approach: the court may only choose between the possible meanings of the word. If there is only one, then that must be taken. • Wide approach: where the words only have one clear meaning which would lead to an absurd result, the court will use the golden rule to modify the words in order to avoid the absurdity.	• *Adler v George* (1964) • *Re Sigsworth* (1935)
Mischief rule	• Originating from *Heydon's Case* (1584), this rule looks back to the gap in the previous law and interprets the Act so as to cover the gap. • Use the mischief rule if it 'is possible to determine from the Act the precise "mischief" the Act was to remedy [and it] is possible to say with certainty what additional words would have been inserted' – Lord Diplock in *Jones v Wrotham Park Settled Estates* (1980).	• *Smith v Hughes* (1960) • *Royal College of Nursing v DHSS* (1981)

Rule	Explanation	Cases
Purposive approach	<ul><li>This is currently popular and recommended by the Law Commission and the EU. The judges look to see what the purpose of the law is.</li><li>This is an extension of the mischief rule because the judges are not just looking to see what the gap was in the old law but deciding what they believe Parliament meant to achieve with the new law.</li></ul>	<ul><li>*R v Registrar-General, ex parte Smith* (1990)</li><li>*R v Coleman* (2013)</li></ul>

Aids to statutory interpretation

REVISED

In addition to the rules above, there are also a number of 'aids' judges can use.

Rules of language

Table 3.3.2 **Rules of language to aid statutory interpretation**

Rule	Explanation	Case example
Ejusdem generis	<ul><li>Covering things of the same type, e.g. 'Cats, dogs and other animals' would only include domestic animals.</li><li>There must be a list of at least two specific words before the general word for this rule to operate.</li></ul>	In *Talbot v Oxford City Magistrates' Court* (2000), the court refused to interpret 'any enclosed yard, garden or area' under s 4 of the Vagrancy Act 1824 to include an office.
Expressio unius est exclusio alterius	<ul><li>The expression of one thing implies the exclusion of the other.</li><li>This rule applies where there is a list of words which is not followed by general words, e.g. 'Persian cats' excludes other types of cat.</li></ul>	In *Tempest v Kilner* (1846), the court decided that the Statute of Frauds 1677, which required a contract for the sale of 'goods, wares and merchandise', did not apply to a contract for the sale of stocks and shares because the list was not followed by any general words.
Noscitur a sociis	<ul><li>The meaning of the word can be gathered from its context.</li><li>This requires examination of other words in the same Act, e.g. 'cat baskets, toy mice and food' would mean cat food.</li></ul>	In *Inland Revenue v Frere* (1964), the court decided that for 'interest, annuities or other annual interest', 'interest' could only mean annual interest.

Intrinsic aids

Intrinsic aids are 'inside the Act' and include:

- preamble/introductory text/long title, which may give some clues that will help with the mischief rule or purposive approach
- explanatory notes included in the margin to show what a section is about
- a glossary of key terms in some Acts.

Extrinsic aids

Extrinsic aids are 'outside the Act' and include:

- the historical context of the Act, for example the Offences Against the Person Act 1861 uses the word 'grievous'; this word is no longer in common usage, but it was when the law was drafted
- dictionaries and textbooks; in *R v Jewell* (2014), Lady Justice Rafferty referred to Smith and Hogan's *Criminal Law* textbook

> *Ejusdem generis*: covering things of the same type.
>
> *Expressio unius est exclusio alterius*: the expression of one thing implies the exclusion of another.
>
> *Noscitur a sociis*: the meaning of a word can be gathered from its context.

- previous commercial practice
- treaties with international law – in order to give continuity to the meaning of words
- Hansard, after Lord Denning's debate with Lord Diplock, culminating with the decision in *Pepper v Hart* (1993) regarding tax on perks; see also *Tuppen v Microsoft* (2000)
- the Interpretation Act 1978, which gives some statutory guidance – 'he' will always include 'she' and singular will always include plural.

Table 3.3.3 **Key cases for statutory interpretation**

Case	Facts	Relevant rule
Fisher v Bell (1961)	Ambiguous words: statute made it a criminal offence to 'offer' flick knives for sale. Goods on display are an 'invitation to treat'.	Literal rule
R (Miranda) v Home Secretary (2016)	Words used are too broad: stop powers under Schedule 7 of the Terrorism Act 2000.	Purposive approach
Royal College of Nursing v DHSS (1981)	The Abortion Act 1967: the progress of technology means the words may need to be considered in light of new advances – nurses are now included in legislation.	Mischief rule
R v Burstow (1997)	There has been an error in drafting – 'inflict' in s 20 of the Offences Against the Person Act 1861 simply means cause.	Golden rule
Whiteley v Chappell (1868)	D used the vote of a dead man; he was not guilty as a dead person was not a person entitled to vote.	Literal rule – example of an absurd result
London and North Eastern Railway Co. v Berriman (1946)	A railway worker killed while oiling the track was denied compensation as this did not count as 'relaying or repairing'.	Literal rule – example of an absurd result
Adler v George (1964)	The defendant was actually in the prohibited place, rather than 'in the vicinity' of it, at the time of the obstruction.	Golden rule – narrow
Re Sigsworth (1935)	A son murdered his mother, who had not made a will; as her only child he was entitled to inherit her entire estate under the literal rule. The golden rule was applied and he inherited nothing.	Golden rule – wide
Smith v Hughes (1960)	Ds were prostitutes soliciting from private premises in windows or on balconies rather than a public place but could still be seen by the public.	Mischief rule
R v Registrar-General, ex parte Smith (1990)	The applicant had statutory right to a birth certificate at age 18, but it was suspected that he wanted this in order to find and murder his mother.	Purposive approach
R v Coleman (2013)	D burgled a narrow boat. The Power of Criminal Courts (Sentencing) Act 2000 was interpreted to mean the same as s 9(4) of the Theft Act 1968.	Purposive approach
Pepper v Hart (1993)	The court had to decide whether a teacher at a private school had to pay tax on the perk he received in the form of reduced school fees. A relevant statement was made in Hansard at this time.	Use of Hansard

Impacts on statutory interpretation

EU law

The purposive approach is preferred by most EU countries when interpreting their own legislation. It is also the approach adopted by the European Court of Justice in interpreting EU law.

Therefore, UK judges having to use the purposive approach for EU law for over 40 years has made them more likely to apply it to UK law.

Where the law to be interpreted is based on EU law, the UK courts have to interpret it in the light of the wording and purpose of the EU law – see s 2(4) of the European Community Act 1972. The European Court of Justice in the *Marleasing* case (1992) ruled that this included interpreting national law in the light and the aim of the EU law.

When the UK leaves the EU, this will no longer apply. However, judges are likely to continue to use the purposive approach.

Human Rights Act 1998

Section 3 of the Human Rights Act 1998 states that, as far as it is possible to do so, legislation must be read and given effect in a way that is compatible with the rights in the European Convention on Human Rights. See *Mendoza v Ghaidan* (2002), which involved interpreting the Rent Act 1977 in terms that were compatible with Convention rights.

Evaluation of the rules and aids for statutory interpretation

Table 3.3.4 Evaluation of the different rules for statutory interpretation

Rule	Advantages	Disadvantages
Literal rule	<ul><li>It respects parliamentary sovereignty.</li><li>It provides certainty, as the law will be interpreted exactly as it is written. This makes it easier to know what the law is and how judges will apply it.</li></ul>	<ul><li>Where it leads to unjust results, such as in *London and North Eastern Railway Co. v Berriman* (1946), it can hardly be said to be enacting the will of Parliament.</li><li>It assumes every Act will be perfectly drafted.</li><li>Zander calls it 'irresponsible'.</li></ul>
Golden rule	It provides a way of avoiding the worst problems created by the literal rule while attempting to respect parliamentary sovereignty.	<ul><li>Two approaches could lead to further inconsistency.</li><li>There is no definition of an absurd result.</li><li>Zander calls it a 'feeble parachute'.</li></ul>
Mischief rule	<ul><li>It responds positively to loopholes in the law.</li><li>It is more likely to produce a 'just' result because judges try to interpret the law in the way that Parliament meant it to work.</li></ul>	<ul><li>Judges are going beyond their authority by filling in gaps, i.e. contradicting parliamentary sovereignty.</li><li>It may lead to uncertainty, as it is impossible to know when judges will use the rule and what result it might lead to. This makes it difficult for lawyers to advise clients on the law.</li></ul>

Rule	Advantages	Disadvantages
Purposive approach	<ul><li>It is most likely to lead to justice in individual cases.</li><li>It allows judges to respond to new technology, as in *R (Quintavalle) v Human Fertilisation and Embryology Authority* (2003).</li><li>It gives judges discretion on when and how to avoid the absurdity of the literal rule.</li></ul>	<ul><li>How can judges know what Parliament's intentions were?</li><li>It allows unelected judges to 'make' law, as they are deciding what they think the law should be rather than using the words that Parliament enacted.</li><li>It leads to the same uncertainty as the mischief rule.</li></ul>

Table 3.3.5 Evaluation of intrinsic aids

Intrinsic aid	Advantage	Disadvantage
Preamble/introductory text/long title	Explains specifically and unequivocally the Act's purpose, e.g. the Female Genital Mutilation Act 2003	Can be vague or non-specific, e.g. the Criminal Justice Act 2003
Explanatory notes	Provides a specific super-summary of a section	Can be too brief, ambiguous or vague
Glossary of key terms	Useful *aide-memoire* of specific terms or definitions	Not consistently included in all Acts of Parliament

Table 3.3.6 Evaluation of extrinsic aids

Extrinsic aid	Advantage	Disadvantage
Historical context	Provides a social or political context behind an Act	Can become over-analysed, or outdated as society changes
Textbooks	Readily available and provide academic authors' opinions on judgments or legal rules	Provide a specific author's commentary which can be disputed by other authors or academics
Hansard	Undisputable verbatim reports of parliamentary discussions	Over-analysis of the literal conversations of parliamentary discussions

Revision activity

Find out who Zander is. Why is his opinion respected?

Exam tip

Use the cases throughout this section to illustrate your discussion of the advantages and disadvantages of different methods of statutory interpretation.

Revision activity

The UK Supreme Court has published its judgment in the controversial case of *Isle Of Wight Council v Platt* (2017).

Using all the information you have learned in this chapter, research this case. Consider the Act and the words that were interpreted, how the justices went about reaching their decision, and the rules they used to do so.

Now test yourself

TESTED ☐

1 Why do statutes need to be interpreted?
2 Why is the literal rule used?
3 Which rule evolved from the literal rule?
4 Which case allowed the use of Hansard?
5 Why does the purposive approach contradict the principle of parliamentary supremacy?

Answers online

Exam summary

In the exam, you MAY be asked to:

- explain one or more of the different rules of statutory interpretation
- describe the different aids to statutory interpretation
- explain the impact of the EU and the Human Rights Act 1998 on statutory interpretation
- discuss the advantages and disadvantages of:
  - one or more of the different rules of statutory interpretation
  - the different aids to statutory interpretation
- explain advantages and disadvantages of the impact of the EU and the Human Rights Act 1998 on statutory interpretation.

These types of question will generally require mid-length answers and be worth 10 or 15 marks.

3.4 Judicial precedent

Judicial precedent will be assessed in Paper 1.

Judicial precedent: where past decisions of judges create law for future judges to follow.

> **Exam tip**
>
> All the cases you learn about in this course are precedents. Use as many as you can to illustrate your points, but remember it is the point of law that is important, not necessarily the facts of the case.

Doctrine of precedent

English law has developed from custom and the decisions of judges in cases. This system of law is known as common law.

The decisions of judges in cases are known as precedents. Therefore, precedent is an important source of law, where past decisions of judges create law for future judges to follow.

The doctrine of precedent means that courts must follow decisions of the courts above. This is known as **stare decisis** (see below).

So, where the point of law in a previous case and current case is the same, the court hearing the current case should follow the decision in the previous case. This concept of treating similar cases in the same way promotes the idea of fairness and provides certainty.

Stare decisis: 'let the decision stand'.

Ratio decidendi: 'the reason for the decision'.

Obiter dicta: 'other things said'.

Stare decisis

Stare decisis is the fundamental principle of precedent, and simply means that a decision in an early case will stand as guidance for all future cases.

The decision made by the court is known as the 'judgment'. This contains the decision and an explanation of how it was reached.

Ratio decidendi

Ratio decidendi is the part of the judgment which forms the precedent for future cases.

All of the points of law you learn throughout the substantive sections that come from cases are the *ratio decidendi*. For example, that words can prevent an action from being an assault can be found in the *ratio decidendi* of *Tuberville v Savage* (1669).

Obiter dicta

Obiter dicta comprises the rest of the judgment apart from the *ratio decidendi*. Judges in future cases do not have to follow it, but it can give useful guidance.

A key case is *Hill v Baxter* (1958), where the example of being attacked by a swarm of bees gives useful guidance for the need for a voluntary act and the defence of automatism.

Hierarchy of the courts

Table 3.4.1 Hierarchy of the courts

Court	Bound by	Binding on	Cases
Judicial Committee of the Privy Council	No one, not even itself	All domestic courts of the Commonwealth, including England	• *Grant v Australian Knitting Mills* (1936) • *The Wagon Mound* (1961)
Supreme Court	European Court of Justice on EU issues Not itself	All other UK courts	• *R v Brown* (1993) • *Donoghue v Stevenson* (1932)
Court of Appeal (Civil Division)	Supreme Court (1) Itself with exceptions (2)	All lower courts and itself (2)	(1) *Broome v Cassell* (1971) and *Miliangos v George Frank (Textiles) Ltd* (1976) (2) *Young v Bristol Aeroplane Co. Ltd* (1944) gave the three rules on when it need not follow its own decisions
Court of Appeal (Criminal Division)	Supreme Court Itself	All lower courts Itself	
Queen's Bench Division of the High Court	Supreme Court Court of Appeal Itself	High Court generally Lower courts Itself	
Chancery and Family Divisions of the High Court	Supreme Court Court of Appeal Themselves	High Court generally Lower courts Themselves	
High Court	Supreme Court Court of Appeal Divisional courts Not itself	Lower courts Not itself	

County Courts, Crown Courts and Magistrates' Courts do not create precedents as:

- there are far too many cases going through them
- they do not publish judgments that could be used.

Practice Statement 1966

When the Supreme Court replaced the House of Lords in 2009, the Constitutional Reform Act 2005 transferred the House of Lords' powers to the Supreme Court.

In *Austin v London Borough of Southwark* (2010), the Supreme Court confirmed that the power to use the Practice Statement had been transferred to it. It said:

> 'Rigid adherence to precedent may lead to injustice in a particular case and also unduly restrict the proper development of the law. They [the Law Lords] therefore propose to modify their present practice and while treating former decisions of this House as normally binding, to depart from a previous decision when it appears right to do so.'

Therefore, the Supreme Court does not have to follow its own previous decisions, but it must explain why if it chooses not to.

Types of precedent

Binding precedent

For this system to work, there has to be a hierarchical court structure. This means the courts are tiered or ranked according to their seniority, and the higher ones bind the lower ones.

Therefore, a **binding precedent** is a decision in an earlier case and a higher court which must be followed in later cases.

Persuasive precedent

There is also **persuasive precedent**, a decision which does not have to be followed by later cases but which the judge may decide to follow. Persuasive precedents may:
- come from courts that do not bind, such as the Judicial Committee of the Privy Council, or
- come from courts lower down the hierarchy, or
- be a part of the decision known as '*obiter dicta*' (see earlier in this chapter).

Original precedent

An **original precedent** comes about when the point of law in a case has never been considered before. There are no past cases upon which the judge can base a decision, so the normal doctrine of judicial precedent cannot apply as there is no precedent to follow:
- *Donoghue v Stevenson* (1932) is an example of an original precedent.
- Original precedent is mostly likely to arise with the development of new technologies, meaning new situations come before the courts.
- The concept of original precedent raises an issue about whether judges create law or are merely declaring it.

> **Binding precedent:** a case decision from a senior court that must be followed in future cases.
>
> **Persuasive precedent:** usually in the form of *obiter dicta*, persuasive precedent is part of the judgment that should be followed in similar cases but is not binding. However, a reason for deciding not to follow it must be given.
>
> **Original precedent:** arises if the point of law in a case has never been considered before so judicial precedent cannot apply.

Operation of judicial precedent

When faced with a precedent set in an earlier case, judges have a number of options. The precedent can be:
- overruled, or
- reversed, or
- distinguished.

These options are explained in Table 3.4.2 below.

Table 3.4.2 Options for dealing with precedents

Option	Explanation	Example
Overruling	• The court in a later case states that the decision in an earlier case is wrong. • Overruling may occur when a higher court overrules a decision made in an earlier case by a lower court. • For example, the Supreme Court overrules a decision of the Court of Appeal, or the Supreme Court uses the Practice Statement to overrule a past decision of its own.	*R v Jogee* (2016) overruled *R v Powell* and *R v English* (1999)
Reversing	A higher court overturns the decision of a lower court on appeal: i.e. the same case moves higher up the court structure.	*Re Pinochet* (1999)

Option	Explanation	Example
Distinguishing	<ul><li>A judge avoids following a precedent.</li><li>If a judge finds that the material facts of the current case are sufficiently different from the case setting a precedent for a distinction to be drawn between the two, they are not bound by the previous case.</li></ul>	*Merritt v Merritt* (1971) distinguished *Balfour v Balfour* (1919)

Typical mistake

Remember that the Practice Statement and rule in *Young v Bristol Aeroplane Co. Ltd* (1944) are methods of avoiding precedent. You can use them in a question about ways of avoiding.

Evaluation of judicial precedent

REVISED

Table 3.4.3 **Evaluation of judicial precedent**

Advantages	<ul><li>**Certainty** – it allows the law to be predictable, which in turn promotes alternative dispute resolution (ADR) in civil cases.</li><li>**Consistency** – like cases are decided alike, promoting a sense of justice.</li><li>**Fairness** – the certainty and consistency allow parties involved in cases to see how the decision was arrived at, and that it is fair in the circumstances.</li><li>**Precision** – the exact details of the law are known by all parties.</li><li>**Flexibility** – bad precedents can be avoided using the Practice Statement, e.g. *Young v Bristol Aeroplane Co. Ltd* (1944).</li><li>**Time-saving** – the predictability makes ADR more likely, thus saving parties (and the courts) time and money.</li><li>**Details** can be added to statutory provisions, such as *R v Clinton* (2012) clarifying the position on sexual infidelity.</li><li>The law can **evolve** to meet changing social attitudes, as it did by establishing an offence of rape within marriage in *R v R* (1991).</li></ul>
Disadvantages	<ul><li>**Rigidity** – binding decisions can restrict decisions made in the interests of individual justice.</li><li>**Complexity** – judgments are long and difficult to read, and it is not always easy to identify the *ratio decidendi* and *obiter dicta*.</li><li>**Illogical distinctions** – some cases are distinguished on very minor or controversial points. This could be argued in *R v Brown* (1993) and *R v Wilson* (1996); the defence of consent was allowed in *Wilson* but not in *Brown*, arguably on the basis of sexuality.</li><li>**Slowness of growth** – the development of precedent depends on accidents of litigation, i.e. waiting for a similar case to come along in order to develop the law further.</li><li>A **bad precedent** needs another case or an Act of Parliament to correct it, as in *DPP v Smith* (1961), and the Criminal Justice Act 1967 which reset intention as a subjective test.</li></ul>

Table 3.4.4 **Key cases for judicial precedent**

Case	Use as an example of:
Grant v Australian Knitting Mills (1936)	Persuasive nature of decisions of the Judicial Committee of the Privy Council
The Wagon Mound cases (1961)	Persuasive nature of decisions of the Judicial Committee of the Privy Council
R v Brown (1993)	House of Lords/Supreme Court precedent; also for distinguishing with *R v Wilson* (1996)
Donoghue v Stevenson (1932)	House of Lords/Supreme Court precedent creating the test for duty of care; it has never been overruled, but it has been restricted

Case	Use as an example of:
Young v Bristol Aeroplane Co. Ltd (1944)	The judgment in this case gave the exceptions to the rule that the Court of Appeal must follow itself
Conway v Rimmer (1968)	First use of Practice Statement 1966, avoided following *Duncan v Cammell Laird* (1942)
R v Shivpuri (1986)	First use of Practice Statement 1966 in a criminal case, avoided following *Anderton v Ryan* (1985)
Herrington v British Railways Board (1972)	Use of Practice Statement 1966 to overrule *Addie v Dumbreck* (1929) and establish a duty to trespassers
Pepper v Hart (1993)	Use of Practice Statement 1966 to allow the use of Hansard in statutory interpretation
Knuller Ltd v DPP (1973)	House of Lords deciding not to use the Practice Statement 1966
R v G and R (2003)	House of Lords establishing the current definition of recklessness, overruling *MPC v Caldwell* (1982)
Michael v Chief Constable of South Wales (2015)	Followed *Hill v Chief Constable of West Yorkshire* (1988) in that it is not fair, just and reasonable to impose a duty on the police to protect future victims of crime
R v Jogee (2016)	Overruled *R v Powell* and *R v English* (1999) on the use of the principle of joint enterprise in criminal law
Merritt v Merritt (1971)	Distinguished *Balfour v Balfour* (1919) in relation to the binding nature of financial arrangements between spouses

Now test yourself

TESTED ☐

1 What does *stare decisis* mean?
2 Which of the following kinds of statement made in a case judgment would best be described as '*obiter dicta*'?
   A Statements about the application of the law to the important facts in the case
   B Statements about the important facts in the case
   C Statements about the result of the case
   D Statements about the application of the law to facts which are a little different from those in the case
3 What does the Practice Statement 1966 do?
4 What is a binding precedent?
5 If a judge is not following a persuasive precedent, what should they do?

Answers online

Exam summary

In the exam, you MAY be asked to:
● explain:
  – one or more of the different ideas of judicial precedent, such as *stare decisis*
  – the different types of judicial precedent, such as binding precedent
● describe:
  – the hierarchy of the courts
  – the impact of the use of judicial precedent, such as overruling or reversing
● discuss the advantages and disadvantages of judicial precedent.

These types of question will generally require mid-length answers and be worth 10 or 15 marks.

3.5 Law reform

There are three main methods of law reform in England and Wales:
- through Parliament passing legislation or via the common-law decisions of judges
- the Law Commission
- Royal Commissions.

Law Commission

The Law Commission was set up in 1965 by the Law Commissions Act 1965. It is a full-time body, consisting of a Chair (who is a High Court Judge), four other Law Commissioners and support and research staff.

Its stated aim is to ensure that the law is:
- fair
- modern
- simple
- cost-effective.

> **Revision activity**
>
> Section 3 of the Law Commissions Act 1965 sets out the role of the Law Commission. Find this section and make some notes on it.

Table 3.5.1 **Work of the Law Commission**

Task	Explanation
Reform	To 'reform' the law means to update it. The Law Commission can choose areas that it considers need updating, or areas can be referred to it by the government via the Lord Chancellor: • Its first step is to open a consultation, which sets out the current law and why it needs to be reformed. For example, a consultation was launched in July 2017 regarding wills. • The consultation invites responses from interested parties and will include the problems with current law, suggestions for reform, questions for interested parties to consider, and examples of how the area of law operates in other countries. • After the consultation, the Law Commission will issue a report. This often contains a draft Bill that Parliament could begin to put through the formal process of creating an Act.
Codification	Codification means reviewing all the law on one topic and creating a complete code of law: • When the Law Commission was first set up, its aim was to codify – i.e. rewrite – all of family law, contract law, landlord and tenant laws and the law of evidence. However, the enormity of this task meant the idea was shelved. • In 1985, the Law Commission published a draft criminal code which included all of the main general principles of criminal law. However, governments have never implemented it, and the Law Commission stated in 2008 that in future it would concentrate on smaller areas, as there is more chance the government will then adopt these.
Consolidation	Consolidation means drawing all the existing provisions in an area of law together into one Act. It is different to codification, as the law is not reviewed or changed; it is simply brought together. In July 2017, a new consultation was launched by the Law Commission to tidy up sentencing law – to 'modernise the law, bring greater transparency and improve efficiency'.
Repeal	The repeal of an Act of Parliament means that the Act ceases to be law. Only Parliament can repeal an Act of Parliament, but the Law Commission can advise Parliament about which Acts should be repealed. Its job is to identify which Acts are no longer needed – such as the Statute of Marlborough 1267 passed during the reign of Henry III! This is the area of the Law Commission's work where it has seen most success: 19 Bills have been enacted since 1965, which repeal more than 3,000 Acts.

Royal Commission

Royal Commissions are temporary, *ad hoc* committees set up to investigate and provide a report on a specific area of law. They are generally set up following a scandal or a public outcry. Some important examples include:

- the Phillips Commission – the Royal Commission on Police Procedure in 1981 which led to the Police and Criminal Evidence Act 1984
- the Runciman Commission – the Royal Commission on Criminal Justice in 1993 which looked at how miscarriages of justice were handled and made recommendations including the referral of appropriate cases to the Court of Appeal.

Royal Commissions: temporary, *ad hoc* committees set up to investigate and provide a report on specific areas of law.

Evaluation of law reform bodies

Table 3.5.2 **Advantages of reform through the Law Commission**

Advantage	This means:	Evidence
It saves Parliament's time.	Parliament has time to deal with political matters, leaving this time-consuming and vital work to a separate body.	Over 3,000 Acts have been examined, found to be redundant and repealed.
Law is researched by legal experts.	Practical recommendations are made.	The Chair is a High Court Judge or an Appeal Court Judge, appointed to the Commission by the Lord Chancellor and Secretary of State for Justice for up to three years. The other four Commissioners are experienced judges, barristers, solicitors or teachers of law.
There is consultation before drawing up proposals.	All interested parties have a chance to have their say.	Publication: *The Sentencing Code* Publication date: 27 July 2017; response date: 26 January 2018
Whole areas of law are considered.	The impact of any new law on related areas is fully explored.	In 2012, the Law Commission published a paper on contempt of court, which covered: <ul><li>contempt in the face of the court</li><li>court reporting</li><li>juror misconduct and internet publications</li><li>scandalising the court.</li></ul>
It can bring the law on one topic together in one Act.	The law is easier to find and therefore more accessible to all.	Powers of the Criminal Courts (Sentencing) Bill
It simplifies and modernises the law.	The law is easier to understand and therefore more accessible to all.	*Simplification of Criminal Law: Public Nuisance and Outraging Public Decency* (Law Com No. 358)

Table 3.5.3 Disadvantages of reform through the Law Commission

Disadvantage	This means:	Evidence
The government is slow to implement the reforms.	Large areas of work can be wasted as they are not politically important.	*Offences Against the Person* (Law Com No. 218)
Some reforms may never be implemented	A great amount of time and public money has been wasted on research and preparation which is not put into place, despite experts identifying a need.	*Liability for Psychiatric Illness* (Law Com No. 249)
There is a lack of parliamentary time to discuss the proposed reforms.	Suggestions for reform may not be thoroughly debated and discussed before being enacted.	The Coroners and Justice Act 2009 selected elements of Law Com No. 290, and Parliament did not properly scrutinise what the implications of this would be.
Parliament may make changes to the proposed reforms without the benefit of legal expertise.	The legal expertise that went into the suggestions for reform is ignored.	Link to the evaluation of the homicide reforms contained in the Coroners and Justice Act 2009

Table 3.5.4 Advantages of reform through Royal Commissions

Advantage	Explanation
Ad hoc	They are quick to establish following an issue or scandal.
Reports on specific area of law	Their remit is clear, with a set agenda and timescale.
Independent	They are used by the government where independent, non-political opinions and/or recommendations are required.

Table 3.5.5 Disadvantages of reform through Royal Commissions

Disadvantage	Explanation
Expensive	It can cost millions of pounds to run and finance, e.g. often many witness testimonies are taken.
Lack of enforceable judgment	Governments can simply ignore the decisions of commissions or, as in the 1980s, simply not use them.
Length of enquiry	In many cases, due to the complex nature of the enquiry, commissions can take many years to report.

Typical mistake

Do not confuse a 'statement' with an actual advantage/disadvantage. You need to explain why your statement is positive or negative, and support it with evidence – a case, an example or a statistic, where possible.

Revision activity

The Criminal Justice and Courts Act 2015 is a good example of an Act coming about as a result of Law Commission proposals.

Look up this Act and make a note of its provisions – link these to the material in Section 1. Then answer the following:
- Do you agree with the provisions?
- Why do you think the Law Commission suggested them?
- Why do you think Parliament enacted them?
- Can you find any prosecutions under these provisions?

Now test yourself

1 What is the Law Commission and what is its remit?
2 When and how was the Law Commission established?
3 Give an example of a Law Commission success.
4 Give an example of where the Law Commission's work has not been implemented.

Answers online

Exam summary

In the exam, you MAY be asked to:
● explain what is meant by law reform
● describe the workings of the Law Commission
● discuss the advantages of law reform bodies, such as the Law Commission.

These types of question will generally require mid-length answers and be worth 10 or 15 marks.

3.6 European Union law

European Union law will be assessed in Paper 3.

Typical mistake

It is a mistake to think EU law is imposed upon the UK. At the moment, the UK is a senior member of the EU and has at least as much say in new EU law as other Member States.

The EU was formed in 1957. The UK joined the EU in 1973 by signing the Treaty of Rome.

Permission for the UK government to adopt the principles of this treaty was given by Parliament passing the European Communities Act 1972, which followed a referendum. There are now 28 Member States.

In 2016, the UK voted by referendum to leave the EU; known as Brexit, this is likely to take place in 2019.

Revision activity

How is a referendum different from other national elections? Can you think of any other significant referendums in recent UK history?

EU institutions

REVISED

Table 3.6.1 EU institutions

Institution	Function	Make-up

Council	• Principal law-making body of the EU
	• Voting in the Council is by qualified (or double) majority, which is reached if:
	  – 55 per cent of Member States vote in favour, and
	  – the proposal is supported by Member States representing at least 65 per cent of the total EU population.
		• The government of each nation sends a representative to the Council, usually the Foreign Minister.
		• A minister responsible for the topic under consideration often attends, so the precise membership will vary with the subject being discussed, e.g. the Minister for Agriculture will attend if the issue involves agriculture.

Commission	• Proposes new laws to be adopted by the Parliament and the Council • Responsible for the administration of the EU • Ensures that treaty provisions etc. are properly implemented by Member States • Can refer the matter to the Court of Justice of the European Union where there is a failure to do so • Responsible for the EU's budget and supervises how the money is spent	• Each Member State has one Commissioner, who must act independently of their national origin. • They are appointed for a five-year term and can only be removed during their term of office by a vote of censure by the EU Parliament. • Each Commissioner heads a department with responsibility for an area of EU policy, e.g. agriculture.
European Parliament	• MEPs form political groups with those of the same political allegiance • Meets once a month • Has standing committees which discuss proposals made by the Commission and then report to the full Parliament for debate • Can now co-legislate on an equal footing with the Council and can approve or reject proposals made by the Commission • Decides on international agreements • Decides on whether to admit new Member States • Reviews the Commission's work programme and asks it to propose legislation	• There are 751 members of the European Parliament (MEPs). • It is directly elected by the electorate of the Member States, in elections which take place every five years. • The number of MEPs from each country is determined by the size of the population of the country.

Institution	Function	Make-up
Court of Justice of the European Union	• Decides whether a Member State has failed in its obligations, e.g. *Re Tachographs: The Commission v United Kingdom* (1979) • Hears references from national courts for preliminary rulings on points of EU law; this is very important, as rulings made by the Court of Justice of the European Union are binding on courts in Member States, ensuring the law is uniform throughout the EU – see *Factortame v Secretary of State for Transport* (1990)	• The court sits in Luxembourg, with one judge from each Member State. • For a full court, 11 judges will sit. • For other cases, the court sits in chambers of five judges or three judges. They are assisted by 11 Advocates General, who take a case, research it and impartially present the issues that arise to the court.

Revision activity

Find the treaties and Articles that create the powers and roles in Table 3.6.1.

Sources of EU law

REVISED

There are three sources of EU law:
• treaties
• regulations
• directives.

These are outlined in the table below.

Table 3.6.2 Sources of EU law

Source	Effect	Cases to research
Treaties	• Primary legislation • Automatically part of a Member State's law • Until it is repealed as part of Brexit, see s 2(1) of the European Communities Act 1972, which allows individuals to rely directly on treaty provisions	• *Van Duyn v Home Office* (1974) • *Macarthys Ltd v Smith* (1980) • *Diocese of Hallam Trustee v Connaughton* (1996)
Regulations	• Binding on Member States • Automatically apply in each Member State	• *Re Tachographs: Commission v UK* (1979)
Directives	• Member States have to pass their own laws to implement directives, within a time limit set by the European Commission • Delegated legislation usually used in the UK	• **Vertical direct effect**: *Marshall v Southampton and South West Hampshire Area Health Authority* (1986) • **Horizontal direct effect**: *Francovich v Italian Republic* (1991)

Vertical direct effect: an individual can claim against the state even if the directive is not yet implemented.

Horizontal direct effect: directives give an individual rights against other people, provided they have been implemented.

Impact of EU law on the law of England and Wales

EU law applies to the court structure in England and Wales. While the UK remains a member of the EU, the Supreme Court must refer questions of EU law to the Court of Justice of the European Union.

The Court of Justice of the European Union is also important because its attitude to interpretation is now being followed by English courts. In *Von Colson v Land Nordrhein-Westfalen* (1984), it was said that 'national courts are required to interpret their national law in the light of the wording and the purpose of the directive'.

Section 2 of the European Communities Act 1972 provides that where EU law exists on a particular subject, it can override any inconsistent UK law, including Acts of Parliament. The *Factortame v Secretary of State for Transport* (1990) cases held the Merchant Shipping Act 1988 to be contrary to EU law.

On the face of it, this is a major limitation on the doctrine of parliamentary supremacy. However, as we have seen through the process of Brexit, Parliament preserves its supremacy by retaining its ability to repeal the European Communities Act in what is currently known as the Great Repeal Bill.

> **Exam tip**
>
> Look out for any guidance from OCR as and when the UK exits the EU – keep up to date with developments.

Table 3.6.3 Key cases on EU law

Case	Facts	Relevant area	*Ratio decidendi*
Re Tachographs: The Commission v United Kingdom (1979)	Regulations to fit tachographs to certain vehicles were not being enforced.	Role of the ECJ	The regulations were enforced by the EU.
Factortame v Secretary of State for Transport (1990)	Multiple cases related to fishing rights and the restrictions of free movement of trade.	Supremacy of EU law	The Merchant Shipping Act 1988 had to be repealed, as it conflicted with EU law.
Van Duyn v Home Office (1974)	A Dutch national wished to enter the UK to take up work with the Church of Scientology.	Effect of treaties	A state is precluded from refusing its own nationals the right of entry or residence.
Macarthys Ltd v Smith (1980)	A woman claimed equal pay with a male counterpart who was not currently employed but had been previously.	Effect of treaties	The principle that men and women should receive equal pay for equal work, enshrined in Article 119 of the Treaty of Rome, is not confined to situations in which men and women are contemporaneously doing equal work for the same employer.
Diocese of Hallam Trustee v Connaughton (1996)	This involved very similar facts to *Macarthys Ltd v Smith* (1980).	As above	As above
Marshall v Southampton and South West Hampshire Area Health Authority (1986)	This involved a challenge to the different retirement ages of men and women.	Conflict of law between a national legal system and EU law	There is no horizontal effect of treaties.

Case	Facts	Relevant area	*Ratio decidendi*
Francovich v Italian Republic (1991)	Italy had not implemented directives to protect workers in insolvency cases.	Effect of directives	The state must impose directives to avoid being liable for the consequences.
Von Colson v Land Nordrhein-Westfalen (1984)	A female German national was refused employment at a prison on the basis of her gender, contrary to the Equal Treatment Directive.	Effect of directives	A national court's duty to interpret national law in accordance with EU law means directives become almost horizontally effective.

Now test yourself

TESTED ☐

1 Explain two forms of EU law.
2 Which institution is made up of members elected directly by the people of the Member States?
3 Which institution's membership varies depending on the topic under discussion?
4 Explain the impact of membership of the EU on the law of England and Wales.

Answers online

Exam summary

In the exam, you MAY be asked to:
● explain one or more of the different types of EU institution
● describe the sources of EU law
● discuss the advantages and disadvantages of the impact of EU law on the law of England and Wales.

These types of question will generally require mid-length answers and be worth 10 or 15 marks.

4 The law of tort

The law of tort is one of the four main substantive areas of law in the OCR A Level Law H415 specification and is assessed in Section B of the Component 2 exam paper. It comprises a series of topics which examine both common-law rules and statutes relevant to the English legal system, where although there is no contractual relationship, the civil law holds that a person or organisation owes a legal responsibility to another. Following a breach of that responsibility, the party causing the 'wrong' or injury can be sued.

You will need to be able to:
- define and explain the principles, defences and remedies in tort law, and be competent in applying these
- understand the rules and theory in tort before carrying out an examination of the key principle of negligence
- understand the statutory impact where damage is suffered by a visitor or trespasser to an occupier's land
- understand the land-based torts of nuisance and *Rylands v Fletcher*
- apply defences such as those of contributory negligence or those specific to nuisance, while considering whether the tortfeasor was employed and acting in the course of employment, thus warranting a claim in vicarious liability.

4.1 Rules and theory

Tort law rules

REVISED

Torts are established by both common-law rules and Acts of Parliament. They form part of what is known as private law, because the state does not get involved in them: i.e. they are not crimes that are investigated and prosecuted by public bodies to protect us all, rather they provide redress when we suffer damage to our person, property or enjoyment of our land through the non-criminal actions of others.

Civil law is concerned with settling disputes between parties. It is not to punish wrongdoing.

Tort law allows a person to claim compensation when they have been injured or their property has been damaged. The individual parties involved in a civil claim are the 'claimant' and the 'defendant'.

The state is not usually concerned with tort law, as the action is between the persons involved in the incident. If the claimant is successful in proving their case, they will ask the court to award a remedy.

> **Tort law:** an area of the law that allows a person to claim compensation when they have been injured or their property has been damaged.

> **Revision activity**
>
> The defendant is not called 'guilty' in civil law. What word do we use instead?

> **Typical mistake**
>
> Do not mix up the terminology used in criminal and civil law, such as the tests in negligence!

Establishing liability: burden and standard of proof

In civil law, the burden of proving that the defendant is liable is on the claimant. The standard of proof in civil cases is 'on the balance of probabilities'. This means that it is more likely than not that the claimant is telling the truth.

The claimant merely has to establish that the defendant was at fault for the incident and responsible for the damage.

The civil courts of first instance are different from those that deal with criminal law.

Revision activity

Identify the civil courts and determine how the appropriate court is selected.

Fault or no fault

Fault was first introduced into negligence law in *Cambridge Water v Eastern Counties Leather* (1994). Before that, fault was not always necessary for damages to be paid.

Fault means that there is some wrongdoing by the defendant, and is a requirement in torts such as:
- negligence
- occupiers' liability.

However, it is not needed in torts such as:
- nuisance
- *Rylands v Fletcher*
- vicarious liability.

In these, the claimant does not need to show how and why the incident happened – simply that it did, and then establish a causal link to the damage suffered.

Fault: there is some wrongdoing by the defendant.

Defences

As in criminal law, there are ways for a defendant to refute a claim. However, there are far fewer defences in civil law than in criminal law.

Defences generally divert blameworthiness away from the defendant back to the claimant, suggesting they were, to some degree, responsible for their own damage.

Remedies

Remedies for successful action can be:
- **damages** – money calculated to return the claimant to their original position before the tort had taken place (in so far as it is possible to do so with money), or
- **injunction** – a court order to stop; this is most common in torts such as trespass and nuisance.

In civil cases, the general rule is that the loser pays the winner's legal costs in addition to their own costs, so it is a risky business. See Section 1 and make the link.

Damages: money calculated to return the claimant to their original position before the tort had taken place (in so far as it is possible to do so with money).

Injunction: a court order to stop; this is most common in torts such as trespass and nuisance.

Tort law theory

REVISED

This is background material for what will be assessed in Paper 2. Chapters 4.2–4.8 give the substantive detail, including case information.

Policy decisions and duty of care

Most of the law relating to negligence is common law, which means it is developed by judges when deciding cases. When deciding whether to impose liability in an area not previously dealt with, judges exercise caution so as not to create an avalanche of new claims.

These types of decisions are known as 'policy decisions' – they are not made simply to achieve individual justice, but to create a precedent that is fair, just and reasonable.

The factors judges take into consideration are:
- loss allocation – who can afford to bear the loss? Is there any insurance? Is either body funded by the taxpayer?
- floodgates – will imposing liability lead to a high volume of new claims? What would the impact of this be on insurance, the courts, public-funded bodies?
- the practical impact of imposing liability – will standards be raised as a consequence of this deterrent, or will essential funds be diverted away from front-line activities to defend legal claims?

These issues often arise in the context of public-funded bodies and in particular in relation to the police, the CPS, local authorities and the emergency services.

Key cases in this area include *Caparo v Dickman* (1990), *Hill v Chief Constable of West Yorkshire* (1988) and *Michael v Chief Constable of South Wales* (2015).

However, in the recent Supreme Court judgment in *Robinson v Chief Constable of West Yorkshire* (2018), Lord Reed (para. 55) reiterated that *Hill* is not:

> '... authority for the proposition that the police enjoy a general immunity from suit in respect of anything done by them in the course of investigating or preventing crime ... [but in fact] the liability of the police for negligence or other tortious conduct resulting in personal injury, where liability would arise under ordinary principles of the law of tort, was expressly confirmed.'

Also, in *Robinson* Lord Mance stated (para. 84):

> 'It would be unrealistic to suggest that, when recognising and developing an established category, the courts are not influenced by policy considerations.'

Landmark examples are *Donoghue v Stevenson* (1932) in relation to physical injury and *Hedley Byrne and Co. Ltd v Heller and Partners Ltd* (1963) in relation to economic loss.

Factors governing the objective standard of care in an action for negligence

In *Vaughan v Menlove* (1837), the defendant built a haystack near his property line, adjacent to the claimant's property. The haystack caught fire and spread to the claimant's barns, stables and cottages. The court said:

> 'If the standard was that the defendant only needed to act "*bona fide* to the best of his own judgement", that would leave so vague a line as to afford no rule at all, the degree of judgement belonging to each individual being infinitely various. We ought to adhere to a standard which requires in all cases a regard to caution such as a man of ordinary prudence would observe.'

Hence, the test that compares the defendant to the reasonable person was born.

Now test yourself

1 Why is the burden in civil law lower than in criminal law?
2 Where is fault not always necessary in tort?
3 Where is fault required in civil law? Which case brought about this change?
4 What is the aim of damages?
5 When might damages be paid in lieu of an injunction?
6 What are policy decisions, and why do they exist?
7 Why is it preferable to sue the employer rather than the employee?
8 Why would a subjective test for negligence be inappropriate?

Answers online

Exam summary

In the exam, you MAY be asked to discuss (in outline) in a full-length essay question:

● any of the rules of the law of tort, such as establishing liability and fault
● any of the theory of the law of tort.

These types of question will each be worth a maximum of 25 marks.

4.2 Liability in negligence

Liability for injury to people and damage to property

Personal injury (which includes death) has recently been discussed by the Supreme Court in *Dryden v Johnson Matthey Plc* (2018), and now, for the first time, has a legal definition in order to be actionable.

To amount to actionable personal injury, the following requirements must be satisfied:

- There must be an impairment of a person's physical condition.
- The impairment damage must be more than trivial.
- The person must be worse off, physically or economically, so that compensation is an appropriate remedy.

This includes an injury sustained to a person's physical capacity of enjoying life, and the absence of symptoms does not prevent a condition amounting to actionable personal injury.

Damage to property relates to personal property, so in the exam look out for things like damage to a claimant's house, car, mobile phone etc. For example, if a car accident is caused by someone's negligence, they will be liable for the injuries caused and the damage caused to the car.

> **Exam tip**
>
> For this part of the course, you need to apply the law to given scenarios.

Duty of care

If a duty does not already exist in law, such as that between road users, between teachers and pupils, and between doctors and patients, then the tests shown in Table 4.2.1 are used to decide whether a new duty should be created.

Table 4.2.1 Tests to decide whether a duty of care should be created

Original test (known as the 'neighbour principle')	New test
Donoghue v Stevenson (1932)	*Caparo v Dickman* (1990)
<ul><li>You must take reasonable care to avoid acts or omissions you can reasonably foresee are likely to injure your neighbour.</li><li>Your neighbour is anyone so closely and directly affected by your actions that you ought reasonably to have them in your contemplation.</li></ul>	<ul><li>The damage must be reasonably foreseeable.</li><li>There must be a relationship of proximity between the parties.</li><li>It must be fair, just and reasonable to impose a duty of care.</li></ul>

You can see that the new test updates the language from *Donoghue* and adds a new element.

Table 4.2.2 explains the new elements of the *Caparo* test that the new Supreme Court case of *Robinson v Chief Constable of West Yorkshire* (2018) tells us should be used 'only in a novel type of case, where established principles do not provide an answer'. Established principles means 'the courts will consider the closest analogies in the existing law, with a view to maintaining the coherence of the law and the avoidance of inappropriate distinctions'.

Therefore, the *Caparo* test will be used only if there are no previous cases that are sufficiently similar.

> **Revision activity**
>
> For a light-hearted moment on this area of law, see www.youtube.com/watch?v=zWia3GCzyLQ

Table 4.2.2 *Caparo* test

Caparo test	Explanation
1 The damage must be reasonably foreseeable.	An objective test
2 There must be a relationship of proximity between the parties.	Close in terms of time, space and relationship
3 It must be fair, just and reasonable to impose a duty of care.	A policy test restricting the imposition of a duty, particularly where imposing a duty might place an unreasonable burden on the operations or budgets of the public services, or might open the floodgates to an avalanche of claims

Exam tip

It is vital to use the facts of the case to illustrate the point of law for all areas of negligence, for example in relation to *Jolley v Sutton* (2002) 'it is reasonably foreseeable that a child will be injured by a boat left abandoned on a park'.

Table 4.2.3 Key cases for duty of care

Case	Facts	Point of law
Dryden v Johnson Matthey Plc (2018)	C worked in a factory making catalytic converters which involved the use of platinum salts that caused illness.	Actionable personal injury was defined for the first time.
Donoghue v Stevenson (1932)	A snail was found in ginger beer.	This created the 'neighbour principle'.
Caparo v Dickman (1990)	Shares were mis-valued.	This updated the neighbour principle with a three-part test, which includes a narrowing of the test.
Robinson v Chief Constable of West Yorkshire (2018)	C, an elderly lady, was injured by a drug dealer who was resisting arrest by the D officers.	*Caparo* is only used if there are no similar cases and there is no policy blanket immunity for the police.
Kent v Griffiths (2000)	An ambulance was late in attending a patient.	The damage was reasonably foreseeable.
Jolley v Sutton LBC (2000)	C, a child, was injured by a boat left abandoned in a park.	'It is reasonably foreseeable that a child will be injured by a boat left abandoned on a park.'
Bourhill v Young (1943)	The nosy fishwife case: she chose to view the scene of an accident.	There was no proximity.
McLoughlin v O'Brian (1983)	C saw the aftermath of a serious accident involving her family and suffered psychiatric loss as a consequence.	There was proximity in this case, as C had no choice.
Hill v Chief Constable of West Yorkshire (1988)	C sued the police for failing to catch the serial killer who murdered her daughter.	It was not fair, just and reasonable for the police to owe a duty in the detection of crime. This was followed in *Michael v Chief Constable of South Wales* (2015).

Breach of the duty of care

Objective standard of care and the reasonable man

An objective test comes from *Blyth v Birmingham Water Works* (1856): 'omitting to do something a reasonable man would do, or doing something a reasonable man would not do'.

Although this is an objective test, an appropriate degree of knowledge may be added to the **reasonable person**. So, a professional will be judged not by the standard of a reasonable person, but by the standard of a reasonable person of that profession. Key cases in this area include *Bolam v Frien Hospital Management Committee* (1957) (although this has now changed for advice given by health care professionals) and *Montgomery v Lanarkshire* (2015).

However, this does not apply to trainees in any skill; therefore the learner driver will be judged by the standard of a reasonable driver – see *Nettleship v Weston* (1971).

A child will be judged by the standard of a reasonable child – see *Mullin v Richards* (1998).

> **Reasonable person:** an objective test, i.e. how a hypothetical person would behave sets a standard against which the defendant is compared; sometimes known as the 'man on the Clapham omnibus' or 'law's ghost God'.

Risk factors

In determining whether the defendant acted reasonably, the court will consider four further factors, outlined in Table 4.2.4 below.

Table 4.2.4 Factors to ascertain whether the defendant acted reasonably

Factor	Explanation	Key case
Degree of risk involved	The greater the risk, the more precautions a defendant will have to take in order for their conduct to be judged as acting at the standard of a reasonable person.	*Bolton v Stone* (1951)
Cost of precautions	The court will not expect the cost of precautions to outweigh the risk involved. Therefore, a defendant does not have to take excessive measures to guard against minor risk. A reasonable person would take reasonable precautions given the circumstances.	*Latimer v AEC* (1952)
Potential seriousness of injury	The more serious the potential injury, the greater the level of care required in order to be judged as acting at the standard of a reasonable person.	*Paris v Stepney Borough Council* (1951)
Importance of the activity	Some risk may be acceptable if the risk undertaken is socially important.	*Watt v Hertfordshire County Council* (1954)

> **Typical mistake**
>
> Your exam answer will not score highly if you fail to make the link between the factors and the impact they have on the standard of the reasonable person.

Table 4.2.5 Key cases for breach of the duty of care

Case	Facts	Point of law
Bolam v Frien Hospital Management Committee (1957)	C was undergoing ECT as treatment for his mental illness. The doctor did not give any relaxant drugs and C suffered a serious fracture.	A professional will be judged not by the standard of a reasonable person, but by the standard of a reasonable person of that profession.
Nettleship v Weston (1971)	D was a learner driver who injured C, her instructor.	Trainees will be judged by the standard of the competent professional.
Mullin v Richards (1998)	Two 15-year-old school girls were fighting with plastic rulers. A ruler snapped and a splinter went into one girl's eyes, causing blindness.	A child will be judged by the standard of a reasonable child.
Bolton v Stone (1951)	Should a cricket club have taken precautions to prevent the injury of a person outside the cricket ground from being hit by a cricket ball?	The greater the risk, the more precautions a defendant will have to take in order for their conduct to be judged as acting at the standard of a reasonable person.
Latimer v AEC (1952)	C worked at D's factory and slipped on the factory floor. D had put up warning signs, mopped up and placed sawdust in the most-used places to make it as safe as possible.	The court will not expect the cost of precautions to outweigh the risk involved.
Paris v Stepney Borough Council (1951)	At work, a splinter of metal went into C's one sighted eye, causing him to become completely blind. The employer did not provide safety goggles.	The more serious the potential injury, the greater the level of care required in order to be judged as acting at the standard of a reasonable person.
Watt v Hertfordshire County Council (1954)	C was injured by equipment not secured due to the rush to save a life.	Some risk may be acceptable if the risk undertaken is socially important.

Damage

REVISED

The resulting damage must be:
- caused by the breach, and
- not too remote from the breach.

Factual causation and the 'but for' test

This means the injury or damage to property must have been caused by the breach of the duty of care, i.e. it would not have happened 'but for' the breach – see *Barnett v Chelsea Hospital* (1969).

> **'But for' test:** the injury or damage to property must have been caused by the breach of the duty of care, i.e. it would not have happened but for the breach.

Legal causation

This means that the loss must be foreseeable as a consequence of the breach. If it is not foreseeable, it is regarded as being too remote from the breach – see *The Wagon Mound* (1961).

However, the precise chain of events from the breach to the damage need not be foreseeable – see *Hughes v Lord Advocate* (1962).

It is not necessary for the extent of the damage to be foreseeable; this is the thin-skull test being used in negligence – see *Smith v Leech Brain* (1962).

Table 4.2.6 Key cases on damage

Case	Facts	Point of law
Barnett v Chelsea Hospital (1969)	A doctor failed to examine a man who had been poisoned. If he had done so, he still could not have saved his life.	Damage must have been caused by the breach.
The Wagon Mound (1961)	A ship leaked oil into Sydney Harbour which led to a fire, destroying a wharf and boats.	Damage must be of a foreseeable type.
Hughes v Lord Advocate (1962)	Two boys went to explore a manhole. An unforeseeable explosion occurred, causing them serious injury.	The precise chain of events leading to the damage need not be foreseeable.
Smith v Leech Brain (1962)	As a result of D's negligence, C incurred a burn to his lip. The lip contained pre-cancerous cells which were triggered by the injury sustained. He died three years later from cancer.	It is not necessary for the extent of the damage to be foreseeable.

Now test yourself

TESTED ☐

1 How and why did *Caparo v Dickman* (1990) change the neighbour principle?
2 What is the difference between *Bourhill v Young* (1943) and *McLoughlin v O'Brian* (1983)?
3 What impact would a highly dangerous situation have on the standard of a reasonable person?
4 How is factual causation tested?
5 What does 'remoteness of damage' mean?

Answers online

Exam tip

Consider using the IDEA method for scenario-based exam questions:
● **I**dentify the point of law.
● **D**escribe the point of law.
● Give a case **E**xample.
● **A**pply the point/case to the facts of the scenario.

Exam summary

In the exam, you MAY be asked to:
● respond to a scenario question based on negligence by advising a:
  – claimant whether they will be successful in a claim under the law of tort against the tortfeasor
  – a defendant, or defendants, whether they can raise any defences to their act or omission
● discuss a key topic or topics of negligence in a full-length essay question relevant to the law of tort.

These types of question will each be worth a maximum of 25 marks.

4.3 Occupiers' liability

Occupiers' liability refers to the duty owed by occupiers to those who come onto their land. There is no requirement for the occupier to also be the owner, or for them to physically occupy the land.

The test applied is one of 'occupational control', and there may be more than one occupier of the same premises. A key case in this area is *Wheat v E. Lacon and Co. Ltd* (1966).

Liability in respect of lawful visitors (Occupiers' Liability Act 1957)

REVISED

Under s 1(3)(a) of the Occupiers' Liability Act 1957, the premises occupied applies not only to land and buildings but also extends to fixed and movable structures, including any vessel, vehicle or aircraft.

In s 2(2), the Act imposes a common duty of care on occupiers to lawful **visitors**:

> 'The common duty of care is to take such care as in all the circumstances of the case is reasonable to see that the visitor will be reasonably safe in using the premises for the purposes for which he is invited or permitted by the occupier to be there.'

The claimable damage under the Occupiers' Liability Act 1957 includes death, personal injury and damage to property.

Lawful visitors

Lawful visitors include:
- invitees – s 1(2): those who have been invited to come onto the land and therefore have express permission to be there; the invitation must not be exceeded
- licensees – s 1(2): those who have express or implied permission to be there; this includes where a licence would be implied at common law (see below)
- those who enter pursuant to a contract – s 5(1), for example paying visitors to see a film at a cinema
- those entering in exercising a statutory right – s 2(6), for example a person entering to read the gas or electricity meters
- implied licence at common law, where there is repeated trespass and no action taken by the occupier to prevent it; this requires an awareness of the trespass and the danger – see *Lowery v Walker* (1911); the courts are more likely to imply a licence if there is something on the land which is particularly attractive and acts as an allurement to draw people on to the land – see *Taylor v Glasgow City Council* (1922).

Standard of care

The standard of care is of the 'reasonable occupier' (a failure to reach the given standard will amount to a breach). However, there are two situations where the standard may vary, outlined in the table below.

Occupiers' liability: the duty owed by occupiers to those who come onto their land.

Exam tip

You will need to apply the law to given scenarios for occupiers' liability.

Visitors: in law, adult visitors are those who have been invited or licensed to enter, or who have a statutory right to enter, or have contractual permission.

Revision activity

Research the relevant (and quite amusing) quote from Scrutton LJ in *The Calgarth* (1927).

Table 4.3.1 Variations on the standard of care under the Occupiers' Liability Act 1957

Situation	Explanation	Key case
Section 2(3)(a) – an occupier must be prepared for children to be less careful than adults.	The court will take into account the age of the child and level of understanding a child of that age may be expected to have.	*Jolley v Sutton* (2000)
Section 2(3)(b) – an occupier may expect that a person in the exercise of his calling will appreciate and guard against any special risks ordinarily incident to it.	This applies where an occupier employs an expert to come onto the premises to undertake work. The expert is expected to know and protect themselves against any dangers that arise from the premises in relation to the calling of the expert. For example, if an occupier calls on a roofing specialist to repair a damaged roof, that roofer would be expected to know the dangers inherent in the work they are engaged to do.	*Roles v Nathan* (1963)

Warnings and warning signs

It may be possible for an occupier to discharge their duty (i.e. reach the standard of a reasonable occupier) by giving a warning of the danger.

However, s 2(4)(a) provides that a warning will not be treated as absolving the occupier of liability unless in all the circumstances it was enough to enable the visitor to be reasonably safe. The warning must cover the danger, but there is no duty to warn against obvious risks – see *Darby v National Trust* (2001).

Dangers arising from actions undertaken by independent contractors

Under s 2(4)(b), an occupier is not liable for dangers created by an independent contractor if the occupier:
- acted reasonably in all the circumstances in entrusting the work to the independent contractor, and
- took reasonable steps to satisfy themselves that the work carried out was properly done and the contractor was competent.

A key case here is *Bottomley v Todmorden Cricket Club* (2003).

Defences

There are a few defences applicable to the Occupiers' Liability Act 1957:
- *Volenti non fit injuria* – s 2(5): the common duty of care does not impose an obligation on occupiers in respect of risks willingly accepted by the visitor.
- Contributory negligence – damages may be reduced under the Law Reform (Contributory Negligence) Act 1945 where the visitor fails to take reasonable care for their own safety.
- Exclusion of liability – s 2(1): allows an occupier to extend, restrict, exclude or modify their duty to visitors, in so far as they are free to do so.

See Chapter 4.6 for more detail on *volenti non fit injuria* and contributory negligence.

Table 4.3.2 Key cases for the Occupiers' Liability Act 1957

Case	Facts	Point of law
Wheat v E. Lacon and Co. Ltd (1966)	C's husband died in a fall while staying in a public house.	Both the brewery and the managers owed a duty.
Lowery v Walker (1911)	C was injured by a dangerous horse when taking a commonly used shortcut.	Licence was implied through repeated trespass, of which D was aware.
Taylor v Glasgow City Council (1922)	A child was poisoned by berries in a public park.	The council was liable: it knew children would be there and it knew the berries were poisonous.
Jolley v Sutton (2000)	Boys were injured while attempting to repair an abandoned boat in a park.	The council had failed to move the boat which was in a park and it knew would be attractive to children.
Roles v Nathan (1963)	Chimney sweeps died of carbon dioxide poisoning while unblocking D's chimney.	D was not liable, as Cs were experts.
Darby v National Trust (2001)	C's husband drowned in a pond commonly used for paddling and swimming. D had taken no steps to prevent this.	As the risk was obvious, D did not need to give warnings.
Bottomley v Todmorden Cricket Club (2003)	C was injured at a firework display held on D's land but run by a contractor.	D was still liable as they had not checked the contractor's insurance and therefore had not taken reasonable steps.

Liability in respect of trespassers (Occupiers' Liability Act 1984)

REVISED

This Act imposes liability on occupiers with regard to persons other than 'visitors'. This includes **trespassers** (and burglars) and those who exceed their permission – see *Revill v Newbery,* (1996).

Section 1(8) states that death and personal injury are the only protected forms of damage; therefore occupiers have no duty in relation to the property of trespassers.

Section 1(3) states that an occupier owes a duty of care to a non-visitor if:
(a) the occupier is aware of a danger or has reasonable grounds to believe that it exists, and
(b) the occupier knows or has reasonable grounds to believe the other is in the vicinity of the danger or may come into the vicinity of the danger, and
(c) the risk is one in which, in all the circumstances of the case, the occupier may reasonably be expected to offer the other some protection.

A key case here is *Donoghue v Folkestone Properties Ltd* (2003).

Standard of care

This is objective, so if not met it will amount to a breach.

Section 1(4) states that the duty is to take such care as is reasonable in all the circumstances of the case to see that the other does not suffer injury on the premises by reason of the danger concerned – see *Ratcliff v McConnell* (1997).

> **Trespassers:** persons on the occupier's land who have no permission or authority to be there.

> **Revision activity**
>
> The origins of this Act can be found in *British Railways Board v Herrington* (1972), which overruled *Addie v Dumbreck* (1929). Can you make the link with the information on judicial precedent in Chapter 3.4?

This also means that it must be the premises themselves that are dangerous, not the activity the claimant chooses to engage in – see *Keown v Coventry Healthcare NHS Trust* (2006).

Warnings and warning signs

Under s 1(5), the duty may be discharged (i.e. reach the standard of a reasonable occupier) by giving a warning or discouraging others from taking the risk – see *Tomlinson v Congleton* (2003).

Defences

There are some defences applicable to the Occupiers' Liability Act 1984:
- *Volenti non fit injuria* – s 1(6): the common duty of care does not impose an obligation on occupiers in respect of risks willingly accepted.
- Contributory negligence – damages may be reduced under the Law Reform (Contributory Negligence) Act 1945 where the trespasser fails to take reasonable care for their own safety.
- Exclusion of liability is not expressly forbidden by the Act so it *may* be possible.

See Chapter 4.6 for more detail on *volenti non fit injuria* and contributory negligence.

Table 4.3.3 Key cases for the Occupiers' Liability Act 1984

Case	Facts	Point of law
Revill v Newbery (1996)	C was a burglar, shot by D.	D was liable, but contributory negligence was taken into consideration and reduced the damages.
Donoghue v Folkestone Properties Ltd (2003)	C was seriously injured by diving into Folkstone harbour on Boxing Day.	It would be reasonable to guard against that in the summer but not at that time of year, so D was not liable.
Ratcliff v McConnell (1997)	C was seriously injured by diving into a college pool late at night.	Locks and warnings were sufficient, so D was not liable.
Keown v Coventry Healthcare NHS Trust (2006)	C, a child, fell from a fire escape he had been climbing.	The premises were not dangerous; therefore D was not liable.
Tomlinson v Congleton (2003)	C was seriously injured by diving into a lake.	The state of the premises was not inherently dangerous; what the claimant chose to do in them was. D was not liable.

Revision activity

There is no obligation in relation to the warning to enable the trespasser to be reasonably safe. How does this contrast with the provision under the 1957 Act?

Exam tip

Look out for scenarios where children trespass regularly and the occupier knows about them. Have they become visitors?

Typical mistake

Do not carelessly lose marks by forgetting to deal with breach, damage and defences. There will be more to the questions than just the duty owed by the occupier.

1 Why are there different statutory provisions for occupiers' liability?
2 Show all the different ways in which children are taken into account by these statutory provisions.
3 How is the claimable damage different between these statutory provisions?
4 Why was Todmorden Cricket Club liable, even though the injuries were caused by an independent contractor?
5 When might a trespasser be treated as a visitor for the purpose of these statutory provisions?

Answers online

Exam summary

In the exam, you MAY be asked to:
● respond to a scenario question based on the Occupiers' Liability Act 1957 or 1984 by advising a defendant, or defendants, whether they:
  – are liable for their acts or omissions
  – can raise any defences to their acts or omissions
● discuss in a full-length essay question a key topic or topics relating to the Occupiers' Liability Act 1957 or 1984.

These types of question will each be worth a maximum of 25 marks.

Liability in respect of trespassers (Occupiers' Liability Act 1984)

4.4 Torts connected to land

For torts connected to land, you need to apply the law to given scenarios in Paper 2. This topic also links well with 'balancing conflicting interests', which is assessed in Paper 3.

Private nuisance

Private nuisance is concerned with protecting the rights of an occupier against 'unreasonable interference with the enjoyment or use of his land'. This often involves disputes between neighbours.

The courts attempt to balance the competing rights of the land owner to use their land as they choose and the rights of the neighbour not to have their use or enjoyment of land interfered with.

In order to bring a claim in private nuisance, a claimant must have an interest in the land in which they claim their enjoyment or use of has been unreasonably interfered with. This means a legal interest, but not necessarily ownership. Key cases here include *Malone v Laskey* (1907) and *Hunter v Canary Wharf* (1997).

However, the defendant – the creator of the nuisance – does not need to own or occupy the land that the nuisance is emitting from; they just need to have used the land. A key case here is *Jones Ltd v Portsmouth City Council* (2002).

'Interference' can be:
- flooding – *Sedleigh-Denfield v O'Callaghan* (1940)
- smells – *Wheeler v JJ Saunders* (1996)
- encroachment – *Lemmon v Webb* (1894)
- noise – *Kennaway v Thompson* (1981)
- balls – *Miller v Jackson* (1977)
- a brothel – *Thompson-Schwab v Costaki* (1956)
- physical damage – *St Helen's Smelting Co. v Tipping* (1865).

> **Private nuisance:** unreasonable interference with the enjoyment or use by the occupier of their land.

> **Revision activity**
>
> Research these cases online.
>
> Do you think the use of the land in *Miller v Jackson* (1977) was unreasonable?

Unlawful interference

This means an unreasonable use of land by the defendant which leads to an unreasonable interference with the claimant's use or enjoyment of their own land – see *London Borough of Southwark v Mills* (1999).

In determining whether or not the use of the land and the interference were reasonable or not, the courts will consider:
- nature of the locality/neighbourhood
- duration
- sensitivity
- malice.

Table 4.4.1 **Factors to consider when deciding whether interference is reasonable**

Factor	Explanation	Key cases
Locality/ neighbourhood	The reasonableness of the use of land will depend on the nature of the locality.	*Hirose Electrical v Peak Ingredients* (2011)
	Planning permission may change the nature of the locality but cannot give permission for a nuisance.	*Coventry v Lawrence* (2012)
	Where the nuisance causes physical damage, the nature of the locality is irrelevant.	*St Helen's Smelting Co. v Tipping* (1865)

Factor	Explanation	Key cases
Duration	Most nuisances consist of a continuing interference, so the claimant seeks an injunction to prevent the reoccurrences. The longer a nuisance lasts, the greater the interference and the more likelihood of it being held to be an unlawful interference. Nevertheless, a temporary activity may still constitute a nuisance.	*De Keyser's Royal Hotel v Spicer Bros* (1914)
Sensitivity	If the claimant is abnormally sensitive or their use of land is particularly sensitive, the defendant will not be liable – unless the activity would amount to a nuisance to a reasonable person using the land in a normal manner.	*Robinson v Kilvert* (1889) *McKinnon Industries v Walker* (1951)
Malice	If the defendant's actions are malicious, they are more likely to be held unreasonable.	*Christie v Davey* (1893) *Hollywood Silver Fox Farm v Emmett* (1936)

Typical mistake

Do not assume that the public benefit of the thing creating the nuisance is a defence; it is not – see *Miller v Jackson* (1977). 'Coming to the nuisance', i.e. the thing creating the nuisance was there before the claimant, is not a defence either.

Revision activity

Find and read Lord Justice Jackson's four-point summary in *Coventry v Lawrence* (2012).

Foreseeability

The foreseeability of the type of damage is important in claims for nuisance. It applies as it does for claims based in negligence. A key case here is *Cambridge Water v Eastern Counties Leather Plc* (1994).

The Wagon Mound No 1 case applies to determine remoteness of damage.

In *Hunter v Canary Wharf* (1997), the judges, in holding that a claimant must have an interest in the land affected by the nuisance, appear to have ruled out the possibility of a claim for purely personal injury arising from nuisance.

Table 4.4.2 **Key cases on private nuisance**

Case	Facts	Relevant area	*Ratio decidendi*
Malone v Laskey (1907)	C was injured when the cistern fell on her in the lavatory.	Legal interest in land	She was unsuccessful in her claim as she did not have a proprietary interest in the house.
Hunter v Canary Wharf (1997)	Cs lived in the Isle of Dogs and complained that the erection of Canary Wharf Tower interfered with their television reception.	Legal interest in land	Many Cs had no proprietary interest: children living with parents, relations, lodgers or spouses of the tenant or owner of the property. The claim failed.
Jones Ltd v Portsmouth City Council (2002)	The roots of trees encroached on C's property and led to subsidence of the property.	Legal interest in land	Portsmouth City Council was liable as it had lawful exercise of control over the trees, even though it did not own the land.

Case	Facts	Relevant area	*Ratio decidendi*
London Borough of Southwark v Mills (1999)	Complaints related to the lack of soundproofing, meaning C could hear the day-to-day activities of their neighbours.	Must be unreasonable	There was no nuisance. Nuisance is based on the concept of a reasonable user.
Hirose Electrical v Peak Ingredients (2011)	D manufactured ingredients for curries in an industrial estate, close to C's business. C complained about the smells from D's premises.	Neighbourhood	Significance to the location of the premises and the character of the industrial estate. D's food additive manufacturing was permitted.
Coventry v Lawrence (2012)	Motor sports expansion was becoming noisier.	Planning permission changing the neighbourhood	If the character of a locality is changed as a consequence of planning permission, then: (a) nuisance must be decided against the background of its changed character (b) otherwise offensive activities in that locality cease to constitute a nuisance.
St Helen's Smelting Co. v Tipping (1865)	Smelting works caused damage to crops, trees and foliage.	Physical damage	Where there is physical damage to property, the locality principle has no relevance.
De Keyser's Royal Hotel v Spicer Bros (1914)	Building work was carried out at night.	Duration/ timing	Interference was considered unreasonable, since it interfered with C's sleep.
Robinson v Kilvert (1889)	D let out the ground floor of the premises to C. The heat generated from D's work damaged brown paper belonging to C.	Sensitivity	D was not liable.
McKinnon Industries v Walker (1951)	Noxious fumes and smuts had deposited over C's shrubs, trees, hedges and flowers, causing them to die.	Sensitivity	Although the flowers were sensitive, the others were not, so there was still unlawful interference.
Hollywood Silver Fox Farm v Emmett (1936)	D objected to a fox farm. He fired a gun on his own land with the intention to scare the foxes and impede breeding.	Malice	D was liable despite the abnormal sensitivity of the foxes, because he was motivated by malice.
Cambridge Water v Eastern Counties Leather Plc (1994)	Solvents seeped through the floor of the building into the soil below. They made their way to the water company borehole.	Foreseeable type of damage	It was not reasonably foreseeable that the spillages would result in the closing of the borehole.

Public nuisance

REVISED

The 'nuisance' element is exactly the same as in private nuisance, so the 'interference' material above applies here too.

The public element was defined in *Attorney General v PYA Quarries* (1957) as a nuisance 'which materially affects the reasonable comfort of life of a class of Her Majesty's subjects'.

> **Public nuisance:** a nuisance which materially affects the reasonable comfort of life of a class of Her Majesty's subjects.

This tort requires there to be a class or group of people affected, and the action will be taken on their behalf by either their local authority or the Attorney General. No minimum number has been set for a 'class', so we can assume it just means the nuisance must interfere with more than one person.

Also, there is no requirement for proprietary interest in the land, so this can include traffic and road access issues if they interfere with comfort as unreasonable interferences as outlined above.

As a rule, individuals cannot claim for public nuisance unless they can show 'special damage' which is 'peculiar, direct and substantial' – see *Benjamin v Storr* (1874).

However, it is possible for one problem to give rise to actions in both types of nuisance – see *Halsey v Esso* (1961).

Table 4.4.3 Key cases on public nuisance

Case	Facts	Relevant area
Attorney General v PYA Quarries (1957)	The quarry caused noise, dust and vibration interference to a local community.	It defines 'public'.
Benjamin v Storr (1874)	Frequent loading of D's wagons blocked the light of the plaintiff's coffee house and detracted from his enjoyment of his dwelling.	The damage suffered was above that of the class (the rest of the street).
Halsey v Esso (1961)	C suffered sleepless nights and damage to his vehicle caused by a petrol depot and not suffered by the rest of the class.	C suffered special damage, and damage to his washing gave rise to private nuisance. One problem may cause both types of nuisance.

Rylands v Fletcher

REVISED

Although named after a case, this is now a tort in its own right. It is a form of strict liability, because the defendant may be liable without being negligent.

Consequently, it is controversial and therefore a restrictive approach has been taken to imposing liability under *Rylands v Fletcher*.

Rylands v Fletcher: where the escape of non-naturally stored material onto adjoining property damages or destroys that property.

Case details: *Rylands v Fletcher* (1868)

The defendant constructed a reservoir on his land, above a disused mine. Water from the reservoir filtered through to the disused mine shafts and then spread to a neighbouring working mine owned by the claimant, causing extensive damage.

Lord Cranworth said:

> 'If a person brings, or accumulates, on his land anything which, if it should escape, may cause damage to his neighbour, he does so at his peril. If it does escape, and cause damage, he is responsible, however careful he may have been, and whatever precautions he may have taken to prevent the damage.'

Therefore, the requirements for an action in *Rylands v Fletcher* are:
- accumulation on the defendant's land
- a thing likely to do mischief if it escapes
- escape
- non-natural use of land
- damage that is not too remote.

Accumulation

Table 4.4.4 Requirements and key cases for 'accumulation'

Requirement	Key cases
The defendant must bring a hazardous thing onto their land and keep it there.	*Giles v Walker* (1890) *Ellison v Ministry of Defence* (1997)
The thing must be accumulated for the defendant's own purposes.	*Dunne v North West Gas Board* (1964)
The thing that escapes need not be the thing accumulated.	*Miles v Forest Rock Granite* (1918)

A thing likely to do mischief if it escapes

The thing need not be inherently hazardous. It need only be a thing likely to cause damage if it escapes, for example:

- a flag pole – *Shiffman v The Grand Priory of St John* (1936)
- branches from yew trees – *Crowhurst v Amersham Burial Board* (1879)
- a fairground ride – *Hale v Jennings Bros* (1938)
- electricity – *Hillier v Air Ministry* (1962).

However, in *TransCo. v Stockport* (2004), Lord Hoffmann referred to the fact that claims for personal injury had been admitted in the past but stated:

> 'The point is now settled by [*Cambridge Water*] which decided that *Rylands v Fletcher* is a special form of nuisance and *Hunter v Canary Wharf* ... which decided that nuisance is a tort against land. It must, I think, follow that damages for personal injuries are not recoverable under the rule.'

Revision activity

Which of the two cases mentioned here would Lord Hoffman's comment affect?

Escape

There must be an escape from the defendant's land. An injury inflicted by the accumulation of a hazardous substance on the land itself will not invoke liability. A key case on escape is *Read v Lyons* (1947).

In *British Celanese v AH Hunt Ltd* (1969), the judge said the escape should be 'from a set of circumstances over which the defendant has control to a set of circumstances where he does not'.

Non-natural use of land

This means the use must be 'extraordinary and unusual'. A use may be extraordinary and unusual at one time or in one place, but not so at another time or in another place.

A key case for this is *TransCo. v Stockport MBC* (2004).

Remoteness of damage

As in nuisance, liability is subject to the rules on remoteness of damage – see *Cambridge Water v Eastern Counties Leather* (1994) above.

There is no liability for pure economic loss under *Rylands v Fletcher*. A key case here is *Weller v Foot and Mouth Disease Research Institute* (1966).

Table 4.4.5 Key cases for *Rylands v Fletcher*

Case	Facts	Relevant area	*Ratio decidendi* (if not stated above)
Giles v Walker (1890)	Thistles from D's land blew into neighbouring land and damaged C's crops.	Accumulation	D had not brought the thistles onto his land, and there can be no liability for a thing which naturally accumulates on land.
Ellison v Ministry of Defence (1997)	Bulk fuel installations at an airfield caused rainwater to run off and flood neighbouring land.	Accumulation	The rainwater accumulated naturally and was not kept there artificially.
Dunne v North West Gas Board (1964)	Gas escaped from a gas main caused by a burst water main. It travelled along a sewer and was ignited, causing explosions which resulted in injuries.	Accumulation	The Gas Board had not accumulated gas for its own purposes.
Miles v Forest Rock Granite (1918)	D was blasting rocks using explosives. Some rocks flew onto the highway, injuring C.	Accumulation	The explosives were accumulated and caused the rocks to escape.
Shiffman v The Grand Priory of St John (1936)	D's flag pole fell and hit C.	Mischief	This amounted to an escape.
Read v Lyons (1947)	C worked in D's factory, making explosives for the Ministry of Supply. An explosion killed a man and injured C. There was no evidence that negligence had caused the explosion.	Escape	There was no escape.
TransCo. v Stockport MBC (2004)	Water supply pipes leaked and caused damage to gas supply pipes.	Non-natural	Although strictly speaking they are not natural, in this day and age they are not extraordinary and unusual either, so D was not liable.
Weller v Foot and Mouth Disease Research Institute (1966)	A virus escaped, affecting cattle and making them unsaleable.	Remoteness	There is no liability for pure economic loss.

Exam tip

To prepare for exam questions in this area, use the IDEA/ILAC method.

Now test yourself

1 What does a claimant need in order to make a claim in private nuisance?
2 What is interference?
3 What can make interference unreasonable?
4 How many people must be affected for a nuisance to become public?
5 Does the 'thing' need to be dangerous in *Rylands v Fletcher*?
6 What does 'escape' mean in *Rylands v Fletcher*?

Answers online

Exam summary

In the exam, you MAY be asked to:
- respond to a scenario based on public nuisance/private nuisance/*Rylands v Fletcher* by advising a:
  - claimant whether they will be successful in bringing a claim against a tortfeasor
  - defendant, or defendants, whether they can raise any defences to their acts or omissions
- discuss in a full-length essay question a key topic or topics of public nuisance/private nuisance/*Rylands v Fletcher*.

These types of question will each be worth a maximum of 25 marks.

4.5 Vicarious liability

For the topic of **vicarious liability**, you will need to apply the law to given scenarios in Paper 2. Vicarious liability is usually assessed alongside negligence, and not on its own.

> **Vicarious liability:** a third person has legal responsibility for the unlawful actions of another.

> **Typical mistake**
>
> This area of law changes frequently – it is 'on the move', according to Lord Phillips in *Various Claimants v Catholic Child Welfare Society* (2012). Do not take the law for granted: check on new developments, as they happen all the time.

Nature and purpose of vicarious liability

REVISED

Employers are vicariously liable for the torts of their employees that are committed during the course of employment. The reasons for this were reiterated by Lord Phillips:

- The employer is more likely to have the means to compensate the victim than the employee, and can be expected to have insured against that liability.
- The tort will have been committed as a result of activity being performed by the employee on behalf of the employer.
- The employee's activity is likely to be part of the business activity of the employer.
- The employer, by employing the employee to carry out the activity, will have created the risk of the tort committed by the employee.
- The employee will, to a greater or lesser degree, have been under the control of the employer.

Three questions must be asked in order to establish liability:

1. Was a tort committed? (For the purposes of this course it is likely to be negligence, but the same principles can also be used in criminal law.)
2. Was the tortfeasor an employee?
3. Was the employee acting in the course of employment when the tort was committed?

Liability for employees

REVISED

Testing employment status

The rules for establishing whether a relationship is one of employment can be found in *Ready Mixed Concrete v Minister of Pensions* (1968) and require the following:

- The work is provided in consideration of a wage.
- The tortfeasor is under the other party's control.
- The other terms of the agreement are consistent with it being a contract of employment; for example there are provisions for holidays etc.

See *Cox v Ministry of Justice* (2016) below and the rules for contractors.

An employer will only be liable for torts which the employee commits in the course of employment. An employer will usually be liable for:

- wrongful acts which are actually authorised by the employer, and
- acts which are wrongful ways of doing something authorised by the employer, even if the acts themselves were expressly forbidden by the employer.

Where there is doubt about this, the courts use the 'close connection test'. This examines the closeness of the connection between the work the employee was employed to do and the tortious conduct:

1 What function or field of activities has been entrusted by the employer to the employee (i.e. what was the nature of the job)? This is to be viewed broadly.
2 Was there a sufficient connection between the position in which the employee was employed and the wrongful conduct to make it right for the employer to be held liable?

A key case here is *Mohamud v WM Morrison Supermarkets Plc* (2016).

Where a defendant is held to be acting outside of the course of employment, they are described as being 'on a frolic of their own' – Parke B in *Joel v Morison* (1834).

Liability for the crimes of employees

The principle of vicarious liability is clearly where no fault has to be proved by the claimant on the employer at the time of the commission of the tort.

If the person who commits the tort is employed and acting in the course of employment, the employer will be liable without further proof.

It could be said that the employer is at fault in a number of ways:
- The employer has chosen an employee who is liable to, or who could, commit a tort at work.
- The training for the job may be inadequate or inappropriate.
- The employer should have supervised the employee more effectively.

However, on this last point, employers are likely to want to allow employees, especially more experienced ones, greater freedom to do their work, as otherwise an army of supervisors will have to be employed to closely monitor every employee for every minute of work.

Liability for independent contractors

Traditionally, employers will only be liable for the torts of their employees, not for the torts of their independent contractors. However, in *Cox v Ministry of Justice* (2016), the Supreme Court set out the following (author's bullets):

'A relationship other than one of employment is, in principle, capable of giving rise to vicarious liability where:

- harm is wrongfully done by an individual

- who carries on activities as an integral part of the business activities carried on by a defendant and for its benefit (rather than his activities being entirely attributable to the conduct of a recognisably independent business of his own or of a third party),

- and where the commission of the wrongful act is a risk created by the defendant by assigning those activities to the individual in question.'

This may now mean that organisations are vicariously liable for the torts of anyone who carries out activities on their behalf, provided the third bullet point is also satisfied.

Revision activity

In light of the decision in *Mohamud v WM Morrison Supermarkets Plc* (2016), examine these older cases and decide whether the employees would now be held to be acting the course of their employment or on a frolic of their own:
- *Limpus v London General Omnibus Co.* (1862)
- *Smith v Crossley Brothers* (1951)
- *Rose v Plenty* (1976)
- *Lister v Helsey Hall* (2001)
- *N v Chief Constable of Merseyside Police* (2006).

Table 4.5.1 Key cases for vicarious liability

Case	Facts	Relevant area	*Ratio decidendi*
Ready Mixed Concrete v Minister of Pensions (1968)	A driver's contract declared him an 'independent contractor' but he had to purchase his own vehicle which was painted in company colours and driven complying with company rules.	While not a vicarious liability case, it provided a definition used in vicarious liability.	It provided a definition of an employee under a 'contract of service'.
Various Claimants v Catholic Child Welfare Society (2012)	Children were abused while in the care of a residential institution.	Wholescale review of the current law	It laid the foundations for the more detailed principles in *Cox* and *Mohamud* – see below.
Cox v Ministry of Justice (2016)	C worked in a prison kitchen and was injured by the negligence of a prisoner 'working' in the kitchen.	Was the prisoner an 'employee' of the MoJ for this purpose?	Yes – see above.
Mohamud v WM Morrison Supermarkets Plc (2016)	C was assaulted by a member of staff in a Morrison's petrol station.	Was the employee acting in the course of his employment?	Yes. It does not matter whether he was motivated by personal racism rather than a desire to benefit his employer's business.
Joel v Morison (1834)	Joel was struck down by a horse and cart, whose driver was Morison's agent. The driver had detoured to visit a friend when the accident occurred.	Was the employee acting in the course of his employment?	The driver was doing Morison's business, so he was not on a 'frolic'.

Now test yourself

TESTED ☐

1 What does a claimant need in order to establish vicarious liability?
2 What is the 'close connection test'?
3 What is a 'frolic of his own'?
4 If my employer asks me to collect some provisions from warehouse A, but I decide I prefer warehouse B, will my employer be liable for any torts I commit while in warehouse B?
5 Why does the identity of the defendant in *Cox v Ministry of Justice* (2016) make this interesting in light of *Caparo v Dickman* (1990) and *Hill v Chief Constable of West Yorkshire* (1988)?

Answers online

Exam summary

In the exam, you MAY be asked to:
- respond to a scenario based on vicarious liability by advising a:
  - claimant whether they will be successful in bringing a claim against a tortfeasor
  - defendant, or defendants, whether they can raise any defences to any act or omission of their employee (or alleged employee)
- discuss in a full-length essay question a key topic or topics on vicarious liability.

These types of question will each be worth a maximum of 25 marks.

4.6 Defences

You will need to apply the law for defences to given scenarios in Paper 2. Defences will not be assessed on their own but with the most appropriate substantive tort.

Contributory negligence

The Law Reform (Contributory Negligence) Act 1945 provides that contributory negligence is a partial defence. That means the courts can apportion loss between the parties, making a fairer outcome than a complete defence. A key case here is *Revill v Newbery* (1996).

Section 1(1) of this Act provides that 'where a person suffers damage as a result partly of his own fault and partly the fault of another(s), a claim shall not be defeated by reason of the fault of the person suffering damage'.

> **Exam tip**
>
> This is a great example of balancing conflicting interests and substantive justice.

Requirements of contributory negligence

The burden of proof is on the defendant to demonstrate the following:

1 The claimant failed to take proper care in the circumstances for their own safety. Lack of proper care for own safety is not the same as 'breach of the duty of care'. It varies, and all circumstances are taken into account, including the age of the claimant. A key case here is *Gough v Thorns* (1966).

2 The failure to take care was a contributory cause of the damage suffered. This has included:
   ○ failure to wear a seat belt – *Froom v Butcher* (1976)
   ○ failure to wear a helmet on a motorcycle – *O'Connell v Jackson* (1971)
   ○ failure to fasten a helmet on a motorcycle – *Capps v Miller* (1989)
   ○ exposing oneself to danger by inappropriate use of a vehicle – *Davies v Swan Motor Co.* (1949) and *Jones v Livox Quarries* (1952)
   ○ suicide – *Reeves v Commissioner of Police of the Metropolis* (2000)
   ○ failure to follow safety instructions – *Stapley v Gypsum Mines* (1953).

> **Revision activity**
>
> Research these case details online.

There is considerable overlap between contributory negligence and consent (below) which is a complete defence. However, since 1945 the courts have been less willing to make a finding of consent. Instead they prefer to apportion loss between the parties, rather than taking the 'all or nothing' approach of consent.

Volenti non fit injuria (consent)

Volenti non fit injuria, also known as consent, is a complete defence. It requires a freely entered and 'voluntary agreement by the claimant, in full knowledge of the circumstances', to absolve the defendant of all legal consequences of their actions.

Elements of *volenti non fit injuria*

Voluntary

● The agreement must be voluntary and freely entered.
● If the claimant is not in a position to exercise free choice, the defence will not succeed.
● This element is most commonly seen in relation to employment relationships, rescuers and suicide.

Agreement

This may be express or implied. An implied agreement may exist where the claimant demonstrates a willingness to accept the legal risks as well as the physical risks.

Lord Denning in *Nettleship v Weston* (1971) said:

'Knowledge of the risk of injury is not enough. Nothing will suffice short of an agreement to waive any claim for negligence. The [claimant] must agree expressly or impliedly to waive any claim for any injury that may befall him due to the lack of reasonable care by the defendant: or more accurately due to the failure by the defendant to measure up to the duty of care which the law requires of him.'

A key case here is *Smith v Charles Baker and Sons* (1891).

Knowledge

- The claimant must have had knowledge of the full nature and extent of the risk that they ran – see *Morris v Murray* (1991).
- A rescuer is not regarded as having freely and voluntarily accepted the risk – see *Haynes v Harwood* (1935).
- A participant in sporting events/games is taken to consent to the risk of injury which occurs in the course of the ordinary performance of the sport – see *Condon v Basi* (1985).

Volenti non fit injuria and occupiers' liability

Section 2(5) of the Occupiers' Liability Act 1957 and s 1(6) of the Occupiers' Liability Act 1984 provide that occupiers owe no duty in respect of risks willingly accepted by a person. There is no need to establish an agreement. A key case here is *Titchener v British Railways Board* (1983).

Table 4.6.1 **Key cases for *volenti non fit injuria***

Case	Facts	Relevant area	*Ratio decidendi*
Revill v Newbery (1996)	C shot a burglar and sued for damages relating to his injuries.	Contributory negligence	He was two-thirds responsible for own injures.
Gough v Thorns (1966)	A lorry slowed down so that children could cross a road. D's car came through the gap and crashed into a child, causing serious injury.	Contributory negligence	A very young child cannot be guilty of contributory negligence. An older child may be, but it depends on the circumstances.
Smith v Charles Baker and Sons (1891)	Workers were putting stones into a steam crane which swung where C was working. A stone fell out of the crane and struck him on the head.	Consent – agreement	C may have been aware of the danger of the job but had not consented to the lack of care. In an employment situation, knowing a danger exists is not to be equated with agreeing to it.
Morris v Murray (1991)	C and D had been drinking all day. D, a pilot, suggested they took an aircraft for a flight. They took off but crashed shortly after. C was seriously injured.	Consent – knowledge of the risk	The risk in accepting a ride in an aircraft from an obviously heavily intoxicated pilot was so glaringly dangerous that C could be taken to have voluntarily accepted it.
Haynes v Harwood (1935)	D left a horse-drawn van unattended in a crowded street. The horses bolted. A police officer was injured when he tried to stop the horses to save a woman and children in their path.	Consent – rescuers	A rescuer does not 'freely' accept risk.

Case	Facts	Relevant area	*Ratio decidendi*
Condon v Basi (1985)	C's leg was broken after a tackle in a football match.	Consent – sports injuries	A participant accepts the risks of injury in sporting activities, but not if this occurs outside the rules of the game.
Titchener v British Railways Board (1983)	C was injured while trespassing on a train line.	Consent and Occupiers' Liability Acts 1957 and 1984	C was fully aware of the danger of crossing a train line, so she must be taken to have consented to assuming the risk.

Defences to nuisance

REVISED

Table 4.6.2 **Defences to nuisance**

Defence	Explanation	Key case
Ordinary use of the land	Ordinary noises do not constitute nuisance.	*Southwark London Borough Council v Mills* (2001)
Statutory authority	Nuisances can be caused by public authorities acting under statutory powers, e.g. roadworks to improve the access to a water main. This is a defence provided the 'nuisance' does not exceed that which was authorised.	*Allen v Gulf Oil Refining Ltd* (1981)
Act of God and nuisances arising naturally	This refers to an event that happens independently of any human action, such as a storm. It is a complete defence.	*Nicholls v Marsland* (1875)
	However, once the occupier becomes aware of the nuisance and fails to remedy it within a reasonable time, they may be liable for damage.	*Goldman v Hargrave* (1967)
Prescription	This rarely succeeds in practice.	
	If D can show that they have been committing the nuisance for 20 years and that C has been aware of this and done nothing about it, then D has a defence.	*Coventry v Lawrence* (2014)
	The 20 years will not start to run until C becomes aware of the nuisance.	*Sturges v Bridgman* (1879)

Typical mistake

Remember that planning permission does not authorise nuisance, but it may change the nature of the 'locality'.

Table 4.6.3 Key cases for defences to nuisance

Case	Facts	Relevant area	*Ratio decidendi*
Southwark London Borough Council v Mills (2001)	C complained about normal household noises.	Ordinary use of land defence to nuisance	It was not a nuisance, as the noises complained of were merely ordinary.
Allen v Gulf Oil Refining Ltd (1981)	C lived near an oil refinery and claimed the operation of the refinery was a nuisance.	Statutory authority defence to nuisance	Gulf Oil was entitled to statutory immunity in respect of nuisance. The refinery conformed with Parliament's intention in the Gulf Oil Refining Act 1965.
Nicholls v Marsland (1875)	D made a reservoir by damming a stream. An extraordinarily heavy rainstorm caused the dam to burst and wash away C's bridges.	Act of God defence to nuisance	The defence applied.
Goldman v Hargrave (1967)	A tree growing on D's land was struck by lightning and set on fire. D failed to extinguish the fire, which spread to C's property and caused damage.	Act of God defence to nuisance	The defence did not apply.
Coventry v Lawrence (2014)	Speedway and stock-car racing had taken place since the 1970s.	Prescription as a defence to nuisance	This established a prescriptive right.
Sturges v Bridgman (1879)	D's premises adjoined those of C (a doctor). For over 20 years, D had used noisy machinery without complaint. C built a consulting room in his garden and then complained of the noise.	Prescription as a defence to nuisance	It failed, since the nuisance commenced only when the new building was erected. Before then, there was no right of action as there had been no nuisance.

Defences to *Rylands v Fletcher*

REVISED

Table 4.6.4 Defences to *Rylands v Fletcher*

Defence	Explanation	Key case
Act of a stranger	D has a complete defence if the escape was caused by the act of a stranger over which D had no control and whose actions could not have been reasonably foreseen.	*Perry v Kendricks Transport Limited* (1956), in contrast with *Ribee v Norrie* (2000)
Act of God	This has the same meaning as under private nuisance, but there is a different case example.	*Carstairs v Taylor* (1871)
Statutory authority	This has the same meaning as under private nuisance, but there is a different case example.	*Green v Chelsea Waterworks Co.* (1894)
Consent/ benefit	If C receives a benefit from the thing accumulated, they may be deemed to have consented to its accumulation.	*Peters v Prince of Wales Theatre* (1943)

Table 4.6.5 Key cases for defences to *Rylands v Fletcher*

Case	Facts	Relevant area	*Ratio decidendi*
Perry v Kendricks Transport Limited (1956)	D kept an old coach. C, a young boy, approached two other boys near the coach. As he got close, the boys lit and threw a match at the coach's petrol tank. It exploded, causing injury to C.	Act of stranger defence to *Rylands v Fletcher*	An occupant of land cannot be held liable under the rule if the act bringing about the escape was the act of a stranger.

Case	Facts	Relevant area	*Ratio decidendi*
Ribee v Norrie (2000)	C's neighbouring property was owned by D and had been converted into a hostel. A fire broke out in the hostel, caused by a discarded cigarette, which spread to C's home. She was injured and her property damaged.	Act of stranger defence to *Rylands v Fletcher*	It was within the power of D to prohibit smoking in the property, so he had control over the third party's actions.
Carstairs v Taylor (1871)	C stored rice in the ground floor of a warehouse which he leased from D, who used the upper floor. A rat gnawed through a gutter box. Heavy rainfall then caused the roof to leak, damaging C's rice.	Act of God defence to *Rylands v Fletcher*	D was not liable under *Rylands v Fletcher*. The heavy rain and actions of the rat were classed as an act of God.
Green v Chelsea Waterworks Co. (1894)	A water main burst, causing damage to C's land. D was under a statutory obligation to maintain high pressure in the water main. Any escape would inevitably cause damage.	Statutory authority as a defence to *Rylands v Fletcher*	D was not liable under *Rylands v Fletcher* as they had the defence of statutory authority.
Peters v Prince of Wales Theatre (1943)	C's shop was damaged when pipes from the theatre's sprinkler system burst.	Consent/benefit as a defence to *Rylands v Fletcher*	The sprinkler system was equally for the benefit of C.

Now test yourself

TESTED ☐

1 Why do the courts favour contributory negligence over consent?
2 How may 'agreement' be communicated?
3 Why is a rescuer not regarded as having freely and voluntarily accepted the risk?
4 How much injury does a boxer consent to?
5 What is the effect of planning permission?
6 How would Heathrow airport defend itself against a nuisance claim regarding the building work?
7 How long does it take to acquire a prescriptive right?
8 What is the impact of an act of a stranger?
9 What amounts to an act of God?
10 Why were the Chelsea Waterworks not liable to Green under *Rylands v Fletcher*?

Answers online

Revision activity

Create a grid showing which defences are appropriate for each tort.

Exam summary

In the exam, you MAY be asked to:
● respond to a scenario based on contributory negligence/*volenti non fit injuria*/defences to nuisance/defences to *Rylands v Fletcher* by advising either the claimant or defendant
● discuss in a full-length essay question the topic or topics of:
  – contributory negligence
  – *volenti non fit injuria*
  – defences to nuisance
  – defences to *Rylands v Fletcher*.

These types of question will each be worth a maximum of 25 marks.

4.7 Remedies

This area requires you to apply the law to given scenarios in Paper 2. It will not be assessed on its own but with the most appropriate substantive tort.

Compensatory damages

The aim of damages in tort is to put the claimant back in the position they would have been in if the tort had not been committed, in so far as it is possible to do so with money. In Latin, this is known as *restitutio in integrum*.

Lord Blackburn in *Livingstone v Rawyards Coal Company* (1880) said:

'It being a general rule that where any injury is to be compensated by damages ... you should as nearly as possible get at that sum of money which will put the party who has been injured, or who has suffered in the same position as he would have been in if he had not sustained the wrong.'

In *British Transport Commission v Gourley* (1956):

'It is manifest that no award of money can possibly compensate a man for such grievous injuries as the Respondent in this case has suffered ... in fixing such damages the Judge can do no more than endeavour to arrive at a fair estimate, taking into account all the relevant considerations.'

These considerations are also known as the 'heads of damage'.

General damages

These are 'unliquidated' or 'non-pecuniary'. This means that they cannot be calculated exactly, and it is for the judge to decide how much to award.

These damages are awarded for:
- pain and suffering: this covers past, present and future physical pain and mental anguish, including fear of future treatment or anguish caused by life expectancy being shortened; however, the claimant must be aware – see *Wise v Kaye* (1962)
- loss of amenity: the loss of things a claimant used to enjoy doing, for example where a claimant had a particular skill or hobby, including loss of senses and reduced marriage prospects
- future loss: for example pension rights and future expenses such as nursing care
- specific injuries: there is a standard tariff for most types of injuries supplied by the Judicial Studies Board called the *Kemp and Kemp Quantum of Damages*.

Post-trial loss of earnings

Post-trial loss of earnings is considered general damages, as it is not possible to calculate the amount precisely, so a formula has been developed by the courts:

Multiplicand x multiplier = future loss of earnings

Multiplicand is the court's assessment of the claimant's net annual loss; multiplier is the period of future loss.

Revision activity

Create a grid showing which remedies are appropriate for each tort.

Restitutio in integrum: putting the claimant back in the position they would have been in if the tort had not been committed, in so far as it is possible to do so with money.

Typical mistake

Do not confuse 'damage' and 'damages'. The former is the 'harm' that the tort has caused; the latter is monetary compensation for the loss or harm suffered.

Exam tip

It is probably wisest to think of the heads of damage as headings under which different types of damage can be assessed.

If C's life expectancy is shortened by the accident, future loss of earnings is adjusted.

A key case here is *Pickett v British Rail Engineering Ltd* (1980).

Special damages

This is loss which can be assessed with some accuracy, for example:
- medical expenses (these are not limited to NHS)
- loss of earnings.

Pre-trial expenses

Pre-trial loss of earnings is considered special damages, as the precise figure can be calculated.

The claimant may claim special damages for loss of earnings up to the date of the trial, as well as for expenses up to the date of the trial, for example medical or travel expenses.

Property

Where property is destroyed, damages are generally assessed by reference to the market value of the property at the time of its destruction.

Where property is damaged but not destroyed, damages are usually assessed by reference to the cost of repair, unless the repair cost is greater than the market value, when the latter is then used.

Interim and periodical payments

Damages are generally awarded in a lump sum, although not always.

Interim payments

Part 25 of the Civil Procedure Rules provides for interim payments, i.e. payments made before the full settlement is awarded. These are most commonly used in personal injury claims, and most especially so in claims for substantial damages arising out of catastrophic injuries.

In such cases, immediate money is required before the final calculation of the claim, in order to pay for things such as adapted housing, equipment or expensive care.

Periodical payments

Section 2 of the Damages Act 1996 provides that a court awarding damages for future pecuniary loss in respect of personal injury 'may order that the damages are wholly or partly to take the form of periodical payment', i.e. regular payments in the future.

Types of damages

Damages may be nominal, contemptuous or aggravated.

Table 4.7.1 Types of damages

Nominal damages	Often paid when no damage has been suffered, for example £1
Contemptuous damages	May be awarded where the court feels that the action should never have been brought, often because C's behaviour has been reprehensible
Aggravated damages	Awarded if the court feels that C's injury has been aggravated by D's conduct and may therefore increase the amount of damages

Table 4.7.2 Key cases on damages

Case	Facts	Relevant area	Ratio decidendi
British Transport Commission v Gourley (1956)	An eminent civil engineer suffered severe injuries while travelling in a train.	*Restitutio in integrum*	Judicial comment showed how difficult it can be to 'restore' C.
Wise v Kaye (1962)	C was left permanently unconscious and unaware of her surroundings.	Pain and suffering	C can only claim for pain and suffering if aware of their injuries (subjective test). There was no claim for the period when C was unconscious.
Pickett v British Rail Engineering Ltd (1980)	C, a 51-year-old, inhaled asbestos causing mesothelioma.	Reduced life expectancy	C's life expectancy was one year. Damages were calculated on the basis that C would have been expected to work until 65 years old.

Mitigation of loss

It is a general principle of the law of damages that the claimant must do everything reasonable to mitigate their loss. The defendant will not be liable for damage resulting from the claimant's unreasonable failure so to do.

The duty to mitigate is not a demanding one as 'it is the party in breach which has placed the other party in a difficult situation'.

This translates to a duty only to do what is reasonable in the circumstances, and the burden is on the party in breach to demonstrate the other side's failure to act reasonably. For example, if you are injured by another's negligence and require numerous trips to the hospital, it would be reasonable for you to claim the cost of taxi fares, but not to hire a limousine and claim the costs.

Revision activity

Boost your knowledge of this area by reading the Law Commission report *Aggravated, Exemplary and Restitutionary Damages* (1997), available online.

Injunctions

REVISED

An injunction is a court order, either to prevent a defendant from doing something or to force a defendant to do something. Injunctions are equitable remedies, and so are at the discretion of the court:

- Injunctions are most commonly used in torts such as nuisance and trespass, in order to stop the tort from continuing.
- The Supreme Court of Judicature Act 1925 (now repealed) stated in s 45 that 'an injunction may be granted … in all cases in which it shall appear to the Court to be just or convenient'.
- Where the public interest outweighs the claimant's interest, the court may decide to award damages in lieu of an injunction – see *Miller v Jackson* (1977) and *Kennaway v Thompson* (1981).
- Lord Neuberger in *Coventry v Lawrence* (2014) set out when this would be appropriate, updating the original tests from *Shelfer v City of London Electric Lighting Co.* (1895).
- Be aware that damages may be awarded in addition to an injunction.

There are a number of different types of injunction, including those shown in the table below.

Table 4.7.3 **Types of injunction**

Type	Explanation	When used	Key case
Prohibitory injunction	An order from the court preventing D from committing a tort or from continuing it	Usually sought in nuisance cases where C wants the activity to stop	*Watson v Croft Promo-Sport Ltd* (2009)
Mandatory injunction	An order from the court to compel D to act in a particular way	Usually sought where C wants D to rectify the damage caused	*Jacklin v Chief Constable of West Yorkshire* (2007)
Partial injunction	An order to limit D's activities or reduce them	Usually granted where the tort has some public benefit	*Kennaway v Thompson* (1981)

Exam tip

This area is closely associated with balancing conflicting interests, so ensure you can make the link.

Table 4.7.4 **Key cases on injunctions**

Case	Facts	Relevant area	*Ratio decidendi*
Watson v Croft Promo-Sport Ltd (2009)	Cs complained about the noise from a motor-racing circuit.	Prohibitory injunction	An injunction (and damages) was granted.
Jacklin v Chief Constable of West Yorkshire (2007)	C owned land which gave him a right of way over D's land. D placed a container across the relevant stretch that prevented C's passage of vehicles.	Mandatory injunction	A mandatory injunction was granted to remove the container.
Kennaway v Thompson (1981)	C owned property next to a lake used for water sports. The frequency of the races increased over time.	Partial injunction	The injunction was granted to limit the frequency of the use of the lake for competitions without preventing it completely.
Miller v Jackson (1977)	The Millers sought to have an injunction to prevent the playing of cricket on a pitch next to their garden, the court held that damages would be paid instead in order to preserve the playing of cricket and balance the interests of both parties.	Damages in lieu of an injunction	The public interest prevailed over C's private right to quiet enjoyment.

Now test yourself

TESTED

1 What is meant by the Latin phrase *restitutio in integrum*?
2 What 'head of damage' would you claim for a new phone if yours had been damaged by someone's negligence?
3 How are lost earnings calculated?
4 Who bears the burden of proof in determining whether the claimant failed to mitigate their loss?
5 Why were damages preferred over an injunction in *Miller v Jackson* (1977)?
6 What type of injunction would you seek if your neighbour was playing very loud music at 3 a.m. every day?

Answers online

Exam summary

In the exam, you MAY be asked to:
- respond to a scenario question by advising a claimant whether there are any remedies available under compensatory damage, mitigation of loss, or via an injunction
- to discuss in a full-length essay question a key topic or topics of remedies, such as compensatory damage, mitigation of loss, or injunction.

These types of question will each be worth a maximum of 25 marks.

4.8 Evaluation

This chapter provides some suggested critical evaluation of the main torts in the OCR specification. This is not an exhaustive list.

Revision activity

Look through your notes for each tort. Identify any justifications for the torts critically evaluated in this chapter.

Liability in negligence

REVISED

Critical evaluation

Table 4.8.1 Critical evaluation of liability in negligence – duty of care

Area of criticism	Criticism	Justified?	Unjustified?
The imposition of a duty of care	The imposition may not be just and fair.	Imposing a duty of care on persons is of crucial importance in a civilised society.	The judicial flexibility to determine a duty may not be just and fair in the circumstances, causing harshness to C.
Duty of care on lawyers	Historically, judges have refused to impose liability on lawyers for work done in court.	The refusal to impose a duty was out of fear of preventing a barrister from carrying out their work effectively, and the potential floodgates of re-opened claims.	This immunity has since been removed, as there is more effective professional regulation of lawyers to avoid abuse of process. This provides greater fairness for Cs.
Duty of care on judges	Historically, judges have had immunity against claims of negligence in judicial office.	Judges need to operate without fear of being sued and of parties being unhappy with tough decisions made. An independent judiciary is of vital importance in any democracy.	This unfairness is now amended in respect of the work of inferior judges, who can be held liable for acts in excess of their jurisdiction.
Duty of care on the police	Historically, the police have been deemed not to owe a duty of care to the public at large.	This is fair on the grounds that the police would not effectively be able to carry out their duties and that this is not as harsh on the C as it first appears due to alternative routes to compensation, for example through the Criminal Injuries Compensation Authority (CICA).	This rule has been lifted in respect of specific duties.

Table 4.8.2 Critical evaluation of liability in negligence – breach of duty of care

Area of criticism	Criticism	Justified?	Unjustified?
Definition – reasonable man	Objective test – the same standard is expected of everyone.	This provides a level playing field so that, for example, inexperience will not justify innocence.	A purely objective standard is not possible – although is this simply down to the individual judge to decide?
Definition – reasonable man	Objective test – same standard is expected of everyone, unless you are a professional.	Professionals have many years of training and therefore must be more aware of the issues leading to a breach.	This higher standard provides an inconsistency to the original reasonable man rule and, perhaps, was not originally envisaged by Lord Atkin.
Definition – foreseeability and reasonable precautions	Liability is fixed with level of fault, unless you are a professional.	Professionals have many years of training and therefore must be more aware of the issues leading to a breach.	Professionals can therefore set their standards and rules to avoid or reduce liability to suit themselves through codes of practice etc. (or 'closing ranks').

Table 4.8.3 Critical evaluation of liability in negligence – causation of damage

Area of criticism	Criticism	Justified?	Unjustified?
Foreseeability of injury	Principles of causation are aimed at making D liable for foreseeable loss they have caused.	Foreseeability is fair to both sides.	It can be difficult to establish foreseeability exactly in the minds of both parties.
Multiple causes of injury	Despite being in breach, if there are multiple causes of injury then the 'but for' test struggles to establish a single D's liability.	Where there is a single cause of injury, the 'but for' test operates perfectly for D. But if there are multiple causes, then it is unfair to place the total blame on one D's actions.	D who is in breach can escape liability and claimant can go unpunished.
Novus actus interveniens	C goes uncompensated if there is a *novus actus*.	A unique act must break the chain of causation since it will be significant enough to do so.	C will be uncompensated unless there is a negligent third party.

Table 4.8.4 Critical evaluation of liability in negligence – remoteness of damage

Area of criticism	Criticism	Justified?	Unjustified?
Rules on remoteness	The rules are simply a means of limiting liability.	There must be rules on both liability or the amount of compensation to allow for certainty and clarity.	Many of the rules seem arbitrary and in favour of claimant, rather than the injured party who may never be fully compensated following injury.
Different judges – different opinions to remoteness	Depending upon the judge or judges, the rules can be restrictively or very liberally interpreted.	See the apparent unfairness in the decisions of *Doughty v Turner Manufacturing* (1964) and *Tremain v Pike* (1969).	Compare the more liberal and fairer approach of *Jolley v London Borough of Sutton* (2000).

Ideas for reform

As the law is so dynamic and constantly changing, there are suggestions that a statutory code would simplify negligence and its spin–off torts. This would give more certainty, raise standards and therefore reduce the burden on the courts.

Occupiers' liability

REVISED

Critical evaluation

Table 4.8.5 Critical evaluation of occupiers' liability: the 1957 Act

Area of criticism	Criticism	Justified?	Unjustified?
Pre-section 2(1)	Pre-Act, different duties were owed to different types of lawful visitor.	Pre-Act there was a complicated set of common-law rules which caused confusion and injustice.	The 1957 Act is a statutory form of negligence which now creates a common duty of care to *all* lawful visitors.
Explanation of premises	The Act only covers the state of a premises.	The Act limits the liability here, so alternative actions in different torts are necessary.	Alternative actions to those under the Act are possible, e.g. under negligence.

Area of criticism	Criticism	Justified?	Unjustified?
Section 2(2)	An occupier may 'extend, restrict, modify or exclude his duty'.	The Act relies on lawful visitors being prudent to look after themselves at all times, including minors (albeit a higher standard of care is owed by the occupier for children).	An occupier can therefore determine the extent of their duty.
Exclusion clauses/limitation notices	An occupier can still have numerous means of reducing, removing or avoiding liability.	The Act relies on lawful visitors being prudent to look after themselves at all times, including minors (albeit a higher standard of care is owed by the occupier for children).	An occupier can therefore determine the extent of their duty via exclusion clauses.
Exceeding permission to be on premises	Once a lawful visitor exceeds their scope to be on the premises, they become a trespasser.	Acting beyond the scope must be deemed wrong and therefore not prudent and expose the person to the subsequent consequences.	It is unclear as to at what exact point a person acts beyond the scope of their lawful permission. The consequences, if so, are potentially catastrophic.
Children as lawful visitors	A higher standard of care is placed on an occupier to ensure the safety of children than of adults.	Children are less likely to see the risk or danger, or the impact of acting outside the scope of their permission to be on the premises.	To what lengths must an occupier go to avoid injury? If present, parents should be looking after the children, not the occupier. But see *Phipps v Rochester Corporation* (1955).

Table 4.8.6 Critical evaluation of occupiers' liability: the 1984 Act

Area of criticism	Criticism	Justified?	Unjustified?
Pre-84 Act	Pre-84 Act, trespassers were treated harshly.	Trespassers should not be on other people's property.	This should not be an absolute duty, as we should have some responsibility for certain injuries to trespassers, even if a moral duty to take care of others.
The duty itself to trespassers	The duty is unfair to the occupier.	Trespassers enter at their own risk.	Occupiers must take responsibility for injuries that occur on their premises – a trespasser is simply a label and nothing else.
Types of premises	The growth of more dangerous premises required more protection.	An occupier should not allow dangerous premises to exist or operate.	Trespassers should not be on other people's property.
Children as trespassers	There are difficulties of children appreciating danger as a trespasser.	A higher duty must be owed to children who cannot appreciate risk in the same way as an adult.	Children should be under the care and supervision of a parent or guardian. They should understand that trespassing is wrong and can be dangerous.
Compensation	Compensation is only available for injury.	Trespassers are deserving of less protection than are lawful visitors	Occupiers must take responsibility for injuries that occur on their premises – a trespasser is simply a label and nothing else.

Ideas for reform

While arguments remain about the justification of owing a duty to trespassers and the nanny state, greater clarity of the difference between the two areas would improve the perception of the law. A statutory code setting out both duties side by side would be helpful.

Torts connected to land

REVISED

Critical evaluation

Table 4.8.7 Critical evaluation of torts connected to land – nuisance

Area of criticism	Criticism	Justified?	Unjustified?
Private nuisance – the balance of interests	A compromise is made, not a resolution.	We live on a crowded island and total satisfaction may not be possible.	To compromise allows the other party to continue the nuisance in some way.
Private nuisance – 'unreasonable' use of land	It is difficult to establish what is meant by the 'unreasonable' use of land.	One person's opinion of 'unreasonable' use of land can be very different to another's, especially where manufacturing or service industries operate.	There has to be some 'give and take' in society to allow the smoother running of society as a whole.
Private nuisance – proof of damage	It is difficult to prove interference with enjoyment of land.	It is easy to prove actual injury, but much more complicated to prove interference with enjoyment of land.	As this may be a subjective opinion, limits must be placed on what is 'interference with enjoyment of land' or the law could allow for ridiculous decisions.
Private nuisance – limitations inherent in the defences available	(For example) local authority planning permission overrides a claim in private nuisance.	The needs of the majority must outweigh the needs of the minority.	Claiming is made much more difficult post planning permission being granted, when in many cases the reason is to raise funds rather than enhance society.

Table 4.8.8 Critical evaluation of torts connected to land – *Rylands v Fletcher*

Area of criticism	Criticism	Justified?	Unjustified?
Definition of the tort	The tort has developed incorrectly and against the original concept.	The development of the tort has meant the original concept (liability for an accumulation of hazardous things that cause damage) is no longer possible.	The tort has been given great flexibility and many justifiable defences have been allowed.
Definition of the tort	The tort was restricted straight away by the House of Lords.	Lord Cairns placed restrictions to prevent 'floodgate' claims – by the requirement of non-natural use of the land.	There are difficulties in showing non-natural use in a technological age, but see Lord Goff's comments in *Cambridge Water v Eastern Counties Leather* (1994) and the changing nature of 'non-natural use' in *Musgrove v Pandelis* (1919).

Area of criticism	Criticism	Justified?	Unjustified?
Definition of the tort	There is limited meaning of 'escape'.	See *Read v Lyons* ...	... but see contrary tests in *Hale v Jennings* (1938) and *British Celanese v AH Hunt Ltd* (1969).
Defences to the rule	There are a wide range of defences available to Ds.	The unusually wide range of defences available limits the scope of the tort.	The rule cannot exist unchallenged; there must be limitations to avoid frivolous and unjustifiable claims being made.
Definition of the tort – foreseeability	The test of foreseeability is strict.	There must be limitations to avoid frivolous and unjustifiable claims being made.	The test of foreseeability is arguably stricter than that of negligence and therefore probably easier to claim under negligence.

Ideas for reform

The foundations for this area of law are steeped in antiquity, and while all common-law-based laws adapt over time, they do this retrospectively.

It can be argued that with technology and service developments such as mobile phone networks and broadband suppliers, this area of law requires a complete overhaul in the form of a statutory code, to respond to the changing nature of society.

Vicarious liability

REVISED

Critical evaluation

Table 4.8.9 Critical evaluation of vicarious liability

Area of criticism	Criticism	Justified?	Unjustified?
Fault	Vicarious liability is a contradiction to the basic fault principle – take responsibility for your own actions, not those of others.	Employers are in a better position to compensate the injured party than the employee.	An employer is blamed for the actions of an employee.
Employer 'bans' an unsafe practice	An employer can still face liability even if they have expressly prohibited the unsafe practice.	An employer must be consistent in ensuring the unsafe practice does not continue.	An employer cannot watch their entire workforce all of the time and must trust their employees to carry out their work correctly.
The basic rule of vicarious liability	The rule may operate inconsistently or arbitrarily.	See *Rose v Plenty* (1976) ...	... and compare with *Twine v Beans Express* (1961).
Timing of unsafe act etc.	The tort will often have occurred before the employer realises that the employee behaves badly and should be disciplined.	An employer should insist on safe and correct working practices at all times and be able to guarantee those practices.	It is unfair to hold liability for retrospective actions over which the employer had no real control.
Level of carelessness of the employee	The employer may be liable even for mere carelessness on the employee's part.	Carelessness is carelessness and should, where significant enough, be prevented and compensated if not.	Where do you 'draw the line' of limitation? This could lead to near inconsequential acts giving rise to liability.

Ideas for reform

This area of law is changing at an enormous rate, so further suggestion for reform is inappropriate.

More time for consolidation and training for employers, trade unions and employer organisations would be helpful, to ensure that their training, policies and procedures are in line with the latest developments.

Exam practice

Questions 1 and 2 could appear on the AS exam paper. Questions 3–6 could appear on the A Level exam paper only.

1 Explain the way in which a breach of the duty of care is established in a negligence claim.   [10 marks]

2 Penny has just parked her car at the side of the road. Without looking in her mirror, she opens the car door right into the path of Joe, a passing cyclist. Joe is knocked over and suffers a head injury but gets up and continues on his bike. He then falls unconscious and crashes into a wall.
   Advise whether or not Penny owes Joe a duty of care and, if so, whether or not she has breached that duty of care.   [10 marks]

3 Discuss the extent to which the rules of remoteness of damage achieve justice for claimants.   [10 marks]

4 Previously a quiet lake overlooked by a few cottages, Linacre Lake has recently been developed by its new owner, Wetlife Developments, to provide extensive leisure facilities, including swimming and powerboating. In consequence, a cottage owner, Ingrid, has experienced a large increase in noise, especially at weekends and during frequent competition weeks. Additionally, damage to a diesel oil storage tank owned by Wetlife Developments resulted in a leak which caused extensive contamination of Ingrid's vegetable garden.
   Advise whether Ingrid will be successful in claims of both private nuisance and *Rylands v Fletcher* against Wetlife Developments.
                                                                   [25 marks]

5 Some swimmers were in the habit of swimming beneath the surface in an area of Linacre Lake clearly marked out for powerboating only. While doing so, Jon surfaced into the path of a powerboat being driven by Kylie. In the resulting collision, Jon suffered severe facial injuries while Kylie was knocked out of the boat and had her arm severed by the propeller.
   Advise whether Jon and Kylie will be successful in claims of occupiers' liability against the owners of Linacre Lake.   [25 marks]

6 Discuss the extent to which the Occupiers' Liability Act 1984 is fair on occupiers.   [25 marks]

ONLINE

5 The nature of law

The final third component of the OCR A Level Law H415 specification is *Further law*. Here, candidates must sit one compulsory topic, *The nature of law*, and one optional topic: either *Human rights law* or *The law of contract*. The nature of law examines a candidate's ability to appreciate:

- an introduction to the nature of law
- law and morality
- law and justice
- law and society
- law and technology.

It is important not to view this section in isolation, but alongside the other two English legal system sections: *The legal system* and *Law making*. They are complementary topics, and links should be made between them to appreciate how the English legal system operates and ultimately to enhance exam responses.

5.1 Introduction to the nature of law

Law and rules

REVISED

There is a difference between enforceable legal rules and principles, and other rules and norms of behaviour.

The law is made up of rules and regulations that are enforceable by the state. This means they are:

- made by the state, and
- administered by state organisations, for example Her Majesty's Court Service.

We obey laws because we *have* to.

Other rules and norms, such as the rules of football or of social etiquette, are not laws because they are not enforceable by the state. We obey these rules because we *choose* to in certain situations.

There are four categories of legal rules and regulations, as outlined in the table below.

> **Revision activity**
>
> In the context of the UK, to what does the word 'state' refer?

Table 5.1.1 Categories of legal rules and regulations

Category	Purpose	Example
Procedural laws	Prescribe the framework in which other laws are made and enforced	The Police and Criminal Evidence Act 1984 provides a procedure to be followed by the police in order to make a lawful arrest; other procedural laws dictate how a trial is to be run, who can access financial assistance when going to court etc.

Category	Purpose	Example
Substantive laws	Create and define legal rights and obligations	Criminal offences are substantive laws, but so are other laws such as employment rights or the law relating to divorce.
Public laws	Govern the relationship between the state and its citizens	Public laws include criminal laws and most procedural laws, as they define the powers of Parliament, government and other key institutions of the state such as the police and courts.
Private laws	Create rights enforceable between individuals; they are mainly substantive in nature	The law of trespass allows you to restrict access to your property.

Exam tip

These are key issues which you will need to compare and contrast throughout this chapter.

Revision activity

Name as many different law-making bodies as you can.

Normative concepts: concepts which establish standards of normality or acceptable behaviour.

Connections between law, morality and justice

Both law and morality are referred to as **normative concepts** – they specify how people should behave. The aim of adhering to the law and a moral code or rules is to achieve justice.

If morals dictate how laws should be made, then justice is served if someone breaks the law and the injured party is compensated as a result.

However, it is impossible to find a single set of moral values that can be considered acceptable to all members of society.

Revision activity

Research the work of Emile Durkheim, the French philosopher who wrote about morality and society. Start here: **www.azquotes. com/author/4244-Emile_ Durkheim**.

Differences between civil and criminal law

REVISED

Civil law

Civil laws create rights that are enforceable between private individuals. This means that enforcement agencies such as the police do not get involved in these laws. Civil laws therefore do not aim to punish but to compensate those whose rights have been violated.

The **claimant** can **sue** the **defendant**. The defendant may be found **liable** on the **balance of probabilities**.

Claimant: legal term for a person or organisation starting a civil claim in the courts.

Sue: take civil legal proceedings against a defendant.

Defendant: legal term for a person defending or responding to a legal claim (called a respondent in some aspects of civil law).

Liable: held to be legally responsible for a breach of the civil law.

Balance of probabilities: the civil standard of proof which means the claimant must satisfy the court that their version of events is more likely than not.

Civil laws fit into the substantive category shown in Table 5.1.1. There are courts that specialise in civil law (see Chapter 1.1).

Revision activity

Name two of the civil courts.

Criminal law

Criminal laws create criminal offences and punish those who commit them. These laws attract the attention of the Criminal Justice Service (CJS), which includes:

- the police
- the Crown Prosecution Service (CPS)
- the criminal courts
- Her Majesty's Prison Service
- Her Majesty's Probation Service
- the National Offender Management Service.

The Crown **prosecutes** the defendant. The defendant may be found **guilty**, provided the jury/magistrates have no **reasonable doubt**.

Criminal law fits into both the substantive and public categories outlined in Table 5.1.1. There are courts that specialise in criminal law (see Chapter 1.2).

> **Prosecutes:** legal term for bringing a criminal charge against a defendant.
>
> **Guilty:** legally responsible for a specified wrongdoing.
>
> **Reasonable doubt:** the criminal standard of proof which means the prosecution must provide sufficient evidence for the jury or magistrates to be certain of the defendant's guilt – if they are not, then they have reasonable doubt.

> **Exam tip**
>
> Make sure you do not mix up the terminology used in criminal and civil law.

> **Revision activity**
>
> Name two of the criminal law courts.

Development of English law

REVISED

Custom

Rules that come about through custom or practice involve the disapproval of the community rather than formal punishment if they are broken. The individual may also become conditioned to accept the rules, so they are enforced by a feeling of self-guilt.

Some such rules may 'harden into rights' and be so widely accepted that they become the law. The early common law developed out of customs that were commonly accepted.

Common law

'Common law' refers to laws that have been developed by judicial decisions.

An example of a common-law crime is murder. This means it has never been defined in an Act of Parliament, but instead developed from ancient custom and is still developing through the decisions of judges in the highest courts. These decisions are known as 'precedents' (see Chapter 3.4).

Equity

Equity is a set of legal principles which are a distinct part of the law of England and Wales. These principles supplement the strict rules of the common law – they allow a different outcome where applying the common law would be too severe or unfair.

Historically, the common law was developed and administered by the royal courts. The Judicature Acts of the 1870s fused the courts of equity and the common law. This means that a majority of modern courts apply the two sets of rules in their proceedings.

Achieving accepted notions of justice and fairness in equity is notoriously difficult, as the seventeenth-century jurist John Selden said: 'Equity is a roguish thing: for law we have a measure, know what to trust to; equity is according to the conscience of him that is Chancellor.'

Modern equity can be seen in remedies such as injunctions, specific performance and estoppel.

Statute

The UK Parliament is based in the Palace of Westminster and made up of the Queen, the House of Commons and the House of Lords. Laws passed here are known as Acts of Parliament or statutes, and these are superior to any conflicting law.

Most new law – and all law that could attract controversy, for example increased police powers in relation to terror suspects – is made by Parliament.

Statute laws are easy to identify as the clues are in the names, for example the Fraud Act 2006.

Devolved bodies

The UK Parliament has delegated some of its law-making power to other organisations in specific matters, such as:

● the European Union (see Chapter 3.6)
● the Scottish Parliament
● the Welsh Government
● the Northern Ireland Assembly
● local councils, such as local borough or county councils.

Laws passed by local councils often only apply in a small geographical area, for example a by-law banning ball games on an area of parkland (see Chapter 3.2).

Overview of common-law and civil-law legal systems

REVISED

Every country operates either a common-law legal system or a civil-law legal system. The key characteristics, differences and similarities are detailed in the table below.

Table 5.1.2 **Summary of common-law and civil-law legal systems**

Feature	Common law	Civil law
Historical origin	The English monarchy used to issue formal orders called 'writs' when justice needed to be done. Because they did not cover all situations, courts of equity were established to hear complaints and devise appropriate remedies. As these decisions were collected and published, courts looked up previous opinions and applied them to current cases – so the common-law system of precedent developed.	Civil law can be traced back to the code of laws compiled by the Roman Emperor Justinian around 600 CE. Authoritative legal codes with roots in these laws developed over many centuries in various countries, leading to similar legal systems, each with their own codes of law.
Source of law	Case law, in the form of published judicial opinions, is a key source of law.	A legal code is the primary source of law.

Feature	Common law	Civil law
Role of the judge	Legal proceedings are 'refereed' by the judge, who has greater flexibility than in a civil-law system to fashion an appropriate remedy at the conclusion of the case. The court process is known as 'adversarial' – a conflict between two sides.	Judges are often 'investigators'. They generally take the lead in the proceedings by bringing charges, establishing facts through witness examination and applying remedies found in legal codes. The court process is known as 'inquisitorial' – a joint effort to arrive at the truth.
Role of the lawyer	Lawyers make representations to the judge, arguing the application of legal principles, and examine witnesses in order to establish the facts for the judge and, where appropriate, the jury.	A lawyer's tasks include advising clients on points of law and preparing legal pleadings for filing with the court. There is far less importance on oral argument or advocacy in court.
Countries using this system	Approximately 80, e.g.: ● England ● (Scotland is a mixture of both) ● USA ● India ● Canada.	Approximately 150, e.g.: ● China ● Japan ● Germany ● France ● Spain.

Rule of law

REVISED

The rule of law is a symbolic idea, with no single definition but much significance. Lord Bingham, one of the UK's most senior judges, wrote a book on the subject that explores the concept in great depth.

The Constitutional Reform Act 2005 makes reference to it in s 1, saying '[the] Act does not adversely affect the existing constitutional principle of the Rule of Law'.

> **Revision activity**
>
> Read the introductory text for the Constitutional Reform Act 2005 to find out its purpose.

Definition

So, what is the rule of law? In broad terms, it means:
● No person shall be sanctioned except in accordance with the law.
● All shall be equal before the law.
● There shall be fairness and clarity of the law.

The rule of law is therefore a safeguard against dictatorship:
● The government and its officials are accountable under the law.
● No single branch of government can exercise unlimited power.
● There are checks and balances, including an independent judiciary, to maintain these principles.

Law academics have developed different views on the rule of law:

A.V. Dicey

Broadly in line with the points above, Dicey felt there were three elements that created the rule of law:
1 An absence of arbitrary power on the part of the state: the state's power must be controlled by the law and can be challenged by judicial review. This includes preventing the state from having wide discretionary powers, because discretion can be exercised without proper checks and balances.
2 Equality before the law: no one is above the law, regardless of how powerful they are; the law deals with them in the same way as it would anyone else. However, differences in wealth can affect access to justice.

3 Supremacy of ordinary law: this is different from the concept of parliamentary supremacy (see Section 3), which may contradict the idea of arbitrary power above.

F.A. von Hayek

Hayek followed Dicey's principles but felt that the rule of law had become diluted because provided actions of the state are permitted by an Act of Parliament, anything done in accordance with this Act is lawful. He also pointed out that regulating economic activity, as modern governments do, is in conflict with the rule of law.

Joseph Raz

Raz saw the rule of law as acting to minimise the danger of the use of discretionary power in an arbitrary way. He thought the rule of law was that law must be capable of guiding the individual's behaviour.

Some of his key principles are:
- There should be clear rules and procedures for making laws.
- The independence of the judiciary must be guaranteed.
- The principles of natural justice should be observed; these require an open and fair hearing, with all parties being given the opportunity to put their case.
- The courts should have the power to review the way in which the other principles are implemented, to ensure that they are being operated as demanded by the rule of law.

Revision activity

Research these theorists, adding dates and context to their arguments.

Whose position is closest to your own feelings?

Importance of the rule of law

Table 5.1.3 **The importance of the rule of law**

The legal system (procedural law)	Criminal procedure: ● Every defendant has the right to a fair trial. ● There is an independent judiciary. ● Trial is by peer, i.e. by magistrates or a jury. ● No person can be imprisoned without a trial. Civil procedure: ● Disputes are resolved through the civil justice system. ● The system should be free from discrimination and corruption. ● The system should be accessible and affordable. There are alternative ways of resolving civil disputes (see Chapter 1.1).
Substantive law	Human rights: ● Human rights, including the right to a fair trial, are central to the modern interpretation of the rule of law. Criminal law: ● The aim is to maintain law and order by creating criminal offences. The law has to be clear and the prosecution has to prove beyond reasonable doubt that D has committed an offence. ● The aim is also to protect society, which is the justification for punishment and sending offenders to prison. ● All offences have a maximum penalty and the courts cannot impose a higher penalty than this. Civil law: ● Through tort, the aim of civil law is aimed at protecting individual's rights. It gives the right to claim compensation for damage caused by breaches of the law. ● Through contract law, civil law recognises that people should be free to make what agreements they wish and tries to redress the balance of power between consumers and big business.

Now test yourself

TESTED

1 Decide into which type and category the following laws fit:
   - theft
   - rules of evidence
   - conventions that dictate how an Act of Parliament should be made
   - wills
   - health and safety law.
2 What is the aim of criminal law?
3 Is the standard of proof higher in criminal or civil law?
4 Who makes the common law, and how?
5 What does the rule of law safeguard us against?
6 What impact can wealth have on 'equality before the law'?
7 Why is judicial independence important to the rule of law?
8 Show two ways in which criminal procedure complies with the rule of law.
9 What is the relationship between the rule of law and human rights?
10 How does the role of the judge differ between common-law and civil-law legal systems?

Answers online

Exam summary

In the exam, you MAY be asked to consider a specific statement based on one of the nature of law topics and discuss the extent to which you agree or disagree. In doing so, you are required to use examples from your full course of study.

This type of question will be worth a maximum of 25 marks.

Exam tip

To prepare for questions on the rule of law, use the cross-references given here.

When revising, it might help to create spider diagrams showing the rule of law's relationship with other areas of law. Remember to include examples and make that link!

Revision activity

Read the introductory text for the Consumer Protection Act 1987 and the Consumer Rights Act 2015. Make a note of their purpose in bringing equality.

Typical mistake

Do not work on the different areas of this topic in isolation. It is really important to view the rule of law holistically and to use examples from across the substantive chapters to show your understanding.

5.2 Law and morality

Distinction between law and morals

REVISED

- Laws are rules and regulations that are objective and not necessarily fault-based, for example speeding.
- Morals are subjective personal codes of values or beliefs that are based on levels of fault and determine what is right or wrong, for example lying.

In some situations, it is possible for there to be an overlap of the two, such as murder which is both against the law and morally wrong.

However, there are other situations that cause tension between legal and moral rules, for example abortion and euthanasia.

Diversity of moral views in a pluralist society

The UK is a pluralist society, which is where there is more than one:
- culture
- race
- religion
- political party
- language
- ethnic origin
- set of customs and traditions
- social class.

In an effective, progressive pluralist society, diversity should be celebrated, not simply tolerated. However, this can lead to tensions: should the law involve itself in matters of moral importance to some groups?

Relationship between laws and morals and its importance

REVISED

Table 5.2.1 shows the relationship between laws and morals. There are different theoretical opinions about whether law should be influenced by moral values and seek to enforce them.

Table 5.2.1 Relationship between laws and morals

Laws	Morals
Made by formal institutions, e.g. Parliament and the courts *(But think of common law: does this have its basis in morality?)*	Evolve as society evolves, no formal creation *(Were the Ten Commandments in the Bible or the Koran an attempt to create a formal moral code?)*
Can be instantly made or repealed *(This often takes time and public pressure: the Human Rights Act was passed in 1998, years after the Universal Declaration of Human Rights in 1948.)*	Change with society's attitudes; slow transitional period *(Change can be rapid, such as during the 1960s, when contraception, sex outside marriage and the use of recreational drugs became widely acceptable.)*
Existence can be established *(But does this make them right? The defence to many war crimes was that the defendants were merely obeying the law.)*	Only vaguely defined *(There may be general agreement on some issues such as murder, but not on others such as abortion.)*

Laws	Morals
Breaking them attracts some form of sanction/punishment/remedy enforced by the state	Breaching moral standards merely results in social condemnation, as opposed to an organised system of enforcement
Society's attitude to the law is irrelevant (see recent disputes over the 'tampon tax') *(In a democracy this can only be a short-term position.)*	Morals reflect society's values and beliefs
Obligatory	Subjective
Not necessarily fault-based (i.e. strict liability)	Fault-based

Legal enforcement of moral values

REVISED

Lord Devlin devised four key principles for Parliament to bear in mind when deciding which moral 'offences' ought to be prohibited by law and which ought not:

1 The individual freedom to be allowed must be consistent with the integrity of society.
2 The limits of such tolerance are not static, but lawmakers should be slow to change laws which protect morality.
3 Privacy must be respected as far as possible.
4 The law is concerned with minimum rather than maximum standards of behaviour; i.e. the law sets down a minimum standard of behaviour; society's standards should be higher.

There has been much academic and legal debate about whether the law should be used to enforce moral values. Broadly, there are two differing philosophies:

● positivism
● natural law theory.

Positivism

Positivism maintains that laws and morals should be kept separate.

> **Positivism:** theory that maintains that laws and morals should be kept separate.

Table 5.2.2 **Key theorists for positivism**

Aristotle	The law should be reason free from passion.
Jeremy Bentham	Natural law theory is 'nonsense upon stilts'.
John Stuart Mill	'The only purpose for which power can be rightfully exercised over any member of a civilised society against his will is to prevent harm to others. His own good, either physical or moral, is not a sufficient warrant.'
H.L.A. Hart	'Is it morally permissible to enforce morality?' 'Laws that merely enforce morals should cease. Laws should only intervene where immorality causes harm to the society or harm to the individual concerned.'
Wolfenden Report 1978	'There must be a realm of private morality and immorality which is, in brief and crude terms, not the law's business.'

Natural law theory

Natural law theory maintains that the law should be used to enforce moral values.

> **Natural law theory:** theory that maintains that the law should be used to enforce moral values.

Table 5.2.3 Key theorists for natural law theory

St Thomas Aquinas	Natural law theory is a 'dictate of right reason'.
James Fitzjames-Stephens	'The immorality of an action is good reason for it to be a crime and the law should be a persecution of the grosser forms of vice.'
Lord Devlin	'The suppression of vice is as much the law's business as the suppression of subversive activities.'
	'It is an error of jurisprudence to separate crime from sin.'
Lon Fuller	Referring to laws made by Germany under the Nazi regime, some laws are so immoral that they must be invalid.
Nigel Simonds	'[The] purpose of the law [is] to conserve not only the safety and order but also the moral welfare of the state.'

Revision activity

Research these theorists: add dates and context to their arguments.

Whose position is closest to your own views?

Revision activity

Why do you think living in a pluralist society can make these sorts of decisions more difficult?

Revision activity

Consider the recent cases regarding baby Charlie Gard and Tony Nicklinson on the rights to receive treatment or to die.

It is difficult in practice to take a theoretical position on this argument, particularly because we live in a pluralist society. Judges are often faced with tough decisions which are matters of life and death – the arguments then become much more difficult to polarise.

In 2000, the case of conjoined twins Jodie and Mary came before the court. The only way to save Jodie's life was for doctors to perform surgery which would kill Mary. Lord Justice Ward said: 'This is a court of law, not a court of morals.'

Table 5.2.4 Key cases for positivism

Case	Facts	Useful quotes or points
R v Wilson (1996)	D branded his initials on his wife's buttocks with a hot knife, at her request. Her skin became infected; the doctor reported the matter to the police and the husband was charged with ABH.	Russell LJ: 'Consensual activity between husband and wife, in the privacy of the matrimonial home, is not, in our judgement, a proper matter for criminal investigation, let alone criminal prosecution.'
R v Human Fertilisation and Embryology Authority ex parte Blood (1997)	Blood's husband lapsed into a coma. Samples of his sperm were taken for later artificial insemination but he died shortly after the samples were obtained.	As the husband's consent was not given, Blood was not permitted to use the sperm. However, she later used an EU rule and was permitted to use it abroad.
Gillick v West Norfolk and Wisbech Health Authority (1986)	G sought a declaration that it would be unlawful for a doctor to prescribe contraceptives to girls under the age of 16 without the knowledge or consent of the parent.	The court refused to grant it, setting out guidelines for when children can give consent to medical procedures. This is now known as 'Gillick competency'.
Evans v UK (2007)	Evans wanted to use embryos fertilised by her ex-partner; he refused.	Despite the emotional issues at stake, consent must be applied.

Table 5.2.5 Key cases for natural law

Case	Facts	Useful quotes or points
R v Brown (1993)	Ds engaged in sadomasochism including physical torture.	Lord Templeman: 'Pleasure derived from the infliction of pain is an evil thing.'
Shaw v DPP (1961)	D published a ladies' directory of the services offered by prostitutes.	The supreme and fundamental purpose of the law is to conserve not only the safety and order but also the moral welfare of the state.
Knuller v DPP (1972)	D published a magazine in which homosexuals placed advertisements to meet other like-minded individuals and engage in sexual practices.	The House of Lords doubted the correctness of the decision in *Shaw* but declined to depart from it.
R v Gibson and Sylveire (1990)	Ds exhibited a pair of earrings made with freeze-dried human foetuses at the Young Unknowns Gallery in London.	This was the first occasion on which the charge of outraging public decency had been preferred in more than 80 years.
Pretty v DPP (2001)	Pretty attempted to change the law so she could end her own life because of the pains and problems caused by her terminal illness, motor neurone disease.	Lord Bingham: 'The task of the committee in this appeal is not to weigh or evaluate or reflect those beliefs and views or give effect to its own but to ascertain and apply the law of the land as it is now understood to be.'
R v Cox (1992)	Cox was a consultant and had been treating V for years. She pleaded with him to end her life. He administered a fatal injection to stop her heart.	D was found guilty but given a suspended sentence.
R v Dudley and Stephens (1884)	Ds were shipwrecked and stranded in a small boat with a young cabin boy. When food ran out, Ds ate the cabin boy. They were convicted of murder.	Law and morality are not the same, and many things may be immoral which are not necessarily illegal, yet the absolute divorce of law from morality would be of fatal consequence.

Typical mistake

In a question such as 'Explain the relationship between law and morality and whether the law should enforce moral values', remember to answer both parts.

Now test yourself

TESTED

1 What is meant by pluralism?
2 What are the earliest examples of law you can think of? Do they still exist in some form today?
3 Who are the key positivists?
4 Who are the key opponents of positivism? What are their arguments known as?

Answers online

Exam tip

If an exam question contains the words 'should' or 'ought', you need to weigh up the arguments – both the theoretical ones and those presented by the reality of hearing such sensitive matters in court – and write a conclusion.

As long as your conclusion is supported by a balanced analysis of the arguments, it should not matter whether you agree or disagree.

Exam summary

In the exam, you MAY be asked to consider a specific statement based on one of the nature of law topics and discuss the extent to which you agree or disagree. In doing so, you are required to use examples from your full course of study.

This type of question will be worth a maximum of 25 marks.

5.3 Law and justice

Meaning of justice

Justice is the idea that the law is 'fair' in how it seeks to punish wrongs and protect rights. The idea comes from John Rawls' book, *A Theory of Justice* (1971), who put this rather metaphysical concept into words:

1 The social contract: social co-operation relies on a contract which people have made among themselves. The principles of justice are to be viewed as the result of a binding contract among the members of society.
2 Greatest equal liberty: this includes basic freedoms such as speech.
3 Difference principle: social and economic inequalities are fair and just, but only if they work for the benefit of the least advantaged in society. People have different interests and demands but will have some individual conception of 'good'. However, the specific content of 'good' may not be developed.

> **Justice:** the idea that the law is 'fair' in how it seems to punish wrongs and protect rights.

Theories of justice

Philosophers from as early as Aristotle's time have attempted to pin down the meaning of justice, with some similarity between them.

Table 5.3.1 Key theorists for law and justice

Aristotle	For Aristotle, justice was about distribution and proportionality. This is quite close to current ideas about social justice and can be seen in many human rights issues. Key case: *Lindsay v Commissioners of Customs and Excise* (2002)
Aquinas	A natural law thinker, Aquinas was followed by Fuller and Rawls. He had ideas of 'justice as fairness'.
Jeremy Bentham	Bentham coined the idea of utilitarianism, a concept later developed by John Stuart Mill. This works on the principle that the purpose of law is to achieve the greatest happiness for the greatest number of people. This clearly indicates the law's purpose is to create a balance, but that the individual's good may be sacrificed in favour of the good of the whole. Examples of this are clear in policy decisions, such as *R v Brown* (1993) (see Chapter 2.7), where the good of society (i.e. not to be corrupted) outweighed the concerns of the individuals involved (i.e. to consent to whatever activity they choose).
Karl Marx	Marx argued that in a capitalist society all laws are unjust. Justice can only be achieved by redistribution of wealth. This perhaps led to Rawls' simple idea of a social contract.
Robert Nozick	Nozick's theory of 'entitlement' holds that society is just if everyone is entitled to the holdings they possess. Unfortunately, not everyone follows these rules: 'Some people steal from others, or defraud them, or enslave them, seizing their product and preventing them from living as they choose, or forcibly exclude others from competing in exchanges.' This is in sharp contrast with Marx and Rawls.

> **Typical mistake**
>
> It is really important to link theory to practical application. Often candidates only reference the theorists and not cases. Ensure you include both.

> **Revision activity**
>
> Research these theorists, adding dates and context to their arguments.
>
> Whose position is closest to your own views?

> **Exam tip**
>
> You will be rewarded for any attempt to evaluate any particular idea of justice, for example the utilitarian's concern for society rather than the individual.

Extent to which the law achieves justice

In most legal disputes, one party will usually see that justice has been done, while the other may wholeheartedly disagree. Whether or not the legal rules achieve justice is a subjective concept.

Even judges can disagree about the scope of their role in trying to achieve justice. In his autobiography, *The Family Story*, Lord Denning wrote that:

> 'My root belief is that the proper role of the judge is to do justice between the parties before him. If there is any rule of law which impairs the doing of justice, then it is the province of the judge to do all he legitimately can to avoid the rule, even to change it, so as to do justice in the instant case before him.'

In *Tito v Waddell* (No. 2) (1977), Sir Robert Megarry VC took an opposing view:

> 'The question is not whether the plaintiffs ought to succeed as a matter of fairness or ethics or morality. I have no jurisdiction to make an award to the plaintiffs just because I reach the conclusion ... that they have had a raw deal. This is a Court of Law and Equity (using "equity" in its technical sense), administering justice according to law and equity, and my duty is to examine the plaintiffs' claim on that footing.'

Procedural law

Procedural law puts systems in place in an attempt to ensure justice, i.e. it provides a framework in which all should be equal before the law:

- Everyone is entitled to put their case in court.
- Financial assistance should exist for accessing lawyers and the courts.
- The rules of evidence ensure the material presented in court is reliable, for example confession evidence of a defendant intimidated by police will not be admissible – see *R v Miller* (1992).
- The right to trial by jury can ensure justice being done in an individual case rather than a policy or 'floodgates' type verdict – see *R v Ponting* (1985).
- Judges, magistrates and juries must not be biased or appear to be biased – see *R v Bingham JJ ex parte Jowitt* (1974).
- Corrective justice, not the Aristotle theory but rather the notion that there is a right to a 'second opinion', provides a system of appeals, judicial review and the Criminal Cases Review Commission (CCRC) to ensure justice has been done.
- Within this framework, disputes are resolved by applying substantive laws to produce the most 'just' results.

Substantive justice

This kind of law is achieved by the application of legal rules themselves. For example:

- In criminal law, there are defences to justify the actions of the defendant, and the partial defences to murder ensure the defendant still shoulders some responsibility but not all.
- Sentencing: the accused should be treated consistently with their level of fault (see Chapter 2.2).
- In civil law, concepts such as the standard of care owed by a professional above that of an ordinary person help to achieve justice.

Procedural law: puts systems in place in an attempt to ensure justice, i.e. it provides a framework in which all should be equal before the law.

Revision activity

Who said 'the law, like a tavern, should be open to all' and what did they mean by this?

Have a look at the Legal Aid, Sentencing and Punishment of Offenders Act 2012 (LASPO): is the law still open to all?

Revision activity

Research the Criminal Cases Review Commission and briefly explain its role.

Where rules have failed to achieve justice

- The mandatory life term for murders allows no judicial flexibility to recognise different levels of seriousness of offence. *In R v Canning* (2002), the trial judge described his sentence as 'a classic example of injustice'.
- The rules on joint enterprise: *R v Jogee* (2016) corrected a historic mistake which had exposed people to being found guilty of the most serious offences on the weakest legal basis.

Miscarriages of justice

The following cases are notorious instances of where justice was not achieved:

- Timothy Evans
- Alan Turing
- the Birmingham Six
- the Guildford Four
- Stephen Lawrence.

These cases stick in our memory because they are unusual. They are, after all, a tiny minority of the cases that pass through our criminal and civil justice systems. Perhaps it is fair to conclude that most of the system is just and achieves just results most of the time – this is a state of affairs to satisfy most utilitarians.

> **Miscarriage of justice:** where someone is convicted and punished by the courts for a crime that they did not commit.

> **Revision activity**
>
> Research these cases and create a grid 'attaching' them to an idea of justice, for example by showing that there was a denial of natural justice.

Table 5.3.2 **Key cases regarding the law and justice**

Case	Facts	Principle of justice
Lindsay v Commissioners of Customs and Excise (2002)	The practice of customs officials to confiscate cars as well as the goods being smuggled in them was held to be disproportionate.	Aristotle
R v Miller (1992)	The police asked 300 questions of the suspect. The interview was held to be oppressive.	Procedural justice – police powers
R v Ponting (1985)	D, an MOD civil servant, was charged under the Official Secrets Act after leaking documents showing the government had lied about the sinking of the ship *General Belgrano* during the Falklands War. He was acquitted.	Procedural justice – trial by jury
R v Bingham JJ ex parte Jowitt (1974)	D was convicted for speeding. His evidence contradicted evidence from a police officer. The chairman chose to believe the police officer, leading the Divisional Court to quash the conviction because of bias.	Procedural justice – the process must be free from bias
Glynn v Keele University (1971)	A student was fined £10 and suspended for sunbathing nude, without a hearing. He should have been given the opportunity to test the evidence.	Procedural justice – there must be reasonable opportunity to test the evidence
R v Thames Magistrates' Court ex parte Polemis (1974)	A Greek sea captain was not given time to prepare his defence to an allegation of polluting docks with oil. He received his summons at 10.30 a.m. and the case was heard at 4 p.m.	Procedural justice – there must be reasonable opportunity to test the evidence
Re Pinochet (1998)	Chilean dictator Augusto Pinochet tried to evade extradition to Spain. One of the House of Lords judges was associated with a charity that had campaigned to have Pinochet brought to justice.	Procedural justice; natural justice – there can be no suggestion of bias (in Latin, *nemo judex in res sua*)

Case	Facts	Principle of justice
R v B (A-G Ref. No. 3 of 1999) (2000)	This case looked at whether DNA profile evidence, which should have been destroyed under s 64(3B)(b) PACE 1984, could be admitted in evidence. The Court of Appeal ruled that it could not.	Procedural justice – evidence must be obtained fairly
R v Mason (1987)	A confession obtained by deceit was wrongly admitted. An appeal was allowed; confession obtained by deceit should be rejected.	Procedural justice – evidence must be obtained fairly
R v Wilson (1996)	See Table 5.2.4.	Procedural justice; defences must be allowed and there must be an ability to distinguish precedents
Miller v Jackson (1977)	See Chapter 4.4–4.7.	Cumming-Bruce LJ: the court had to 'strike a fair balance'; damages were awarded instead of an injunction
R v Dudley and Stephens (1884)	See Table 5.2.5.	Utilitarianism not used here; individual justice is not sacrificed for the good of the majority – though the sentence was commuted and therefore reflective of Ds' ordeal

Now test yourself

TESTED ☐

1 Define 'justice'.
2 How did Lord Denning and Sir Robert Megarry differ in their opinions about the role of the judge in achieving justice?
3 What is meant by 'substantive justice'?
4 Why are utilitarians happy about the law's efforts in achieving justice? What do you think?

Answers online

Exam summary

In the exam, you MAY be asked to consider a specific statement based on one of the nature of law topics and discuss the extent to which you agree or disagree. In doing so, you are required to use examples from your full course of study.

This type of question will be worth a maximum of 25 marks.

5.4 Law and society

Role of law in society

Emile Durkheim considered law to be a boundary-maintaining device, with two purposes:

● to define sanctions
● to prescribe punishment by way of deterring us from creating social instability.

Durkheim argues social stability is created and maintained by its legal structures. There are two types of legal structure:

1 Repressive – criminal law: the aim of criminal law is to maintain law and order. Therefore, when a person is found guilty of an offence, that offender will be punished. Criminal law also aims to protect society, which is the justification for sending offenders to prison.
2 Restitutive – civil law: the aim of civil law is to uphold the rights of individuals and businesses. The courts can order compensation to put the parties back to the position they would have been in if their rights had not been violated.

Law as a social control mechanism

Law can be described as a mechanism of social control. It comprises rules for controlling our behaviour, to keep order in society.

These rules develop from the behaviour that society has, over time, accepted as 'appropriate' or 'normal'.

A rule is something that determines the way in which we behave. We either:

● submit ourselves to the rule voluntarily, as is the case with moral rules (see Chapter 5.2), or
● have to follow the rule as it is enforceable in some way, as is the case with the law.

How the law creates and deals with consensus and conflict

Each of us has rights or interests, and it is the function of the law to create balance when our rights or interests conflict.

What are rights/interests?

In this context, rights and interests are defined by Rudolf von Jhering and Roscoe Pound as principles identified by individuals and/or states as being of fundamental importance.

Individuals' interests (i.e. private interests) might include:

● survival
● safety
● freedom
● justice
● privacy
● health care
● education.

We now associate many of these areas with human rights law.

The state's interests (i.e. public interests) are less complex – generally just:

● physical security
● financial security.

The state is regarded by Durkheim as our 'collective conscience' and therefore we all have consensus about these interests.

When do interests conflict?

Individuals can conflict with:

- other individuals, for example a starving man's method of survival may be to steal another person's bread
- the state, for example a suspected terrorist's interest in freedom will conflict with the state's interest in security.

Conflict between individuals' interests are generally dealt with by substantive laws, such as theft.

Conflict between an individual's interests and the state's interests are generally dealt with by procedural laws, such as the rule in the Terrorism Act 2006 that allows the police to hold a suspected terrorist for up to 14 days without charge, as in our example above.

Roscoe Pound (1870–1964)

Pound is associated with social engineering, emphasising the importance of social relationships in the development of law.

He stated that a lawmaker acts as a social engineer by attempting to solve problems in society using law as a tool. Therefore, highlighting the law's purpose is to attempt consensus, but be prepared to deal with conflict.

> **Typical mistake**
>
> Do not forget to make reference to theorists when answering questions from this section.

> **Exam tip**
>
> Your exam responses should show that you know how the important areas of substantive and procedural law attempt to balance conflicting interests and can use key cases to illustrate your points.

Table 5.4.1 Key cases for balancing competing interests

Case	Use as an example of:
Miller v Jackson (1977)	Conflict of individual rights: the cricket club wanted to play cricket, its neighbours wanted to stop balls flying into their gardens
Kennaway v Thompson (1981)	The use of partial injunctions and damages in order to strike a balance between the rights of the neighbours and the social interest of sport
Evans v UK (2006)	Individuals' conflicting rights over the destruction or otherwise of embryos created from them both
R v T (1990)	Substantive law, i.e. a defence attempting to balance the conflicting interests of the defendant and the victim
DPP v Majewski (1976)	Restriction of the use of a 'defence' for policy reasons

> **Revision activity**
>
> Identify whether the areas of law listed below are procedural or substantive:
>
> - nuisance (see Chapter 4.4)
> - bail (see Chapter 1.2)
> - treatment of suspects by the police
> - criminal trial process (see Chapter 1.2)
> - automatic disclosure of criminal convictions
> - cautions
> - consent (see Chapter 2.7)
> - intoxication (see Chapter 2.6).
>
> Link them to the cases in Table 5.4.1– does the law successfully engineer a balance of the interests?

Realist approach to law making

The realist school of thought holds that:

- the reason judges disagree and rely so heavily on precedent and legal argument is because there is not really a right answer in most legal disputes; instead there are only different, subjective opinions
- precedents and statutes are not sufficient to determine the correct legal outcome, and often the judgment is a matter of a particular judge's political opinions.

Realists say that this must be the case, or there would be far fewer disputes – results could be far more accurately predicted and disputes settled without having to go to court.

There is a notion that a judge begins with the outcome and works backwards to justify it. The lengthy published judgment simply rationalises the arbitrary nature of the decision which has been made in response to the real human need, rather than by following objective legal rules.

Lord Reid said famously 'There was a time when it was thought almost indecent to suggest that judges make law - they only declare it ... But we do not believe in fairy tales anymore'.

Now test yourself

1 How successful is the law in fulfilling its purpose?
2 Why is it important that the balancing of competing interests is seen to be done?
3 Why do we obey the law?
4 How do legal rules develop?

Answers online

Exam summary

In the exam, you MAY be asked to consider a specific statement based on one of the nature of law topics and discuss the extent to which you agree or disagree. In doing so, you are required to use examples from your full course of study.

This type of question will be worth a maximum of 25 marks.

5.5 Law and technology

This chapter is a new OCR topic. It takes the nature of law beyond its link to morality, justice and society by developing your understanding of how the law interacts with technology (mainly **information technology**) and is modernised by it.

> **Information technology:** the use of systems, especially computers and telecommunications systems, for storing, retrieving and sending information.

Intersection of law and technology

REVISED

The English legal system has been a paper-based system for hundreds of years. The courts and legal services have required the presence of paper documents, paper files and physical appearances in court; failure to provide these has led to many cases being adjourned or 'dropped'.

As technology has developed, the legal services industry has embraced some of the changes, but this has been slow and unenthusiastic in comparison with other areas of the public and private sector.

Nevertheless, the last ten years have seen pressure, most notably from younger lawyers and judges, in demanding change.

Legal firms in the UK have had to:
- adapt to new technology to remain competitive in world markets
- change communication systems to prevent international legal service companies from taking clients through their ability to communicate instantly via email and the internet.

> **Revision activity**
>
> Consider the benefits of the following recent technological advances to the work of a lawyer or judge:
> - smartphone or tablet computer
> - the internet
> - Cloud storage
> - social media
> - eLaw libraries.

> **Revision activity**
>
> Discuss the benefit of FaceTime or Skype to the work of a lawyer or to a judge sitting in court.

Advantages of technology in the law

Table 5.5.1 E-solutions to problems in the legal system

Problem	e-Solution
A lack of efficiency and accuracy in case preparation and research using paper-based law reports, statutes etc.	e-libraries such as Westlaw or LexisNexis, enabling lawyers to become more efficient and accurate in research and case construction
The physical nature of having to appear in court – time off work, travelling expenses etc.	The use of online dispute resolution (ODR) in civil cases Pleading 'guilty' to some minor criminal offences in 'online courts', with sentencing by email and fines payable online
Hugely expensive labour costs in running a legal firm	Reducing labour costs by swapping employees with machine-read or artificial intelligence systems
Lack of innovation in the legal system	Information technology allowing the creation of ideas for further process innovation
Information technology's own flaws and problems around confidentiality and security	Producing work around cyber-security, data protection and new technology laws, creating a further industry of innovation
Consumer demand and expectations	Changes in legal services simply supporting consumer demand and expectation

> **Revision activity**
>
> Research any major online business, such as eBay, Amazon or similar, to see how their in-house online dispute resolution systems operate. Write down their systems' key points. See **www.judiciary.gov.uk/wp-content/uploads/2015/02/ethan_katsh_int2_evo_of_odr.pdf** for eBay's introduction and evolution of ODR.

See Chapter 1.1 for information on online courts and ODR.

Key issues

Privacy, data protection and cyber-crime

While technology can greatly assist with the smooth running of the legal services, information held in electronic means has its own problems, in particular:

- where an individual's privacy is at stake
- breaches of **data protection**
- through the perpetration of **cyber-crime**.

> **Data protection:** the legal control of access to, and the use of, factual and statistical data generally stored in digital or paper-based systems.
>
> **Cyber-crime:** criminal activity carried out by the use of computers, generally via the internet.

Privacy and data protection

While Article 8 of the European Convention on Human Rights guarantees the right to respect for private and family life, the Article is not an absolute right and can be restricted in accordance with the law or where necessary in a democratic society.

Table 5.5.2 **Privacy and data protection issues**

Tools affecting privacy or data protection	Issue
Closed circuit television (CCTV)	While appearing to make society safer, the ability to continuously track people without permission is of major concern.
Automatic number plate recognition (ANPR)	Like CCTV, car registration plates are constantly filmed to check for uninsured cars or wanted drivers, even though the majority of car users are insured and have not committed crimes.
Biometrics	This is the application of statistical information to biological data, which attempts to predict how a person will act and behave without actually testing or even meeting the individual (this is used in job recruitment).
Radio frequency identification	Small location-emitting devices are attached to products so that manufacturers can track their movements and location after production. They are used on hire cars or ID cards in workplaces, tracking the number of times a person uses the toilet etc.
Location data	For example, smart phone technology tracks the location and movement of people so companies can track where people have been and are likely to go.
Investigatory Powers Act 2016	This is a framework for the security services or other relevant bodies to intercept communications and store information. While providing safeguards, the powers are widespread and the ability to store and record any communication is possible.

Cyber-crime

Table 5.5.3 **Key issues and terms for cyber-crime**

Issue relating to cyber-crime	Problem
Computer Misuse Act 1990	It is criticised as being poorly drafted, hastily enacted and, like any criminal law, it does little to prevent cyber-crime.
Hacking	If information is held electronically, it can be accessed illegally for criminal purposes.
Computer viruses	Most viruses are designed to halt or slow the operation of a computer or computer network system, for financial gain or simply to destroy information.
Identity theft and identity fraud	This is a popular and devastating criminal activity where a person's details are used to access confidential information or commit crimes.

> **Exam tip**
>
> Research some statistics to back up arguments about the growth in cyber-crime.

> **Typical mistake**
>
> Do not forget that this is a law exam, so you must use legal authority in your answers, such as Acts of Parliament and cases.

Cross-border issues and future challenges

These include:

- Language barriers – will English remain or become the standard form of communication? Which version of English will be used: UK or US?
- IT formats and platforms – which specific IT hardware or software will be used? Will it be standardised, or will there be many types available that would need to interface and interact?
- Will cost and complexity require further IT/legal training that could prejudice developing countries and simply benefit 'western' countries?
- Over-reliance on IT exposes systems to attack via computer viruses and other intrusions. Certain countries are accused of specific cyber-attacks targeting IT systems in other countries.

See Chapter 1.3 for information on globalisation and its impact on the law and legal education.

Now test yourself

TESTED

1. Why do you think that the legal system in England and Wales has been slow to adopt technology in its working practices?
2. In terms of technology, how would a solicitor's office in 1970 differ from one in 2018?
3. How would an online court benefit a defendant in certain criminal cases?
4. Why would a citizen become concerned with the use of biometrics in the UK?
5. What is meant by the term 'globalisation'?

Answers online

Exam summary

In the exam, you MAY be asked to consider a specific statement based on one of the nature of law topics and discuss the extent to which you agree or disagree. In doing so, you are required to use examples from your full course of study. These questions attract 25 marks.

Exam practice

1. Explain the relationship between legal rules and moral principles. Discuss the extent to which law should be based on moral principles. [25 marks]
2. Discuss the importance of fault-based liability in English law. [25 marks]
3. Discuss the meaning of 'justice' and the extent to which English law succeeds in achieving justice. [25 marks]
4. Explain what is meant by 'balancing conflicting interests'. Discuss whether the law is successful in balancing conflicting interests. [25 marks]
5. 'Cyber-crime and data protection are the greatest technological challenges facing the law.' Discuss the extent to which you agree with this statement. [25 marks]

ONLINE

6 Human rights law

In Component 3 of the OCR A Level Law H415 specification, you are required to choose one of two optional topics: either *Human rights law* or *The law of contract*.

Human rights law explores specific human rights, while also contextualising those rights within the English legal system and beyond. You will be required to understand the restrictions placed upon those rights and the enforcement mechanisms that have been developed.

Exam questions will concentrate on a critical awareness of this topic while requiring you to make informed decisions about human rights laws and their application in scenario-based situations in the following areas:
- rules and theory
- protection of the individual's human rights and freedoms in the UK
- key provisions of the European Convention on Human Rights
- restrictions on human rights law
- enforcement of human rights law.

6.1 Rules and theory

Rules of human rights law

Since the passing of the Human Rights Act 1998 by the UK government in 2000, and the development of its case law, the idea and awareness of having basic human rights have become a crucial part of the way society operates. This area of law has become much more important and controversial.

The Act brought into law, for the first time, many **rights** in a single document that citizens thought already existed but largely did not. Before the passing of this Act, there was no single document or full classification in UK law of human rights.

The law under the Act, and the consequent case law, has been seen as both a benefit and a detriment to UK citizens.

European Convention on Human Rights

Until the Human Rights Act 1998 was passed, UK citizens were protected under the European Convention on Human Rights (ECHR). The Convention had been drawn up after the Second World War, following the atrocities perpetrated by the Nazis, in order to avoid such trauma from occurring in Europe again. It marked a turning point for peace and European diplomacy.

Drafted in 1950 by the newly formed Council of Europe, the Convention came into force in 1953. The Convention has its own specific court, the European Court of Human Rights (ECtHR), which is based in Strasbourg, France.

While a signatory of the Convention, the UK courts were not bound by it. The Human Rights Act's aim was to enshrine the Convention into domestic law in the UK, albeit with restrictions.

> **Rights:** rules or laws which are believed to belong to every person without discrimination.

> **Revision activity**
>
> Explain the difference between a 'right' and a 'freedom'.

> **Exam tip**
>
> To help prepare for the exam, draw up a timeline of the different pieces of human rights legislation – domestic, European and international – and make sure that you can explain why each piece was specifically passed.

Rules and principles of law under the Convention

The original Convention was divided up into Articles, similar to sections of an Act of Parliament, which guarantee certain important rights and freedoms. These include:

- Article 2 – the right to life
- Article 5 – the right to liberty and security of person
- Article 6 – the right to a fair trial
- Article 8 – the right to respect for private and family life
- Article 10 – the right to freedom of expression
- Article 11 – the right to freedom of peaceful assembly and association.

Recognition by the UK

The UK was an original signatory to the Convention in 1953, but the specific detail as laid out by the Convention was not ratified into domestic law until 2000.

Until 2000, UK citizens had to exhaust domestic laws on human rights (if they existed) before they could gain access to those rights under the Convention. This was a complicated and expensive process.

The government introduced the 1998 Act to streamline access to the basic human rights and freedoms under the Convention, so that citizens could access these rights as a first line of uncomplicated protection in any domestic court. However, many of the rights allow the imposition of restrictions, generally asserted as being for the purpose of protecting national security.

The introduction of the 1998 Act has been controversial. Dubbed a 'burglar's charter', many argued it vastly overprotects criminals rather than assisting the victims of crime.

> **Revision activity**
>
> Using A3 paper, begin to create mind maps on the main five Articles of the European Convention on Human Rights.

> **Typical mistake**
>
> It is easy to become muddled with the different Acts and Conventions, so make sure that you understand the differences between each important piece of law.

> **Revision activity**
>
> Using the internet, research the case of *Thompson and Venables v United Kingdom* (1999).

Table 6.1.1 Key case on human rights law

Case	Facts	Outcome
Thompson and Venables v United Kingdom (1999)	The two child-killers of Jamie Bulger argued there had been a breach of Article 6 ECHR (the right to a fair trial) due to the media frenzy that surrounded the case.	Their lawyers successfully argued that the trial and the surrounding media attention undermined the chance of a fair trial. No compensation was awarded but their legal costs were to be paid.

Theory of human rights law

REVISED

This section looks at the different **theories of rights**, how they have developed and been restricted, and how they are contrasted with civil liberties.

> **Typical mistake**
>
> This topic concentrates on the theories of human rights. As theoretical concepts, make sure you do not quote them as being legal fact as opposed to being legal theory (especially natural rights and legal rights). As they are theories, there is room for debate, conjecture and challenge in your answers.

> **Theories of rights:** systems of ideas proposed to explain the rationale of having rights based on general principles.

> **Exam tip**
>
> This topic is more a sociological area than a legal area, but nevertheless it is an important one to understand. It underpins the 'why do we have rights?' rather than the 'what rights do we have?' concept.

The concept and basic theories of human rights can be traced back to ancient civilisations and their influence on the rest of the world:

- The ancient Greeks, through the teachings of the great philosophers, believed that certain rights were above normal laws introduced by man, and that rights came from divine authority and intervention.

- When Cyrus, the King of Persia, conquered the city of Babylon in 539BC, he freed all the slaves, allowed them to return to their homelands and reinstated religious freedom. This idea of having basic human rights spread through Europe and was eventually championed by the Roman Empire through rights and '**natural law**'.

As societies progressed, and revolutions were fought for changes in the way countries were ruled, the idea of human rights replaced divine rule and these rights were incorporated as fundamental to their **constitutions**:

- English Bill of Rights 1689
- American Declaration of Independence 1776 (as amended in 1791)
- French Declaration of the Rights of Man and Citizen 1789
- Universal Declaration of Human Rights 1948.

The table below explains the different theories of human rights.

Natural law: rules which are not necessarily written down as laws but are nevertheless followed by citizens.

Constitutions: sets of rules which state how a country is to be run and the specific rights of its citizens.

Revision activity

Using the internet, research the purpose of the English Bill of Rights 1689.

Table 6.1.2 Theories of human rights

Theory	Explanation
Natural rights	- Each citizen from birth to death has certain fundamental rights that cannot be removed by their government. - Developed from the law of nature, natural order and selection, these rights form the basis of a peaceful and co-existing society, focusing on the rights of individuals. - John Locke's writings stated that individuals were entitled to the rights of life, liberty and property. This theory relies upon citizens being independent from one another and having a government or state which respects such individualism.
Legal rights	- Rights come from the state and not society or the individual or natural law. These rights are formulated by the state in order to run and maintain order in society. - This is a common theory in countries run by despotic regimes or autocrats as opposed to democracies.
Societal rights	- What is desirable to society results in the rights accepted by that society. - Societal rights depend upon the beliefs, views and autonomy of that society, so may differ as beliefs or religions differ. - To be a societal right, the right must be socially useful and achieve the greatest social benefit for the majority of the citizens in order to be accepted.
Historical rights	- This theory applies to the English legal system especially. Custom creates a system of rules and laws common to the country, which evolve and spread with common usage. They are tried and tested, and therefore valued and accepted by a society. - The 'Glorious Revolution' of 1688 reaffirmed the rights, liberties and customs that the English had enjoyed since ancient times but which had been gradually eroded or changed by successive monarchs and not through democratic means. - Many historical rights have their basis in primarily religious beliefs, and then socio-economic beliefs through trade and such practice.

Theory	Explanation
Economic rights	• Karl Marx argued that rights are maintained by laws which simply protect and prop up the dominant group or groups in society. Rights are maintained as a method of controlling production. • These rights create and maintain a class system and divide society into the exploiters and the exploited. Therefore, the most economically powerful group becomes the main influence on the government, or in fact becomes the government. • Therefore, such rights are not from natural law or custom but made and developed to assist the powerful to the detriment of the weak. This leads to inequality and discrimination. • Marx argued against such capitalism as being fundamentally wrong and an affront to democracy. He held that rights can only truly operate in a classless society and that, at the time of his writings, democracy was simply a myth in most western societies.

Revision activity

Using the internet, research in greater detail John Locke's theory of natural rights.

Rights contrasted with liberties

There is a slight difference between rights and liberties:
- Rights are considered universal to all human beings regardless of origin, whereas liberties (or civil liberties) are those specific to a particular country.
- Liberties represent the things that we are free to do in our countries, provided that there is no law against such activities.
- Liberties have been part of our society for centuries and evolve or change as society changes.
- Liberties are 'allowed' in certain societies, whereas rights are guaranteed in certain societies.

In the UK, the Human Rights Act came into law in 2000 and gave effect to the European Convention on Human Rights. This guaranteed a certain number of fundamental rights.

Scope of fundamental human rights

In order for there to be fundamental human rights, there has to be an understanding that they come with responsibilities and restrictions:
- Every right has a responsibility – citizens cannot expect to have total use of a right unless they respect that others also have the same right.
- In order to use a right, it must not be to the detriment of other citizens who co-exist at the same time.
- It may be necessary to restrict our fundamental human rights such as to life, liberty etc. in order to make a society run smoothly.

There are three main ways to categorise rights that are based on restrictions:

1 Absolute rights cannot be restricted in any way, nor can they be removed. For example, we have the right not to be tortured during the investigation of a crime or for any other purpose.
2 Limited rights are more common, and there are many examples under the Human Rights Act 1998. For example, we may have freedom of movement, but this can be restricted if a person is lawfully arrested or imprisoned.

3 Qualified rights need to be balanced against the needs of other people and will be restricted, generally temporarily, for the benefit of society. For example, the police may restrict freedom of movement in order to stop people from entering a certain area during a protest, or they may be detained in a certain area to avoid confrontation with other people, thus avoiding public order issues.

Now test yourself

1 Using key dates from this section, draw a timeline in the formulation of human rights law that has impacted the UK.
2 What do you think is meant by 'the right to life'? Should there be any restrictions, such as a right to die?
3 What do you think is meant by 'the right to liberty and security of the person'? Should there be any restrictions, such as detaining suspected criminals?
4 What do you think is meant by 'the right to a respect for a private life'? Should there be any restrictions, such as media scrutiny of celebrities?
5 What do you think is meant by the term 'freedom of expression'? Should there be any restrictions, such as when religion is criticised?
6 Explain what is meant by the term 'natural law'.
7 How did Karl Marx explain the theory of economic rights?
8 Explain how the right to freedom of movement, for example going for a walk with a friend, has to be balanced with other citizens' rights.
9 Explain how the right to the freedom of expression, for example writing a newspaper article, has to be balanced with other citizens' rights.
10 Explain what is meant by 'absolute right', 'limited right' and 'qualified right'. How might each of these rights be restricted?

Answers online

Exam summary

In the exam, you MAY be asked to discuss, in outline, the rules of human rights law or the theory of human rights law. This question will be worth a maximum of 25 marks.

6.2 Protection of the individual's human rights and freedoms in the UK

Overview of the development of human rights in the UK

This section looks at the existence of human rights in the UK and the enforcement of human rights before the passing of the Human Rights Act 1998 in 2000.

Historically, many countries have written down all the rights of its citizens in a single document. These tend to be 'new' countries, which have been established in more recent times.

Countries such as the USA established a written constitution upon gaining independence, which contained a **Bill of Rights** outlining its citizens' rights and freedoms.

The UK is one of the older established countries that does not have a constitution, but it does have a Bill of Rights. However, this Bill is not like that of other countries, although it does establish certain freedoms.

Not having a constitution or full Bill of Rights did not mean that before 2000 the UK did not protect human rights; it simply meant that such freedoms and rights were found in a variety of different places.

Statute law

As Parliament passed laws, it naturally created rights and freedoms. The main examples of such historic Acts or similar documents are:
- the *Magna Carta* 1215, which importantly guaranteed a right of appeal against unlawful imprisonment through a document called a writ of *habeas corpus*
- the Bill of Rights 1689, which guaranteed freedom of speech in Parliament without the interference of the Crown
- the Human Rights Act 1998, which enshrined into UK domestic law the European Convention on Human Rights.

Common law

This is the law common to the land – laws that have spread through custom and been adopted and developed as the norm around the UK for centuries and ratified by judges in legal cases.

Common law is the basis of the English legal system and of many ex-British colonies such as the USA, Canada, India and Australia. Examples include:
- *Entick v Carrington* (1765): Carrington entered Entick's property, claiming he had a warrant to forcibly enter, search and seize certain papers. The court said that the warrant had no legal effect and established Carrington as a trespasser. The 'police' had no right to enter premises without lawful authority.
- *Bushell's Case* (1670): a judge ordered a jury to be detained in a room without food or water until they brought back a certain verdict against their will. The case decided that such a decision went against the principle of a fair trial and stated that a judge cannot interfere with the decision of a jury.

Revision activity

Make brief notes to explain how human rights or freedoms were maintained in the UK after the Second World War and before the passing of the Human Rights Act 1998.

Bill of Rights: a document which sets out the civil rights of citizens.

Revision activity

Explain the importance of the passing of the *Magna Carta* in 1215.

EU law

The UK has benefitted from its close association with European countries and the influence of EU law in various ways:

- The UK's membership of the European Union has meant that many freedoms, particularly in employment law, have been adopted. Directives under Article 141 of the Treaty of Rome have banned discrimination on the basis of gender, sexual orientation, age and race.
- Membership of the European Convention on Human Rights: the Convention was eventually adopted fully as incorporated by the Human Rights Act 1998.

History of the European Court of Human Rights

The European Court of Human Rights (ECtHR) is an international court which was established in 1959 with a remit to rule on individual or state applications which allege violations of the civil rights established under the European Convention on Human Rights.

Table 6.2.1 **Key dates for the European Court of Human Rights**

Key date	Activity
5 May 1949	Creation of the Council of Europe
4 November 1950	Adoption of the European Convention on Human Rights
3 September 1953	Entry into force of the European Convention on Human Rights
21 January 1959	First members of the European Court of Human Rights elected by the Consultative Assembly of the Council of Europe
23–28 February 1959	Court's first session sitting
18 September 1959	Court adopts its Rules of Court
14 November 1960	Court delivers its first judgment in *Lawless v Ireland*
1 November 1998	Protocol No. 11 – Court now sits as a full-time court
18 September 2008	Court issues its 10,000th judgment

Human Rights Act 1998

This section looks at the domestic impact of the UK's first designated piece of **human rights law**, which has been controversial since its enactment.

The Human Rights Act 1998 (HRA 98) was passed by the UK government in 1998 and became law in 2000. It was the first specific Act passed in the UK that solely enforced basic human rights for its citizens.

The Act was designed to incorporate the majority of the Articles of the European Convention on Human Rights into domestic law.

Human rights law: law governing fundamental rights and freedoms that exist in our legal system simply because we are human beings.

Revision activity

Using the internet, research the timescale of the Human Rights Act 1998 from Green Paper to Royal Assent.

Typical mistake

Do not confuse section numbers of the Human Rights Act 1998 with Article numbers of the European Convention on Human Rights. The documents' section and Article numbers do not correspond.

Purpose of the Act

The purpose is declared at the beginning of the Act as being primarily 'to give further effect to rights and freedoms guaranteed under the European Convention on Human Rights'. The Act incorporates *inter alia* Articles 2 to 12 and 14, as well as Articles 1 to 3, of the First Protocol.

Section 6 of the Act states: 'It is unlawful for a public authority to act in a way which is incompatible with a Convention right.' Therefore, the Act makes it unlawful for any 'public authority' to act in a way that is incompatible with any of the Articles in the European Convention on Human Rights, which were incorporated by the Act.

The term 'public authority' is fairly broad, covering organisations and persons in the public sector, but it does not include government ministers or those connected to Parliament while exercising functions connected to parliamentary business.

Section 7 of the Act states:

> 'A person who claims that a public authority has acted (or proposes to act) in a way which is made unlawful by section 6 may (a) bring proceedings against the authority under this Act in the appropriate court or tribunal, or (b) rely on the Convention right or rights concerned in any legal proceedings.'

Therefore, if an individual believes that a public authority is acting in breach of a Convention right, they can bring proceedings against them in a court or tribunal.

Impact of the Act on UK legislation

Section 2 of the Act states:

> 'A court or tribunal determining a question which has arisen in connection with a Convention right must take into account any … judgment, decision, declaration or advisory opinion of the European Court of Human Rights.'

Therefore, decisions and opinions of the European Court of Human Rights must be taken into account by UK courts, even if there is a conflicting decision of a UK court.

Section 19 of the Act states:

> 'A Minister of the Crown in charge of a Bill in either House of Parliament must, before Second Reading of the Bill … make a statement to the effect that in his view the provisions of the Bill are compatible with the Convention rights.'

This is known as a 'statement of compatibility'. However, s 19 continues by stating that the minister can nevertheless make a declaration of incompatibility and still proceed with the Bill, thus avoiding Convention rights.

Interpretation of UK legislation

Section 3 of the Act states that 'so far as it is possible to do so, primary legislation and subordinate legislation must be read and given effect in a way which is compatible with the Convention rights'. Therefore, any UK legislation should be harmonious and not contravene the Convention's rights.

However, this compatibility is only 'so far as it is possible to do so', which, in effect, allows the UK government to avoid the Convention's rights.

Exam tip

You do not need to memorise the sections of the Human Rights Act 1998. Just make sure that you have a broad understanding of the purpose of the sections as outlined below.

Revision activity

Using the internet, research the case of *R v DPP ex parte Kebilene* (1999).

It is interesting to note that English courts had given precedence to the Convention even before the 1998 Act was passed – see *R v DPP ex parte Kebilene* (1999).

Incompatibility with UK legislation

Section 4 of the Act states that 'if the court is satisfied that the provision is incompatible with a Convention right, it may make a declaration of that incompatibility'. Therefore, a court in determining whether a provision of an Act of Parliament is compatible with the Convention can make a declaration of incompatibility. This brings to the attention of the government the specific incompatibility, but it does not affect either party to that present action.

Under s 10, if an Act is found to be incompatible under s 4, a statutory instrument can be used to amend the Act in question to comply with the Convention.

However, under s 10(2) the relevant government minister 'may by order make such amendments to the legislation as he considers necessary to remove the incompatibility'. This means that they do not have to amend the law to comply with the Convention.

Table 6.2.2 **Key cases on human rights law**

Case	Facts	Outcome
R v DPP ex parte Kebilene (1999)	Three defendants were charged with terrorist offences, but the trial judge stated that s 16A of the Terrorism Act 1989 was contrary to Article 6 ECHR.	The House of Lords agreed with the trial judge.
Re: Medicaments (No. 2), Director General of Fair Trading v Proprietary Association of Great Britain (2001)	The case involved an alleged breach under Article 6 ECHR and the test of bias in UK court cases. Domestic law in relation to bias had been set in *R v Gough* (1993), but this decision was incompatible with several cases decided by the ECtHR.	The Court of Appeal refused to follow the House of Lords' decision in *Gough*.
R v A (2001)	D was charged with rape and wanted the complainant's sexual history to be raised in court. However, this evidence was to be excluded under an Act of Parliament. D argued that s 3 HRA 98 should be interpreted in the light of Article 6 ECHR.	The House of Lords stated that any Act of Parliament should be interpreted where necessary under s 3, but in this case it was a matter for a trial judge. A person's sexual history can be raised, but not to prejudice the fairness of the trial. The issue of Article 6 was not in question here.
H v Mental Health Review Tribunal (2001)	H argued s 72 of the Mental Health Act 1983 placed an unnecessary and incompatible burden to prove that he was not suffering from a mental disorder before a mental health tribunal could order his release.	The Court of Appeal held that certain sub-sections of s 72(1) of the Mental Health Act 1983 were incompatible with ECHR Articles 5(1) and 5(4). However, only Parliament could amend the law.

Human Rights Act and devolution

It has long been considered that the Human Rights Act 1998 is so entrenched in the UK's domestic law that if that Act were repealed by the UK government in favour of a Bill of Rights, the devolved nations of Wales, Scotland and Northern Ireland could potentially block such a move.

The Scottish government has already stated in 2014 that it would not tolerate any UK government attempt to preclude Scotland from the European Convention on Human Rights.

However, the complication facing the UK government is that while it may be able both to repeal the Human Rights Act and to amend the devolution statutes for each of these three countries in the union, each country has the right to consultation.

For example, with regard to Scotland, the Sewell Convention provides that in order to pass decisions on devolved matters, the UK government must seek the consent of the devolved country to do so. Therefore, there is currently a quandary over what permission is required and exactly how it is obtained.

Now test yourself

TESTED

1 Explain the difference between a constitution and a Bill of Rights.
2 How does statute law differ from the common law?
3 If the cases of *Entick v Carrington* (1765) and *Bushell* (1670) were decided today, which Articles of the European Convention on Human Rights could potentially be breached?
4 What was the purpose of the Human Rights Act 1998?
5 What is the main objective of s 2 of the Human Rights Act 1998?
6 How can s 19 of the Human Rights Act 1998 be criticised?
7 In what way does it seem that s 10(2) defeats the overall purpose of s 10(1)?

Answers online

Exam summary

In the exam, you MAY be asked to discuss:
● the development of human rights in the UK, including the *Magna Carta* 1215, the Bill of Rights 1688 and/or the history of the European Court of Human Rights
● the impact of the Human Rights Act 1998.

These types of question will each be worth a maximum of 25 marks.

6.3 Key provisions of the European Convention on Human Rights

The European Convention on Human Rights is divided into Articles and Protocols, which each protect an individual human right.

It is important to note that while the Convention guarantees these rights, a state can still restrict them, even if that state has signed and ratified the Convention and incorporated it into domestic law.

> **Exam tip**
>
> When answering a question on this topic, it is important to understand that rights and freedoms did not begin in the UK with the passing of the Human Rights Act 1998. The Act simply codified much of the European Convention on Human Rights into UK law.

> **Typical mistake**
>
> Do not mix up the European Convention on Human Rights with the Human Rights Act 1998, or the European Court of Human Rights with the European Court of Justice. You need to understand the different purposes of each.

Article 5: the right to liberty and security of person

REVISED

Article 5(1) states:

> 'Everyone has the right to liberty and security of person. No one shall be deprived of his liberty save in the following cases and in accordance with a procedure prescribed by law.'

Liberty means autonomy or independence from arrest or detention and is a fundamental right in a free and democratic society.

Security of person means that an individual cannot have their liberty removed or restricted without just cause.

Therefore, despite having such a right to liberty under Article 5, it is restricted in cases where the law allows arrest or detention.

> **Right to liberty and security of person:** no one without just cause can interfere with your right to live a free life. There may be exceptions, such as arrest or imprisonment.

> **Exam tip**
>
> When evaluating this right, try to understand that there are two separate, but closely linked, rights:
> 1 A citizen is allowed to be 'at liberty', i.e. free to conduct their day-to-day business such as going to college or work.
> 2 A citizen has the right not to have their body touched, held or restrained without just cause.

> **Revision activity**
>
> Make a list of activities that the right to liberty allows you to do during a typical school or college day.

> **Typical mistake**
>
> This is a more specific right than the general right of freedom of movement, as Article 5 protects an individual against unlawful arrest, detention or imprisonment.

Article 6: the right to a fair trial

Article 6(1) states:

'In the determination of his civil rights and obligations or of any criminal charge against him, everyone is entitled to a fair and public hearing within a reasonable time by an independent and impartial tribunal established by law.'

This Article provides that in criminal or civil rights trials an individual is entitled to:

- a fair and public hearing
- the trial being held within a reasonable time
- the trial being heard by an independent and impartial tribunal
- a public judgment, but that the media can be excluded from coverage if necessary.

Article 6(2) states:

'Everyone charged with a criminal offence shall be presumed innocent until proved guilty according to law.'

Article 6(3) states:

'Everyone charged with a criminal offence has the following minimum rights:

(a)   to be informed promptly, in a language which he understands and in detail, of the nature and cause of the accusation against him;

(b)   to have adequate time and facilities for the preparation of his defence;

(c)   to defend himself in person or through legal assistance of his own choosing or, if he has not sufficient means to pay for legal assistance, to be given it free when the interests of justice so require;

(d)   to examine or have examined witnesses against him and to obtain the attendance and examination of witnesses on his behalf under the same conditions as witnesses against him;

(e)   to have the free assistance of an interpreter if he cannot understand or speak the language used in court.'

These rights are in addition to those stated under Article 6(1), given that an individual's liberty is at stake and a term of imprisonment or other incarceration or punishment could be the outcome.

> **Typical mistake**
>
> While this is a more specific right than some of the other general rights, it does not guarantee the correct decision is made by the tribunal. There are many examples of 'miscarriages of justice', where decisions are overturned by subsequent courts.

> **Right to a fair trial:** individuals charged with a criminal offence or involved in cases concerning a civil right have a right to a public hearing with an impartial and independent 'tribunal' or judge within a reasonable time.

> **Typical mistake**
>
> The term 'tribunal' refers, in reality, to a court of law such as a Magistrates' Court, Crown Court or High Court. It does not only refer to the types of tribunal discussed in the legal system component, for example employment tribunals.

> **Exam tip**
>
> When evaluating this right, you can where necessary make links to the rules and theories of rights and to other topics such as the nature of law.

> **Revision activity**
>
> Make a list of guarantees that the right to a fair trial allows an individual, for example an independent judge, and another list of the potential consequences if any of these guarantees are not met.

Article 8: the right to respect for private and family life

> **Typical mistake**
>
> Despite being a fundamental right, this is one of the most heavily restricted. Exam questions will often give clues, sometimes implied, as to a legitimate restriction or restrictions. You must give responses that are based on the law, and not what you feel personally is a correct restriction or not.

> **Right to respect for private and family life:** no one without just cause can interfere with your right to respect for your private and family life, your home or your correspondence.

This Article covers a broad range of rights which were not specifically, or satisfactorily, covered by statute or the common law before the passing of the Human Rights Act 1998.

This has meant that many Acts of Parliament have had to be passed in order to comply with this Article, for example the Data Protection Act 1998 and the Freedom of Information Act 2000.

Specifically, the Article protects citizens from interference with their privacy and can, in certain circumstances, impose obligations on public bodies, such as the government or local authorities, to promote such privacy.

Under Article 8(1), every person has a right to respect of privacy, family life, home and correspondence:

- Privacy – this means that a citizen has the right to live their own life in a way that they choose to do so in private. This could include choosing their own sexuality, appearance (clothes, hair style, having tattoos or piercings, or not so having) or the right not to be interfered with by the media without public interest – see *Douglas v Hello! Ltd* (2001) below.
- Family life – this means respecting a person's choices on how they conduct their family relationships, such as sexual activity, being married or unmarried, having children within or outside of marriage, and allowing those families seeking immigration or settlement to live together until status is granted.
- Home – this covers home owners, tenants and landlords and means respecting a person's right to access and occupy their home without interference from public authorities, for example being evicted without just cause. This includes peaceful enjoyment of one's home without noise or other types of pollution.
- Correspondence – this means respecting a person's post, email, phone calls, texts etc.

Prior to the 1998 Act, there was no general right to privacy. Homes were generally protected under tort law, while several Acts of Parliament protected correspondence in different ways.

Compare the different outcomes of the cases in Table 6.3.1.

> **Exam tip**
>
> Remember that there are four similar, but specifically distinct, parts to this Article: privacy, family life, home and correspondence.

> **Revision activity**
>
> Under what circumstances do you think the right to privacy of a person's correspondence should be ignored by the state?

Table 6.3.1 Key cases on Article 8

Case	Facts	Outcome
Douglas v Hello! Ltd (2001)	Actors Michael Douglas and Catherine Zeta-Jones sued *Hello!* magazine when it had published unauthorised photographs of their wedding.	While upholding the couple's right to privacy, the court said it had to balance this with the magazine's freedom of expression in publishing the photographs under Article 10.
Hatton v United Kingdom (2001)	H sought a declaration that the increase of noise, caused by aircraft landing and taking off from Heathrow Airport in London, was a breach of Article 8.	The court decided that the applicant's right (and the rights of those who lived very close by) to respect for family and private life had been breached.
Laskey, Jaggard and Brown v United Kingdom (1997)	Consenting sadomasochists were convicted of various offences against the person. They argued that their rights under Article 8 had been violated.	ECtHR held there was no violation of Article 8, as state law dictates the level of consensual activity between individuals. The court also questioned whether privacy was a primary concern, as the activities were filmed and the tapes distributed.

Article 10: the right to freedom of expression

> **Exam tip**
>
> Remember that ideas, views and opinions can be expressed not just by individuals in domestic situations but by religions, political organisations, the media and through artistic expression etc. Exam questions may focus on a less common group of citizens (such as painters or dancers expressing opinion) than someone writing for a newspaper.

> **Typical mistake**
>
> In a democratic society, allowing a broad basis to the freedom of expression means accepting another's right to express a view that may be unpopular or unpleasant. Such views may be acceptable, and you cannot simply discount them as offensive in an exam.

Freedom of expression is achieved by different means:

- being able to converse freely with each other on topics or issues
- publishing newspaper or magazine articles, or broadcasting television or radio programmes or via the internet
- through artistic mediums, such as painting or drawings or via theatrical performances.

This is even the case where views may 'offend, shock or disturb the state or any sector of the population' – see *Handyside v United Kingdom* (1976).

Article 10(1) states:

> **Freedom of expression:** being free to express ideas, views and opinions and share them with others without the state interfering.

> 'Everyone has the right to freedom of expression. This right shall include freedom to hold opinions and to receive and impart information and ideas without interference by public authority and regardless of frontiers. This Article shall not prevent states from requiring the licensing of broadcasting, television or cinema enterprises.'

Freedom of expression is commonly misunderstood as being an existing right before the enactment of the Human Rights Act 1998. It is also commonly misunderstood as giving UK citizens the freedom of speech, which it does not due to its restrictions.

> **Revision activity**
>
> Look through a magazine or newspaper, particularly one aimed at teenagers and above. Consider whether any of the content, in your opinion, may 'offend, shock or disturb the state or any sector of the population'.

The freedom is massively restricted by domestic laws, for example those covering racial hatred and criminalising homophobia. Nevertheless, this residual freedom allows a person to:

(a)   receive information and ideas, and

(b)   communicate information and ideas.

Clause (a) would, for example, allow citizens to read/view publications by a free press (newspapers and television).

Clause (b) would, for example, allow a free press to report on issues that it felt were newsworthy and in the public interest.

Compare the different outcomes of the case examples in Table 6.3.2.

Table 6.3.2 Key cases on Article 10

Case	Facts	Outcome
Handyside v United Kingdom (1976)	H published in the UK *The Little Red Schoolbook*, with a chapter on pupils containing information on 'Sex'. H was convicted of having an obscene publication for gain.	ECtHR held there was no violation of Article 10, as the UK's right to interfere with H's freedom of expression was allowed by its domestic law.
The Observer and the Guardian v United Kingdom (1991)	This was called the 'Spycatcher' case, after the name of a book written by a former member of MI5. The UK government tried to ban the book, which revealed MI5 theories and tactics.	ECtHR ruled that the UK government had breached Article 10 by preventing the newspapers serialising the book since it was freely available in other countries (e.g. Scotland) and therefore contained no secrets to suppress.

Case	Facts	Outcome
Steel and Morris v United Kingdom (2005)	Known as the *McLibel* case, two environmental activists published a leaflet criticising McDonald's. Some accusations were false and others true. The UK courts ordered the pair to pay compensation for libel.	ECtHR ruled that UK laws breached Article 10 and did not protect the public's right to criticise companies whose business practices affect people's lives and the environment.

Article 11: the right to freedom of peaceful assembly and association

REVISED

Exam tip

Be aware that there are two similar but specifically distinct parts to this Article:
1 the freedom to come together
2 the freedom to come together with individuals of their choosing.

Right to freedom of peaceful assembly and association: you are able to assemble (gather) with other people for peaceful purposes and associate with (be in the company of) others for the same reasons.

This right was born out of the restrictions of movement and peaceful protest that allowed the Nazi party in Germany, before and during the Second World War, to crush any opposition to its government and policies.

For more modern times, the Article allows citizens to come together for peaceful protest. It disallows forcing people to join an organisation, such as a trades' union, or to take part in a protest against their will. This is something which despotic Middle-eastern countries propagate.

Article 11(1) states:

'Everyone has the right to freedom of peaceful assembly and to freedom of association with others, including the right to form and to join trade unions for the protection of his interests.'

'Assembly' means that citizens can meet and gather with other citizens as a group for lawful purposes.

'Association' means that citizens can form lawful groups, organisations or clubs for their own interests. This freedom includes the forming of trades' unions to protect workers' rights, freedoms and interests.

Compare the different outcomes of the cases in Table 6.3.3.

Typical mistake

This is not an absolute right, although it is often assumed that this is the case. Also, remember that there are reciprocal rights under this Article, so people cannot be forced to associate and assemble.

Table 6.3.3 **Key cases on Article 11**

Case	Facts	Outcome
Wilson and Palmer v United Kingdom (2002)	Applicants failed to secure pay rises because they were members of trades' unions.	There was a clear breach of Article 11. The law changed in 2004, outlawing such action.
ASLEF v United Kingdom (2007)	A trades' union expelled one of its members for being an activist for the British Nationalist Party. The member successfully took the union to an employment tribunal and was readmitted as a member of the union.	ECtHR held that there was a violation of Article 11, stating that just as a person has a right to join a union, a union has a right not to admit a person for legitimate reasons, especially when the views of a member are fundamentally at odds with the union.

Revision activity

Explain the arguments relied upon by the excluded member of the trades' union in *ASLEF v United Kingdom* (2007).

Now test yourself

1 Why is it important to have a right to liberty and security of person?
2 What are the justified exceptions to the right to liberty and security of person? Do you agree with them?
3 Why is it important to have a right to a fair trial? What does 'a fair trial' mean under Article 6(1)?
4 Do you agree or disagree that certain judgments may be censored or restricted from being reported fully in the press? Explain your answer.
5 Using examples, explain the meaning of the right to respect of privacy.
6 Using examples, explain the meaning of the right to respect of family life.
7 Explain how drawings or paintings can contain freedom of expression.
8 Explain why it is acceptable to say, or publish information, that may 'offend, shock or disturb the state or any sector of the population'.
9 Research further the case of *Steel and Morris v United Kingdom* (2005). Do you agree with the ECtHR's decision? Explain your answer.
10 Explain the meaning of freedom of peaceful assembly and association.

Answers online

Exam summary

In the exam, you MAY be asked to:
● respond to a scenario based on Article 5, 6, 8, 10 or 11 by advising a claimant, defendant or defendants whether they will be successful in a claim (the question could be linked with one or more of the right's restrictions and how that restriction could be enforced)
● discuss and evaluate Article 5, 6, 8, 10 or 11 in a full-length essay question.

These types of question will each be worth a maximum of 25 marks.

6.4 Restrictions on human rights law

Restrictions permitted by the European Convention on Human Rights

Table 6.4.1 Key restrictions on human rights law under the European Convention on Human Rights

Article	Restriction
5(1)a–c	Justified deprivation of liberty – lawful arrest or detention: • after conviction in a competent court • after non-compliance with a court order (such as bail) • when a suspect is committing or about to commit a crime.
5(2)	A person must be informed as soon as possible that they are being or have been arrested, the reason for the arrest and all in a language they understand.
5(3)	An arrested person must be brought to trial, bailed (with or without conditions) to appear at a trial, or released within a reasonable period of time.
5(4)	An arrested person is entitled to a swift trial to decide their innocence or guilt. This includes any appeals against conviction and/or sentence.
5(5)	If any of the rights under Article 5 are infringed, the arrested person is entitled to compensation, usually in the form of a financial reward.
6(1)	Restriction on the right to a fair trial – the press and public can be excluded from all or part of a trial: • in the interests of morals and public order, or • in the interests of national security in a democratic society, or • where the interests of juveniles or the protection of the private life of the parties so require, or • in the opinion of the court in special circumstances where publicity would prejudice the interests of justice.
8(2)	The right to respect for family and private life can be restricted if there is a law required in a democratic society and it: • benefits national security, the public's safety or the financial safety of the country, or • prevents disorder or crime, or • protects the health or morals of its citizens, or • protects the rights and freedoms of others.
10(2)	Freedom of expression can be restricted if there is a law required in a democratic society and it: • benefits national security, the country's boundaries or the public's safety – see *R v Ponting* (1985), or • prevents disorder or crime, or • protects the health or morals of its citizens – see *R v Lemon and Gay News* (1979), or • protects the reputation or rights of citizens who are affected by a person exercising their freedom under Article 10(1), or • prevents the revelation of information gained under trust, or • maintains the authority and neutrality of the judiciary.

> **Restriction:** a right or freedom can be limited where it is just and equitable to do so. Each restriction depends upon the exact nature of the right and freedom.

Article	Restriction
11(2)	Freedom of assembly and association can be restricted if there is a law required in a democratic society and it: • benefits national security or the public's safety, or • prevents disorder or crime, or • protects the health or morals of its citizens, or • protects the rights and freedoms of others.

Other restrictions

Section 12 was specifically incorporated into the Human Rights Act 1998 in relation to freedom of expression and adds a further restriction to Article 10.

The section requires courts to have particular regard to the importance of the freedom of expression when granting 'relief'. A court should not impose, for example, an injunction without the respondent being notified, unless there is a strong justification for doing so.

Table 6.4.2 **Key cases on restrictions of the European Convention on Human Rights**

Case	Facts	Outcome
MH v United Kingdom (2013) – restricted Article 5	A woman with Down's Syndrome had been placed in a secure hospital for her own safety.	The ECtHR ruled that the inability of the woman (or her representative, her mother) to be able to challenge her detention under s 2 of the Mental Health Act 1983 had violated her human rights under Article 5.
R v Ponting (1985) – restricted Article 10	D gave opposition MPs documents stating that the government had lied about the sinking of an Argentinian battleship during the Falklands War.	Despite the clear direction of the judge that D's conduct did amount to an offence, the jury found D not guilty.
R v Lemon and Gay News (1979) – restricted Article 10	A poem was published in an issue of *Gay News* describing various sexual acts performed on the body of Christ after the crucifixion, including acts of fellatio.	The magazine and its editor were convicted with the common-law offence of blasphemous libel.

Restrictions permitted by the UK Parliament and courts in line with the ECHR

REVISED

In addition to those restrictions above to the rights and freedoms under the European Convention on Human Rights, the UK Parliament and courts have set restrictions.

Public order offences

The purpose of public order law is to safeguard the balancing of freedom of expression and freedom of assembly against the rights of others to go about their daily lives unimpeded, and the right to respect for family and private life.

The main public order offences are covered under the Public Order Act 1986 and include:
• section 1 – riot
• section 2 – violent disorder

- section 3 – affray
- section 4 – using threatening, abusive or insulting words or behaviour causing fear of or provoking violence
- section 4A – using threatening, abusive or insulting words or behaviour, or disorderly behaviour, intending to and causing harassment, alarm or distress
- section 5 – using threatening, abusive words or behaviour, or disorderly behaviour, likely to cause harassment, alarm or distress.

Other pieces of legislation are:
- section 91 of the Criminal Justice Act 1967 – drunk and disorderly behaviour
- section 1 of the Racial and Religious Hatred Act 2006 (amending the Public Order Act 1986) – the use of words, behaviour or display of written material likely to stir up racial or religious hatred.

Police powers

The purpose of police powers' law is to provide greater clarification of the police's right to restrict the freedom of liberty and security, the right to a fair trial, the right to respect for family and private life and the freedom of assembly.

Police powers' law must balance the need to investigate and prevent crime against the rights of individuals to go about their daily lives unimpeded.

The main police powers are covered under the Police and Criminal Evidence Act 1984 and include:
- section 1 – the power of a constable to stop and search a person or vehicle
- sections 16, 17 and 18 – the power of a constable to enter and search premises
- section 24 – the power of a constable to arrest a suspect
- Part IV of the Act – the power to detain an arrested person.

Interception of communications

The Regulation of Investigatory Powers Act 2000, as amended, provides guidance on the procedures that must be followed before interception of communications can take place.

In order for a public body to intercept communications, it must be authorised as a justifiable interference with an individual's rights under Article 8 – the right to respect for private and family life:
- Under s 1(1), it is a criminal offence for a person without authority to intercept in the UK any communication via a public postal service or public telecommunications system.
- Under s 1(2), it is a criminal offence for a person without authority to intercept in the UK any communication via a private telecommunications system.
- Section 5 gives lawful authority to the interception of communications if a warrant is issued by the Secretary of State.
- Under s 5(2), the Secretary of State will not issue an interception warrant unless it is necessary and proportionate to what it is sought to achieve.
- Under s 6, an interception warrant cannot be issued unless the application is made by, or on behalf of, the persons listed in s 6(2), for example the Director General of the Security Service.

Duty of confidentiality

The duty of confidentiality is essentially a common-law duty, whereby lawyers are bound to respect the confidentiality of matters arising in the course of representing their clients inside and outside of court.

The purpose of the duty is to allow the client to discuss freely and in confidence with their lawyer. It is not an absolute duty, as there may be occasions when confidential information may be disclosed, for example at the client's request. However, statutory provision covering the duty is rare and would need to be balanced against an individual's rights under Article 8.

Obscenity

The Obscene Publications Act 1959 was introduced to amend the laws on obscenity, to prohibit the publication of obscene matter by providing a test for obscenity.

Section 1 states:

> 'An article shall be deemed to be obscene if its effect or ... the effect of any one of its items is, if taken as a whole, such as to tend to deprave and corrupt persons who are likely, having regard to all relevant circumstances, to read, see or hear the matter contained or embodied in it.'

These statutory provisions, which prohibit obscene publications, performances and photographs, must be balanced with the right to freedom of expression set out in Article 10, and any such restriction on this right must be so justified.

Torts of defamation and trespass

Defamation

A defamatory statement injures the reputation of another by exposing them to contempt, ridicule or hatred, or might lower them in the esteem of right-thinking members of society:

- Libel is a defamatory statement in permanent form, for example in a newspaper.
- Slander is a defamatory statement made in transient form, for example via the spoken word.

Holding a statement as defamatory must be balanced with:

- the maker's rights under Article 10, and
- the rights of the person against whom the statement is made under Article 8.

Trespass to land

This is one of the oldest torts and is where there is unlawful and direct interference with the rights of an owner of land. Therefore, this tort necessarily restricts rights under Articles 5 and 11 and enforces Article 8.

Harassment

Harassment is generally covered by the Protection from Harassment Act 1997, as amended. Under the Act, a restraining order may be made prohibiting the defendant from doing anything stated in the order:

- section 2 covers acts 'causing alarm or distress'
- section 4 covers acts 'putting people in fear of violence'.

These offences naturally and necessarily curtail an individual's rights under Article 10, for example making telephone calls or writing letters or articles in newspapers.

Now test yourself

TESTED

1 Explain one reason why it is important that Article 5(1) is restricted under Article 5(1)–(5).
2 Explain one reason why it is important that Article 6(1) is restricted under Article 6(1).
3 Explain one reason why it is important that Article 8(1) is restricted under Article 8(2).
4 Explain one reason why it is important that Article 10(1) is restricted under Article 10(2).
5 Explain one reason why it is important that Article 11(1) is restricted under Article 11(2).
6 Explain the purpose of s 12 of the Human Rights Act 1998.
7 Explain one reason why it is important that human rights law is restricted by public order offences.
8 Explain one reason why it is important that human rights law is restricted by interception of communication.
9 Explain one reason why it is important that human rights law is restricted by obscenity laws.
10 Explain one reason why it is important that human rights law is restricted by harassment laws.

Answers online

Exam summary

In the exam, you MAY be asked to:
● respond to a scenario question based on Articles of the European Convention on Human Rights by advising a claimant, defendant, or defendants whether a right or freedom they may wish to rely upon could be restricted (the question could be linked with one or more of the rights and/or freedoms and how that restriction could be enforced, for example via an injunction)
● discuss and evaluate a restriction to rights or freedoms in a full-length essay question.

These types of question will each be worth a maximum of 25 marks.

6.5 Enforcement of human rights law

This chapter looks at how the rights and freedoms contained in the European Convention on Human Rights are implemented in the UK.

Having rights and freedoms is important in a democratic society, and there must be consequent mechanisms of enforcement. Unless a restriction applies, most rights and freedoms can be enforced through the UK's courts.

More recently, the process of judicial review has allowed citizens to challenge the decisions of public bodies, such as the government, local authorities or their officials.

If a human rights issue is in question, and domestic law does not provide a solution, then a claim can be brought before the European Court of Human Rights (often abbreviated to ECtHR).

Role of domestic courts

REVISED

In some situations, UK law, both common and statute, already protected the rights and freedoms of its citizens before the introduction of the Human Rights Act 1998. However, large parts of the European Convention on Human Rights had not been covered by UK domestic law before the Act.

If a complainant is unsuccessful with domestic law or feels that such laws are incompatible with the Convention, a claim can be made by petition to the European Court of Human Rights.

Under the Human Rights Act 1998, citizens can bring a claim in the domestic courts to argue that a public body has breached one or more of their rights under the Convention and seek redress. If the court agrees that there is a breach, an appropriate remedy can be issued.

If there is an existing domestic law which covers a human right, for example under the Equality Act 2010, then this method of redress must be used first before being challenged.

See Table 6.2.2 for details of the following cases, which demonstrate the conflict between domestic law and the Convention:
- *Re: Medicaments (No. 2), Director General of Fair Trading v Proprietary Association of Great Britain* (2001)
- *R v A* (2001)
- *H v Mental Health Review Tribunal* (2001).

Effect of decisions on states and claimants

The irony is that while the decisions of the domestic courts are binding on the parties to a human rights case, the effect of a decision from the European Court of Human Rights, while binding, is difficult to enforce. Nevertheless, decisions have these effects:

- For states – the European Court of Human Rights may decide the state is in breach and award compensation to a claimant. However, it cannot make the state change its domestic laws, instead relying on the state voluntarily making amendments.
- For claimants – if successful, the most appropriate decision would be to award them compensation, but this is not guaranteed. As with decisions against the state, the European Court of Human Rights has no means of enforcing that the state makes the compensation payment.

Process of judicial review

This process reinforces the canon that everyone is equal before the law, and that includes public bodies or their officials.

The decisions of the lower courts, in particular the Magistrates' Courts, can be challenged under **judicial review**.

Judicial review is carried out by the Queen's Bench Division of the High Court.

> **Judicial review:** process allowing certain decisions of government or other public bodies to be challenged by citizens to see if they are 'reasonable'.

Table 6.5.1 Principles of judicial review and remedies

Principles	There are three main challenges under judicial review: 1 Illegality: the decision by the public body has included a mistake of law or has gone beyond that which the law allows the public body to act. 2 Irrationality: the decision by the public body is so unreasonable that no reasonable public body would have made such a decision. 3 Irregularity: the decision by the public body has not followed the correct procedure.
Remedies	Remedies are possible under private law, e.g. injunction or compensation. Under public law, the following remedies are available by court order: 1 Prohibition – prevents or prohibits the public authority from continuing with the decision or from doing the same act in the future. 2 *Certiorari* – the High Court can quash a decision made by the public body. 3 *Mandamus* – forces a public body to do something, e.g. to hear a case or argument that it has refused to hear.

Table 6.5.2 Key cases on judicial review

Case	Significance	Judgment
Associated Provincial Picture Houses v Wednesbury Corporation (1948)	This case established the 'Wednesbury' unreasonableness test.	A decision by a public body will be deemed unreasonable, and struck out if no reasonable public body could have reached the same decision.
Council of Civil Service Unions v Minister for the Civil Service (1984)	Known as the GCHQ case, it established the three challenges or principles for judicial review.	(See above for the principles for judicial review.)

> **Revision activity**
>
> Research what is meant by GCHQ and explain the purpose behind it.

Role of the European Court of Human Rights

The European Court of Human Rights is based in Strasbourg, France, and includes judges representing each of the Member States. The judges act independently and not in the interests of their own states.

There is usually a panel of seven judges to hear a case. Even if the case is sent to the court, a panel of three judges will first hear its merits before agreeing, or not, to fully hear the complaint.

If they find that a Member State has breached an Article, then they have the power (although difficult to enforce) to award compensation or other 'just satisfaction' to the complainant.

The court relies heavily on the co-operation of the Member State to be bound by its decisions, but the court cannot force the state to change its domestic law if required.

Bringing a claim

1 Once a citizen has exhausted all means of redress for their complaint in their domestic courts, a petition can be made by the citizen to the European Commission of Human Rights. The Commission will investigate whether the citizen's petition has any merits before agreeing to pass the petition on to the full court.
2 The petition must be made within a specific period of time, usually six months, from the time of being denied redress from the last court in their state. In the UK, this would generally be the Supreme Court.
3 If the Commission feels that there is a legitimate petition, it will generally seek the co-operation of the Member State's government to resolve the issue amicably. If the complaint cannot be resolved amicably, then the case will be sent to the European Court of Human Rights to decide whether the citizen's rights have been breached.
4 A Member State is also able to bring a claim for an alleged breach of the Convention committed against another state.

Impact of decisions

The European Court of Human Rights is a very important and powerful court. However, despite its unique purpose, it has been criticised for a variety of reasons:

● It can take years for a case to reach the court, so some breaches of the Convention can simply be abandoned before reaching the court.
● Judges must be independent but can be accused of acting in their own state's interests.
● Usually, having a panel of seven judges in order to avoid bias can slow down the decisions of the court.
● While the court does have sanctions available, such as finding a state in breach of the Convention and ordering compensation to be paid, there is no real way of enforcing its decision.
● A decision of the court relies mainly on the co-operation of the state in breach of the Convention, who could in theory refuse to accept its decision.

> **Revision activity**
>
> Consider some of the problems for an individual in bringing a claim to the European Court of Human Rights.

Now test yourself

1 Describe the features of the European Court of Human Rights.
2 How does a citizen bring a case to the European Court of Human Rights?
3 What is meant by judicial review?
4 Explain the three main challenges available under judicial review.
5 Explain the remedies available under judicial review.

Answers online

Exam summary

In the exam, you MAY be asked to:
- respond to a scenario question based on an Article of the European Convention on Human Rights by advising a claimant, defendant or defendants how rights and freedoms are enforced (the question could be linked with one or more of the rights and/or freedoms and how rights and freedoms could be enforced, for example via judicial review)
- discuss and evaluate one of the methods of enforcing rights and freedoms in a full-length essay question.

These types of question will each be worth a maximum of 25 marks.

6.6 Evaluation

For many citizens, the enactment of the Human Rights Act 1998 was long overdue. It was introduced as a means of 'bringing rights home'. However, its enactment and subsequent enforcement have been heavily criticised. For the first time, the provisions of the European Convention on Human Rights were made directly enforceable in the UK.

The Act was given cross-party support in Parliament when it was passed, and it remains not a political tool, but rather an Act supporting mutual respect and consideration of others.

The horrors of the Second World War led to the European Convention on Human Rights as a means to prevent such atrocities from occurring again. It is unarguable that human rights and freedoms form the foundation of a democratic society.

As legislation in the UK must be compatible with the Act, it not only provides rules and considerations for policy-makers but also provides rules and safeguards for citizens.

Despite support for the Act, laws and rights must adapt to reflect a changing society. While the fundamental tenets of rights and freedoms remain the same, the laws that support such tenets must move with the times.

Human rights protection in the UK   REVISED

Criticisms

- The European Convention on Human Rights was signed by the UK in 1950, but the ability to use and petition under the Convention was not incorporated into domestic law until 2000 by the Human Rights Act 1998.
- Many areas of protection have only recently been covered by the UK's domestic law, for example the Equal Pay Act 1970 and anti-discriminatory legislation on sex, race, disability and sexual orientation.
- The Equality Act 2010 was passed to rationalise anti-discriminatory law, but breaches of human rights law in this area are often ignored by businesses.
- Successful breaches of human rights law involve lengthy and expensive trials, with successful outcomes being awarded damages only if this can 'afford just satisfaction' to a victim.
- Human rights law has been criticised as protecting the perpetrators of crime more than the victims – a 'burglar's charter'.

Ideas for reform

If a Bill of Rights were introduced (which repealed the Human Rights Act 1998), a more UK-friendly set of rights and responsibilities could be set out, rather than the current pan-European viewpoint. This would have the following effects:

- The UK government could pass legislation appropriate to the UK that could not be challenged by EU membership.
- Any potential incompatibility with EU law would be removed, along with any restrictions.
- The UK courts would not have to consider, nor be bound by, decisions of the European Court of Justice in Strasbourg.
- The Supreme Court would be reasserted as the primary court over Strasbourg.
- Civil laws would be more *laissez-faire* and less consumer-focused, which has hampered and restricted the growth of many UK businesses.

European Convention on Human Rights

REVISED

Criticisms

- Before the incorporation into domestic law by the Human Rights Act 1998, the use of the Convention by UK citizens was a time-consuming, expensive and exhausting process.
- To use the Convention specifically, citizens had to use and exhaust all domestic means of challenge.
- Even if the Convention was signed by a Member State, for example the UK, it did not mean that the Convention automatically became incorporated into domestic law.
- The Convention's court, the European Court of Human Rights, is based in Strasbourg, France, which requires further cost for travel and stay for claimants and defendants in order to present a case.
- Each Article under the Convention allows an individual state to impose restrictions, such as to protect national security. This limits the impact of the aims of each Article.
- There is no automatic right to be heard by the European Court of Human Rights, as cases can be rejected.
- The UK has a poor record when it comes to its citizens arguing breaches of the Convention. It is argued that the UK has more breaches than any other signatory country.

Ideas for reform

- Allow national courts to have a greater say over local domestic laws.
- National courts should be given wider interpretation rights under the Convention and from decisions of the European Court of Human Rights.
- Reform of the wording of the Convention would dispel criticism of decisions of the European Court of Human Rights that have prevented terrorists from being deported from the UK and given prisoners the right to vote.
- The European Court of Human Rights should only review decisions taken by national authorities to ensure that they are within EU law; if they are not, then the court should advise but not decide on the matter.
- The European Court of Human Rights should simply be an advisory mechanism, providing guidance to national authorities and allowing them to pass ultimate judgment.

Criticisms

● There are so many loopholes in the Act which allow avoidance of rights under the Convention, that the Act seems no more than an altruistic paper-exercise which only benefits UK's citizens if the government so wishes.

● The Act removes the sovereignty of the Supreme Court and replaces it with a European Court of Human Rights, which allows non-UK judges to decide on UK domestic issues.

● If found incompatible, the UK government does not have to amend UK laws to make them compatible with the Convention.

● The Act relies on individuals, not organisations, to bring an action for a declaration of incompatibility.

● There is no overarching scrutiny committee which monitors an Act's adherence to the Convention. Instead, the Act relies on individuals (or organisations bringing the attention to individuals) pointing out any incompatibilities.

● The Act is seen by many as not 'British', since it introduces 'foreign' rules which have removed Parliament's sovereignty.

● By its very application and interpretation by the courts, the Act is seen as enforcing 'foreign' rules.

● It is generally misunderstood by the public and misrepresented in the media.

Ideas for reform

Table 6.6.1 **Proposals for reforming the Human Rights Act 1998 (HRA 98)**

Date of reform proposal	Origin/name of proposal	Purpose of proposal
2006	Department for Constitutional Affairs: *Review of the Implementation of the Human Rights Act*	The review stated that HRA 98 had been widely misunderstood by the public and misused in a number of situations.
2006	David Cameron, then leader of the Opposition	The Conservatives proposed a British Bill of Rights and Responsibilities to 'define the core values which give us our identity as a free nation', along with a repeal of HRA 98.
2007	Labour Government Green Paper: *The Governance of Britain*	This included a proposal for a British Bill of Rights and Duties, providing explicit recognition that 'human rights come with responsibilities and must be exercised in a way that respects the human rights of others'.
2008	Joint Committee on Human Rights	A report emphasised a need for public consultation before plans were drawn up.

Date of reform proposal	Origin/name of proposal	Purpose of proposal
2009	Labour Government report: *Rights and responsibilities: developing our constitutional framework*	Labour felt HRA 98 had been an important move towards the incorporation of rights and freedoms but that an incorporation of UK values alongside Convention rights would endorse a stronger guarantee of rights and freedoms.
2010	General election manifesto promises	The Conservatives were to replace HRA 98 with a Bill of Rights, while Labour and the Liberal Democrats were committed to protecting the Act.
2011	Commission on a Bill of Rights established	This was established to investigate the creation of a Bill of Rights.
2012	Commission of 2011 report: *A UK Bill of Rights? The Choice Before Us*	As the commissioners could not agree on a common position, each one published their own findings under the one report.
2013	2013 Conservative Party Conference, Home Secretary Theresa May	'The next Conservative manifesto will promise to scrap the Human Rights Act. ... the Conservative position is clear – if leaving the European Convention is what it takes to fix our human rights law, that is what we should do.'
2015	Conservative Party General Election Manifesto 2015 (coalition government in office)	The manifesto promised to scrap HRA 98 and replace it with a Bill of Rights.
2017	Conservative Party General Election Manifesto 2015 (government in office)	The manifesto stated that while Brexit is in progress, HRA 98 would not be replaced and the UK would remain signatories of the European Convention on Human Rights for the duration of the Parliament.

> **Revision activity**
>
> Using the internet, research the purpose of the Commission on a Bill of Rights set up in 2011.

> **Revision activity**
>
> Create your own Bill of Rights. What rights and freedoms would it include?

Now test yourself

TESTED ☐

1 Explain why the Human Rights Act 1998 was introduced into UK law.
2 Explain one reason why the Human Rights Act 1998 is arguably in need of reform.
3 How did the Department for Constitutional Affairs in 2006 criticise the Human Rights Act 1998?
4 Explain why the commission set up in 2011 did not produce definite reform proposals.
5 Explain what is meant by a UK Bill of Rights.
6 Why did the Conservative Government in 2017 decide to suspend its proposals for a UK Bill of Rights?

Answers online

Exam summary

In the exam, you MAY be asked to discuss and evaluate human rights protection in the UK, the European Convention on Human Rights and/ or the Human Rights Act 1998 and suggest any ideas for reform.

These types of questions will be worth a maximum of 25 marks.

Exam practice

1 Yulia, who is from Russia, was arrested on suspicion of shoplifting and had her rights read to her by the arresting officer. However, Yulia does not speak a lot of English and did not understand what was happening.

Yulia was put on remand and her trial date was set for six months' time. She was refused access to a solicitor for the first two weeks. When the date arrived for her trial, the judge was ill, so the trial date was postponed for another six months. At Yulia's trial, she was sent to prison for two years.

Advise Yulia on whether her rights or liberties were breached on her arrest, while on remand or during the trial. [25 marks]

2 Melanie was the leader of an animal rights group that had decided to organise a march through the city centre. The police were concerned about the march, as the group had deliberately caused criminal damage on some, but not all, of their previous marches.

Anne was an undercover police officer who infiltrated the group. She read all of Melanie's letters while staying at her house. One of the letters contained plans about entering a fast-food restaurant and a department store to throw paint during an upcoming march.

Anne took photos of the letters and gave them to the local newspaper, the *Daily Blag*. The newspaper contacted Melanie saying it was going to print a story which contained information about the plans.

Advise Melanie of her rights and remedies against the police and the *Daily Blag* arising from these incidents. [25 marks]

3 Discuss the impact of the Human Rights Act 1998 on the doctrine of parliamentary sovereignty. [25 marks]

ONLINE

7 The law of contract

In Component 3 of the OCR A Level Law H415 specification, you are required to choose one of two optional topics: either *Human rights law* or *The law of contract*. *The law of contract* explores the central elements of the topic, from the formation of a contract, its constituent parts and its enforcement.

Exam questions will concentrate on critical awareness of this topic while requiring you to make informed decisions about laws of contract and their application in scenario-based situations in the following areas:
- rules and theory
- formation
- terms
- vitiating factors
- discharge
- remedies
- critical evaluation of formation and contract terms, including ideas for reform.

> **Exam tip**
>
> You need to be able to define correctly each important term in contract law. For example, definitions of contract, offer and acceptance are crucial in securing marks and providing a foundation for you to explain or analyse a topic for an exam question.

7.1 Rules and theory

Rules

REVISED

Contract law is an area of private law concerned with agreements, which range from the simple purchase of a student textbook to multimillion-pound business deals:
- All contracts contain the same elements of offer and acceptance, consideration and intention.
- The purpose of contract law is to ensure that agreements are formed in a fair way and, if required, enforced by the courts in a fair way.
- The rules of contract have been developed over centuries and adapted as society has changed, through common-law, judge-made decisions, parliamentary intervention and statute law.
- Contract law is particularly important to consumers, as agreements to buy goods and services are for most of us a daily occurrence.

> **Contract:** an agreement between two parties which is binding in law and therefore enforceable in court.
>
> **Breach of contract:** when a party fails to carry out any of their obligations under the contract, or in carrying it out they fail to do what they are supposed to do.

Formation of a contract

A **contract** is an agreement between two parties who are bound by law to carry out their obligations under the contract.

A formal agreement is generally deemed essential between businesses and between businesses and private individuals. If something goes wrong, then the contract should provide an answer.

When a valid contract is formed, both parties have rights that can be enforced or compensated in court, provided that strict rules are adhered to. If either party fails to carry out their obligations under the contract, then they may be in **breach of contract**.

> **Revision activity**
>
> Using a decided case, identify and memorise a definition of a contract.

In civil law, when there is a breach of contract the 'injured' party (claimant) will ask either for:

- the other party (defendant) to carry out the agreement, or
- compensation for any losses in a court of law.

Not every agreement we enter into is meant to be legally enforceable, for example agreeing to meet a friend at the cinema. If the friend fails to arrive, it is unlikely that a breach of contract can be found, because neither party intended to form a legally binding agreement. The 'injured' party will be unable to sue for compensation, however upset or angry they may be.

To fill the courts with cases concerning 'broken promises' would be ridiculous. Therefore, contract law has established the first major element in the formation of contracts, known as 'intention to create legal relations'.

Contract law therefore distinguishes between two key types of contract, to decide whether there is an intention to create legal relations:

- social and domestic arrangements (no intention)
- commercial or business agreements (intention).

Both types are formed with a rebuttable presumption.

In its purest form, a contract is made up of:

- an agreement (a valid offer followed by a valid, unconditional acceptance of the offer)
- intention to create legal relations
- consideration.

See Chapter 7.2 for further detail on these.

Contract terms

Terms form the content or subject matter of the contract. They are the binding part of the contract that the parties to the contract agree to perform in order for the contract to be fulfilled. If either party fails to carry out the term, they will be in breach of contract and legal recourse is possible for the breach.

Terms form the foundation of pre-contractual negotiations or are inserted into the contract by other means. They are either express (from the parties themselves), implied (as a presumption of agreement by the parties) or 'imputed' by process of law, for example for consumer protection.

Terms can be conditions, which go to the root of the contract, or warranties. These are lesser terms and are generally descriptive.

Vitiating factors

Even if a contract has all the necessary constituent parts in its formation – offer, acceptance, consideration and intention – there can still be other defects in the contract unknown to either party. These defects are called vitiating factors and can invalidate a contract, even if at the time the contract is made both parties are happy with the terms of the agreement.

Vitiating factors come into operation either through:

- a void contract, i.e. the contract was not valid from the start, or
- a voidable contract, i.e. the contract may be avoided by either party.

Discharge of a contract

Discharge refers to the ending of a contract.

> **Revision activity**
>
> Think about a typical day in your life. Identify all the agreements you have entered into, for example paying for a bus or train journey. Which of your agreements are legally enforceable?

> **Revision activity**
>
> Think about any agreements you have entered into with close family and friends this week, for example agreeing to meet someone at the cinema. Which are legally enforceable?

> **Revision activity**
>
> Start a contract dictionary. Under V, write 'void' and 'voidable', together with their definitions.

> **Discharge (of a contract):** the ending of a contract.

In the majority of cases, contracts are discharged when both parties complete their obligations under the contract. This is called discharge by performance.

However, a contract can also be discharged through frustration. Here, the contract cannot be performed due to events outside of the party's control. Although there are limits on this doctrine, in effect the contract will end as soon as the intervening event occurs.

A breach of contract occurs if either party fails to perform one or more of their contractual terms. In such situations, primary obligations, where breached, are replaced by secondary obligations, for example having to pay the injured party damages.

Remedies for breach of contract

There are two types of **remedy** available for breach of contract: common-law remedies and equitable remedies.

Table 7.1.1 Common-law and equitable remedies

Remedy	Explanation
Common-law remedy	Damages are the most common remedy in contract law. They involve a payment of money to compensate the other for their loss. If the case is proven, then damages are granted as of right.
	There are three basic types of damages: unliquidated, liquidated and *quantum meruit*.
	Where damages would not properly compensate the injured party, equitable remedies have been developed.
Equitable remedy	These have developed due to the inadequacies of common-law remedies. If the case is proven, then equitable remedies are at the court's discretion but are not automatically granted.
	There are four main types of equitable remedy, which have been developed to assist specific situations: ● specific performance ● rescission ● injunction ● rectification of a document.

Theory

REVISED

This section relates to the concept of contract law and how it has developed over time.

Freedom to contract: the voluntary nature of agreements

The origins of contract law can be traced back to the Middle Ages, but modern contract law developed from the nineteenth-century theory of *laissez-faire* economics, where transactions between parties were free from regulation.

The fundamental basis of contract law is:
● the issue of voluntariness
● the freedom to contract
● the development of rules and principles to formalise these voluntary arrangements.

> **Remedy:** in contract law, this is a way of providing a solution to a breach of contract.
>
> *Quantum meruit*: a reasonable sum of money that is to be paid for services in contracts where an exact sum of money is not stipulated.

> **Typical mistake**
>
> When discussing remedies, do not assume that all remedies are available to the injured party. Common-law damages are available as of right, but equitable remedies are at the discretion of the judge.

> **Revision activity**
>
> Think about the different types of remedy, both common-law and equitable. Identify situations where each type would be appropriate.

> **Typical mistake**
>
> Do not explain at great length your historic knowledge of the growth of contract law in your exam responses when such knowledge is not required.

Modern contract law had to differentiate between formal and informal agreements. Land transfers were made 'under seal' by a document called a deed, and these arrangements were formal and enforceable. Other informal agreements were more commonly made orally, and difficult to prove if either party denied any knowledge.

Protection for the consumer

Contracts are not uniquely formed as part of a business arrangement. Many contracts are formed during the normal routine of life. Private citizens make agreements on many occasions each day.

In most instances, we do not make such agreements formally in writing. For example, on the way to school or college, you may travel by bus or train, buy a chocolate bar or a can of fizzy drink. In each of these cases, without paying much attention to these acts, a contract is formed.

But what if you were injured on the bus due to the fault of the driver? Or the chocolate bar had a foreign body in it? Or the can was empty, or contained another liquid other than fizzy drink? In each case, you would wish to know the implications of not getting what you paid for and be compensated for your loss.

Traditionally, contracts observed the maxim *caveat emptor* – 'let the buyer beware' – and allowed great freedom in making agreements. This was reflected in the master–servant relationship, where big businesses were allowed a stronger bargaining power over the consumer or smaller business.

During the twentieth century, this became unworkable and unfair on the weaker party in the contract, usually the consumer. In consequence, consumer groups were formed to put pressure on governments to make the formation of contracts fairer on such parties.

The courts began to develop contractual rules to protect consumers, and Parliament introduced legislation – statute law – to formalise this protection. Since the UK joined what is now the European Union, further protection has been continuously provided for consumers as part of EU membership.

Revision activity

Read the introductory chapter of a contract law textbook that considers the origins or historic formation of contract law and familiarise yourself with the contents.

Now test yourself

TESTED

1 Give a definition of a contract.
2 List the main constituent parts of a contract.
3 What is a vitiating factor? Name two types.
4 How can a contract be discharged?
5 What are the three basic types of damages available for a breach of contract under the common law?
6 What are the four main types of equitable remedy available for a breach of contract?
7 List any agreements or contracts you have entered into so far today.
8 How many of the agreements that you have identified in question 7 would you consider to be legally enforceable?

Answers online

Exam summary

In the exam, you MAY be asked to discuss the:
- rules of the law of contract in outline, for example, formation, terms, vitiating factors, discharge
- theory of the law of contract, for example, the voluntary nature of contract or protection for the customer.
These types of question will each be worth a maximum of 25 marks.

tp Formation

In its purest form, a contract is made up of:
- an agreement (offer and acceptance)
- an intention to create legal relations, and
- consideration.

Agreement

SEG REVISED

For an agreement to be made, there must be a valid offer followed by a valid, unconditional acceptance of the offer.

Offer

The party making the **offer** is known as the offeror, while the party to whom the offer is made is known as the offeree.

The offeror will usually state verbally or in writing that they will be bound by the terms of the offer following a valid acceptance and that they have an intention to create legal relations.

The contract will not be formed until the offeree accepts the terms in the offer. A simple example of an offer would be if I said to a friend: 'I'll sell you my car for £5,000', or 'Do you want to buy my car for £5,000?'

Invitation to treat

Where problems have arisen is in the difference between a valid offer and what the law calls an '**invitation to treat**'.

> **Exam tip**
>
> Remember that not all offers are in fact offers and they may be invitations to treat – this is an opportunity to form an offer using passive conduct, which invites a party to make an offer.

Since negotiations to strike some sort of agreement may take some time, the early stages of forming the agreement are often not considered to be offers but simply invitations for parties to make offers.

> **Revision activity**
>
> Start to develop and practise your contractual vocabulary by using terms such as 'offeror' and 'offeree', rather than 'buyer' and 'seller' etc.

> **Offer:** an expression of one party's willingness to contract on certain terms, made with the intention that it will be legally binding upon acceptance.
>
> **Invitation to treat:** the early stages of forming the agreement are often not considered to be offers but simply invitations for parties to make offers.

Table 7.2.1 Invitations to treat

Invitation to treat	Explanation
Goods on display	Such items will not be considered to be an offer, and simply picking up an item would not be seen as making an acceptance.
	The law says that the display is an invitation to treat. By picking up the item and taking it to the till, the customer makes an offer to buy and the shop owner can choose whether or not to accept the offer to buy – see *Pharmaceutical Society of Great Britain v Boots Cash Chemists Ltd* (1953).
	The same approach has been taken with goods on display in shop windows. It is for the customer to come into the shop to make the offer to buy. At this point, the shopkeeper can decide whether or not to accept the offer to buy and therefore sell the goods – see *Fisher v Bell* (1961).

OCR A Level Law   213

Invitation to treat	Explanation
Goods or services advertised in the media	The advertisement is not an offer but instead an invitation to treat. It is up to the person who acts on the advertisement to make an offer to buy what is advertised. This can be accepted by the advertiser, forming a contract – see *Partridge v Crittenden* (1968). There are some exceptions to this rule: ● If an advertisement is made where a reward will be paid, e.g. to find a lost cat, and the cat is returned, then the person making the advertisement cannot rely on the reward being an offer to treat. ● Instead, the law will treat it as what is called a unilateral offer – see *Carlill v Carbolic Smoke Ball Co.* (1893).

Typical mistake

Do not confuse an invitation to treat (no offer) with its exceptions, for example a unilateral offer sometimes referred to as a reward.

Counter-offer

If an offeree decides they would like to change the terms of an offer (for example by trying to negotiate/change the price of an item), this would be called a counter-offer.

A counter-offer, in effect, ends the original offer and becomes an offer in itself. Therefore, the counter-offer can be accepted or rejected by the person making the original offer – see *Hyde v Wrench* (1840).

A modern example of a counter-offer would be in using the internet selling site, eBay. A seller can place an item on eBay with a 'Buy it now or best offer' label. Here, the potential buyer can offer a lower price than the 'Buy it now' price, and it is up to the seller to accept the lower offer or counter-offer with a higher price at which they are happy to sell.

Revision activity

Try to find an example of a 'buy it now' item on an internet auction website.

Communication of offers

One of the basic rules of contract is that an offeree cannot accept an offer that has not been communicated to them. Clearly, it would be impossible to accept an offer if the offeree has no knowledge of it – see *Taylor v Laird* (1856).

Table 7.2.2 Key cases on offers

Case	Facts	Element of offer	Legal point
Pharmaceutical Society of Great Britain v Boots Cash Chemists Ltd (1953)	The court was asked to clarify if controlled drugs displayed in a self-service pharmacy were offers (an offence) or invitations to treat (no offence).	Goods on display	The display was an invitation to treat. The contract was formed when the goods were presented at the till.
Fisher v Bell (1961)	D had a flick knife on display in his shop window. Statute made it an offence to 'offer' for sale such an item.	Goods on display	It was not an offer, but an invitation to treat.
Partridge v Crittenden (1968)	P was charged with 'offering for sale' several wild birds, which was a criminal offence, after placing an advertisement in a newspaper.	Goods or services advertised in the media	His advertisement was an invitation to treat and therefore no offer to sell had been made.

Case	Facts	Element of offer	Legal point
Carlill v Carbolic Smoke Ball Co. (1893)	C bought and used a medical product correctly but still caught the 'flu. She sued for £100.	Goods or services advertised in the media	The advert was not a true offer: it was an example of a unilateral offer.
Hyde v Wrench (1840)	W offered to sell his farm for £1,000 and rejected H's offer of £950. W then refused H's higher offer of £1,000 and sold to another party.	Counter-offers	The original offer of £1,000 had been rejected by H's counter-offer of £950.
Taylor v Laird (1856)	T had commanded L's ship but resigned command and worked as an ordinary crew member. On his return to England, T tried to claim his wages.	Communication of offers	T was unable to claim since he had not communicated his offer. There was therefore no contract.

Acceptance

In order for a contract to be formed, the offer must be validly accepted by the offeree and that **acceptance** communicated back to the offeror. This in turn changes an offer into an agreement or contract. It is important, therefore, that the acceptance must:

- 'mirror' the offer
- not change the terms of the offer
- be communicated properly back to the offeror.

Acceptance must be unconditional

It is clear that an acceptance must be unconditional – see *Hyde v Wrench* (1840) above. However, making enquiries about the offer may not amount to a counter-offer and therefore may not be taken as rejecting the original offer – see *Stevenson v McLean* (1880).

Battle of the forms

In the commercial world, businesses will often make the same type of offers to sell their products or services, and other businesses will agree to buy their products or services.

With the similarity of such offers, companies draw up 'standard forms' with the terms and conditions that they wish to contract on. This is usually to their own advantage.

However, if two businesses contract together and both use their own standard forms, one standard form which makes the offer and the other standard form containing the acceptance, the question is – which standard form is to be used if there is a conflict of terms? See *Butler Machine Tool Co. Ltd v Ex-Cell-O Corp.* (1979).

Rules of communication and revocation

If a valid offer has been made, then the contract can only be formed if the acceptance is communicated back to the offeror. Only the offeree can make the acceptance.

The general principle of 'silence does not amount to an acceptance' makes common sense. In general terms, an acceptance can be made in any

> **Exam tip**
>
> You might be faced with a scenario question which involves an enquiry being made after an offer is made. This generally will not be a counter-offer, so the offer will still stand.

> **Acceptance:** unconditional agreement to all the terms of an offer.

> **Revision activity**
>
> Using the internet, identify a typical business contract from a large high-street shop and read through its terms and conditions.

form. However, if a specific method of acceptance is stipulated, then the acceptance must follow that format to be valid.

Usually the offer is accepted through conduct (see *Carlill v Carbolic Smoke Ball Co.* above) or through an agreed method, and this method is communicated to the offeror.

Nevertheless, an offer can be revoked – in other words removed by the offeror – in certain circumstances.

Postal rule

There is an exception to the rule, where the acceptance can be validly made before it reaches the offeror. This is known as the **postal rule** – see *Adams v Lindsell* (1818). Here, the acceptance is valid and the contract is formed when the acceptance letter is posted, and not when it is received by the offeror.

- The postal rule only operates where such acceptance is agreed upon or is in the normal manner that the offeror conducts their business. If this is not stated in the contract, nor is it a common-sense approach to accept, then the courts will look at whether it was reasonable to accept in such a way.
- If it is clear that the acceptance must be communicated to the offeror before a contract is formed, by excluding the rule in the terms of the contract, then the postal rule will not suffice – see *Holwell Securities v Hughes* (1974).
- The postal rule will also form a valid contract even if the letter of acceptance is sent but not received at all by the offeror – see *Household Fire Insurance Co. v Grant* (1879).
- The postal rule does not apply where methods of communication are instantaneous (for example telephone, telex or fax), nor is it clear with electronic communication whether the rule applies when an email is sent or received.

> **Postal rule:** the acceptance is valid and the contract is formed when the acceptance letter is posted, and not when it is received by the offeror.

Table 7.2.3 Key cases on acceptance

Case	Facts	Element of acceptance	Legal point
Stevenson v McLean (1880)	M offered to sell S some iron and S agreed the price and quantity. S asked for four months of credit instead of paying cash. Hearing nothing from M, S sent a letter of acceptance.	Acceptance must be unconditional	The enquiry for credit was not a counter-offer but was instead an enquiry for information. The offer was still able to be accepted.
Butler Machine Tool Co. Ltd v Ex-Cell-O Corp. (1979)	B's standard form of contract contained a price variation clause. E accepted the offer on their own standard form which had conflicting terms and no price variation clause.	Battle of the forms	Lord Denning controversially suggested replacing contested terms by implying reasonable ones.
Adams v Lindsell (1818)	D wrote to C offering a quantity of wool and requiring an acceptance via the post. D's letter was incorrectly addressed, causing delay. C accepted the offer and posted it the same day, but D had already sold the wool.	Communication of the acceptance	The court held that the contract began on the day that the acceptance was returned via the post.

Revocation of an offer

Revocation of an offer means the withdrawal of an offer, and the following rules apply:

- A unilateral offer cannot be withdrawn if the offeree is in the process of performance – see *Errington v Errington and Woods* (1952).
- The offeror withdraws the offer before the offeree has accepted it – see *Routledge v Grant* (1823).
- The revocation must be communicated to the offeree and cannot be withdrawn without warning – see *Byrne v Van Tienhiven* (1880).
- The revocation does not need to come from the offeror, but if not it must come from a reliable third party with whom both parties are well acquainted – see *Dickinson v Dodds* (1876).

> **Revocation of an offer:** the withdrawal of an offer.

Table 7.2.4 Key cases on revocation of offers

Case	Facts	Element of revocation	Legal point
Errington v Errington and Woods (1952)	A father bought a house for his son and daughter to live in. He promised to transfer the title to them if they paid off the mortgage. The father died. The family wanted possession of the house.	Unilateral offer and revocation	The father's promise, the unilateral contract, could not be withdrawn as long as the couple paid the mortgage.
Routledge v Grant (1823)	G offered his house for sale; the offer remaining open for six weeks only. G removed the house from sale before the six weeks expired.	Offer withdrawn before acceptance	Given there was no acceptance of the offer, G was entitled to revoke the offer.
Byrne v Van Tienhiven (1880)	• 1 October – V wrote to B offering to sell B certain goods. • 8 October – V wrote to B revoking the offer. • 11 October – B received the letter from 1 October and accepted by telegram. • 15 October – B confirmed the acceptance by letter. • 20 October – B received V's revocation letter.	Communication of revocation	The second letter was received after B's acceptance on 11 October – the 'postal rule' applying here.
Dickinson v Dodds (1876)	X offered to sell houses to Y, the offer to remain for two days. B, a reliable mutual acquaintance, informed Y that X had revoked the offer; Y quickly accepted.	Third-party revocation of offer	An offeror does not need to revoke the offer in person. However, the third party or agent must be able to be relied upon by both parties.

Intention to create legal relations

REVISED

The intention to create legal relations is important, as the courts will only enforce agreements that are in need of support and not gratuitous promises.

Contract law distinguishes between two key types of contract in determining whether there is an intention to create legal relations. In both, the types are formed with a rebuttable presumption:

- Social and domestic agreements: there is a presumption that there is no intention to create legal relations unless the contrary can be proved, i.e. the rebuttable presumption – see *Merritt v Merritt* (1970). Such promises or agreements are not legally enforceable – see *Balfour v Balfour* (1919) and *Jones v Padavatton* (1969).

Exam tip

Look closely at scenario questions and take note of the parties to an agreement. Are the parties related? If so, could the rebuttable presumption apply? Similarly, a business 'agreement' could fail if there was no intention to create legal relations.

- Commercial or business agreements: there is a presumption that there is intention to create legal relations. Unless the contrary can be proved (i.e. the rebuttable presumption – *Jones v Vernons Pools* (1938)), such agreements are legally enforceable – see *Edwards v Skyways* (1964).

Typical mistake

Do not assume that since there seems to be an agreement with all its constituent parts, there must be a contract. This may not be the case where there are one or two rebuttable presumptions in social or business arrangements.

Table 7.2.5 Key cases on intention to create legal relations

Case	Facts	Element of intention to create legal relations	Legal point
Merritt v Merritt (1970)	After separating, Mr M agreed to pay Mrs M £40 per month. Mr M agreed that Mrs M should pay off the mortgage and that he would transfer the home into her sole name when it was paid off. He then refused to do so.	Social/domestic arrangement or otherwise	When parties are separating, or are separated, there is a presumption of an intention to create legal relations.
Balfour v Balfour (1919)	While married, Mr B, who was working abroad, agreed to send maintenance payments which eventually stopped. Mrs B sought to enforce the payment.	Social/domestic arrangement or otherwise	As the agreement was social and domestic, there was a presumption against an intent to be legally bound.
Jones v Padavatton (1969)	A mother persuaded her daughter to give up a job in the USA to study for the Bar in England. A house was provided by the mother, but later they both quarrelled and the mother sought possession of the house.	Social/domestic arrangement or otherwise	As there was no formality in the agreement, there was no intention to create legal relations and the mother could reclaim the house.
Jones v Vernons Pools (1938)	J claimed to have won a competition run by D. D refused as the form, called 'a coupon', contained the phrase 'binding in honour only'.	'Gentleman's' agreement' or legally enforceable business agreement	There was no contract, as the agreement to pay was based purely upon the honour of the parties.
Edwards v Skyways (1964)	E was told he would receive an *ex gratia* payment (meaning 'no pre-existing liability') as part of a redundancy payment.	'Gentleman's agreement' or legally enforceable business agreement	There was a presumption that the agreement, being a business agreement, was binding.

Consideration

REVISED

Consideration was defined in *Dunlop v Selfridge* (1915) as:

> 'an act or forbearance of one party, or the promise thereof, is the price for which the promise of the other is bought, and the promise thus given for value is enforceable'.

Exam tip

Explain the rationale of the judge's decisions in the consideration cases you use in an exam question, to demonstrate your understanding of the law.

> **Consideration:** 'an act or forbearance of one party, or the promise thereof, is the price for which the promise of the other is bought, and the promise thus given for value is enforceable'.

A contract is not fully formed simply because there is a valid offer, a valid acceptance of the offer and an intention to create legal relations. Historically, consideration was developed to provide further evidence that the parties to an agreement intended a legally binding contract by contributing something in return for the promise of the other party.

So, in order for a contract to be valid, there must be some form of 'consideration'. The simplest and most usual form of consideration is the price of the goods or services.

For example, if A offers to sell his car for £3,000 and B agrees to buy his car for £3,000, the price is the consideration for the offer to sell the car, and the passing of the car is the consideration for the acceptance of the £3,000.

However, contracts may be formed without a cash transaction, so consideration can take other forms.

Consideration is, in effect, the proof that an agreement exists. In *Currie v Misra* (1875), consideration was defined as being in terms of 'benefit and detriment'. In the example above, A gains the benefit of £3,000 but to the detriment of releasing his ownership of the car to B.

As with all parts of contract law, judges have developed a series of rules in relation to consideration.

Table 7.2.6 Rules on consideration

Rule	Explanation
Adequacy	The courts are not necessarily interested in whether parties to the agreement have made a bad or poor agreement. They are more interested in the freedom of contract. Therefore, if the price for goods or services does not reflect the value of the goods, then in the absence of duress or undue influence, the courts will seek to enforce the original agreement's terms – see *Thomas v Thomas* (1842).
Sufficiency	The consideration must be in a form which the courts have accepted as 'sufficient'. This means it must be real, be tangible and have some inherent value – see *Ward v Byham* (1956).
Past consideration	The general rule is that past consideration is unenforceable. So if a voluntary agreement is struck and there was no mention of payment, then a later promise to pay is unenforceable. For example, if A agrees to give B his car for free, then later B agrees to give A £100 for the car, the £100 consideration is not enforceable – see *Roscorla v Thomas* (1842). *Lampleigh v Braithwaite* (1615): there is an exception, when a party has requested a service where there is a reasonable implication that a payment be made, even though such has not been stated in the agreement.

Rule	Explanation
Pre-existing duties	If a party is under an existing obligation to carry out something, they cannot use that promise as consideration for a new agreement – see *Stilk v Myrick* (1809). This rule also applies to persons who are under a legal obligation to carry out an act. In *Collins v Godefroy* (1831), the court rejected a police officer's claim that he was entitled to a payment promised by a defendant in a court case if the police officer gave evidence. The officer was under a legal obligation to attend and no further consideration was present. However, there are some exceptions – if a party does something extra than what was required in the original agreement, that may be considered to be new consideration in return for the new agreement.

Revision activity

Summarise the judicial rules that have been developed in relation to consideration.

Table 7.2.7 **Key cases on consideration**

Case	Facts	Element of consideration	Legal point
Dunlop v Selfridge (1915)	D sold tyres to X, a dealer, who then resold the tyres to S, a retailer, at a price below the agreed price enforced by D.	Definition	This case provided the legal definition of consideration.
Thomas v Thomas (1842)	A widow was allowed to stay in the matrimonial home for a very low rent of £1 per year.	Consideration need not be adequate	This was sufficient consideration for the agreement for her to stay in the house.
Ward v Byham (1956)	The father of an illegitimate child agreed with the mother to pay her £1 a week to keep the child 'well looked after and happy'. He then refused to pay.	Consideration must be sufficient	The court held that as the mother was under no legal obligation to keep the child 'happy', this was sufficient consideration for the £1 per week.
Roscorla v Thomas (1842)	T sold a horse to R, stating that it was 'free from vice'. In fact, the horse was violent. R sued for breach of contract.	Consideration must not be past consideration	There was no consideration for the later promise that the horse was fine. The only consideration, the £30, was in the past, and therefore not relevant to the later promise.
Lampleigh v Braithwaite (1615)	B asked L to get him a King's pardon after B had been accused of killing a man. L did so, at his own expense. B later agreed to pay L £100, which he failed to do.	Rule in *Lampleigh v Braithwaite*	It was implicit that a payment would be made at the time of the agreement, and L was entitled to the £100.
Tweddle v Atkinson (1861)	A father and future father-in-law (D) agreed to pay a sum of money to X. D died before he made the payment. X sued the executors of his estate for the money promised.	Consideration must move from the claimant	Because X had provided no consideration to the original agreement, he could not enforce it.
Stilk v Myrick (1809)	When two members of a ship deserted, the captain promised the remaining crew a share of the deserter's wages if they got the ship home. Once home, the captain refused to pay any extra wages.	Performance of existing obligations	The court rejected C's argument that he was entitled to the extra wages, since he was simply doing what he was contractually obliged to do and had provided no further consideration for the new promise.
Hartley v Ponsonby (1857)	Nineteen ship crew members were left when 17 others deserted. Only four were 'able seamen' on this dangerous voyage. The captain promised to pay the remaining crew extra money if they agreed to sail, but later refused to pay.	The performance of existing obligations	By agreeing to continue in such dangerous circumstances, the remaining crew had provided further consideration to the new agreement.

Privity of contract

Generally, a contract is only enforceable by the parties to the contract – see *Dunlop v Selfridge* (1915).

The basic rule follows common sense, since a third party would generally not wish to be bound by an agreement they had not agreed upon. However, if a benefit is bestowed from such a contract onto a third party, then the basic rule may seem unfair – see *Tweddle v Atkinson* (1861).

Exceptions to the general rule include:

- statute
- third-party trusts
- restrictive covenants – see *Tulk v Moxhay* (1848)
- agency – see *The Eurymedon* (1975)
- collateral contracts – see *Shanklin Pier v Detel* (1951)
- application of s 56 of the Law of Property Act 1925 – see *Beswick v Beswick* (1968).

Contract (Rights of Third Parties) Act 1999

It seems unfair that a third party is unable in contract law to claim the benefit that is intended for them. This led to calls for reform and led to the 1999 Act which provides:

> 'A person who is not a party to a contract may enforce a term of the contract in his own right if the contract expressly provides that he may, or if it purports to confer a benefit on him. The Act also requires that this party is expressly identified in the contract by name, or as a member of a class, or answering a particular description.'

Table 7.2.8 Key cases on privity of contract

Case	Facts	Element of privity	Legal point
Tulk v Moxhay (1848)	C sold land with a restrictive covenant attached, which prevented the land from being built upon. The land was sold several times, until D bought it and wanted to build on the land.	Exception to basic rule: restrictive covenants	D argued there was no privity of contract, but the court held that the covenant was enforceable in equity, as an injunction and not damages was sought by C.
The Eurymedon (1975)	A contract to ship machinery contained a limitation clause of a year to bring a claim for damaged goods. C brought a claim against a stevedore after a year had passed, arguing they were not privy to the contract.	Exception to basic rule: agency	Stevedores were party to the contract as they provided services of unloading – consideration owed to a third party can be valid consideration for a new promise to another party.
Shanklin Pier v Detel (1951)	S employed X to paint a pier. D said a particular paint was suitable. Within three months, the paint began to peel off.	Exception to basic rule: collateral contracts	Established the doctrine of collateral contracts, where a contract may be given as consideration by simply agreeing to enter into another contract.
Beswick v Beswick (1968)	P agreed to sell his coal business to his nephew, D, in return for a sum of money each week, then £5 per week to P's wife after he died. D agreed, but after P died, D made one payment then refused to pay any more.	Exception to basic rule: s 56 of the Law of Property Act 1925	P's wife was able to sue in her capacity as her late husband's administratrix in enforcing D's promise to pay.

Now test yourself

1 How would the courts distinguish between an offer and an invitation to treat?
2 What is the difference between a unilateral offer and an invitation to treat?
3 What impact on the original offer does a counter-offer have?
4 How do the courts decide if there is an intention for an agreement to be legally binding?
5 What were the reasons for the cases of *Balfour v Balfour* (1919) and *Merritt v Merritt* (1970) to be decided differently?
6 Why were the cases of *Stilk v Myrick* (1809) and *Hartley v Ponsonby* (1857) decided differently?
7 Explain the rule that consideration need not be adequate.
8 Explain the rule in *Lampleigh v Braithwaite* (1615).

Answers online

Exam summary

In the exam, you MAY be asked to:
- respond to a scenario question based on formation of contract by advising a claimant whether there was:
  - a valid offer and acceptance made
  - an intention to create legal relations
  - valid consideration
- discuss and evaluate in a full-length essay question the topics of:
  - offer and acceptance
  - intention to create legal relations
  - consideration.

These types of question will each be worth a maximum of 25 marks.

7.3 Terms

In negotiations to form a contract, both parties may discuss a variety of issues before committing to the agreement.

Many of the issues that are discussed will form the basis of the contract's terms. However, some of the issues discussed may not. Therefore, contract law makes a distinction between what are called:

● terms, which form part of the contract, and
● mere **representations** – statements of opinion/fact or what are known as trade 'puffs', which are unlikely to form part of the contract.

When problems arise after the contract is made and a party wishes to rely on a matter discussed before the agreement, the courts will have to decide whether the issue is a term or a non-contractual (mere) representation. The former will create contractual obligations, while the latter simply encourages one party to enter into the initial agreement and is not binding.

Therefore, the terms are the subject matter of the contract and bind both parties to perform them in order for the contract to be complete.

Terms are decided upon during negotiations or inserted into the contract, for example on a party's standard form contract. They can be:

● expressly stated, and therefore included into the contract by the parties, or
● implied as a matter of fact from what was the intention of the parties or by statute law.

An example of terms implied into a contract through statute law is the Consumer Rights Act 2015.

> **Representations:** statements made before the contract which may or may not become one of the main terms of the contract.

> **Revision activity**
>
> Create a contract, including all of its terms, for the following situation: you agree to buy your friend's A Level Law revision guide. Tip: include who, what, why, where and how.

> **Revision activity**
>
> In order to understand trade puffs, watch advertisements on television and read advertisements in magazines or newspapers and pick out any boasts or pretention that the business makes which would be unlikely to be legally binding.

Express terms

REVISED

If matters that were discussed at the negotiation stage are clearly written into a contract, this makes it easier to understand and therefore determine which matter becomes a term of the contract.

However, if this is not the case, the common law has created a series of tests to determine whether a matter previously discussed is included in the contract.

> **Exam tip**
>
> An express term will be a clear point that expresses the subject matter of the contract. However, remember that terms can also be implied by the presumed intention of the party and by statute.

Table 7.3.1 Determining whether a term is included in a contract

How important was the representation?	Clearly, if either party attaches great importance to a statement made during negotiation, then it is more than likely it will be considered a term – see *Birch v Paramount Estates (Liverpool) Ltd* (1956).
Did the party rely on the skill of the other making the representation?	If one party makes a specific representation due to their level of expertise and the other party relies upon it, this is more likely to become a term of the contract – see *Dick Bentley Productions Ltd v Harold Smith (Motors) Ltd* (1965) and *Oscar Chess Ltd v Williams* (1957).

Was the written agreement signed?	If a written contract is signed, the courts will usually take it that both parties have read and agreed its contents. The courts agreed in *L'Estrange v Graucob* (1934) that the term was 'in regrettably small print but quite legible'. Such terms would nowadays be subject to scrutiny under the Unfair Contract Terms Act 1977.
Are the parties aware of the term when making the contract?	Generally, if a party is unaware of a 'term' which is relied upon later by one of the parties who knew of the term, then the term is unlikely to be actionable. This depends on the term and the likely impact of its operation.

Exam tip

Support any description or evaluation of the law with relevant and accurate case citations.

Table 7.3.2 Key cases on express terms

Case	Facts	Element of express terms	Legal point
Birch v Paramount Estates (Liverpool) Ltd (1956)	A married couple bought a house on the basis that they were told it would be 'as good as the show house'. They sued when it was not so.	How important was the representation?	The Court of Appeal stated that the statement was so crucial to forming the contract that it became a term.
Dick Bentley Productions Ltd v Harold Smith (Motors) Ltd (1965)	C asked D to find him a 'well-vetted' Bentley car. D found a car, but falsely stated it had done 20,000 miles, when in fact it had done 100,000 miles.	Did the party rely on the skill of the other making the representation?	The Court of Appeal held the mileage was a term of the contract and C could successfully sue for breach in relying on D's expertise.
Oscar Chess Ltd v Williams (1957)	W, a motorist, sold his car to O, a motor dealer. Without any specialist knowledge, W stated it was a 1948 Morris 10. However, it was a 1939 Morris 10. O sued W.	Did the party rely on the skill of the other making the representation?	W's statement was an innocent representation and as a dealer, O should have spotted the error. The statement was held not to be a term of the contract.
L'Estrange v Graucob (1934)	L bought a cigarette-vending machine from G. L signed the written contract without reading its exclusion term. The machine stopped working, so L sued under the Sale of Goods Act as to the fitness of purpose.	Was the written agreement signed?	G was held to be protected by the clause and L failed in her action since she had signed the contract.

Implied terms

REVISED

Typical mistake

Do not ignore presumed implied terms and statutory implied terms in the rush to consider only what a scenario question has made explicit.

Not all terms may have been expressed, or written, in the contract. It could be that an event occurs where the express terms do not cover the eventuality and therefore terms can be implied into a contract to cover such – see *Grant v Australian Knitting Mills Ltd* (1936).

The law implies terms into a contract in one of two possible ways:
● implied by fact during a dispute to see what the unexpressed intentions of the parties were, or
● implied by statute, regardless of what either party may have intended.

Revision activity

What would be the implied terms in a contract for the sale of a pair of running shoes which cost £150?

Terms implied by fact

There are a variety of ways such terms are incorporated into the contract, where the courts, through the common law, attempt to give the presumed intention of the parties in cases of dispute. These are:

- through custom – where common practices will over a long period of time allow an actual and enforceable implied term
- through common trade practices – specific to the type of industry and how that commonly operates through professional custom
- to preserve business efficacy – the implication here is that where two parties contract, the effectiveness of the agreement must be adhered to; here, terms can be implied to allow this to operate – see *The Moorcock* (1889).

The courts will not simply imply a term because the term is reasonable.

In *Liverpool City Council v Irwin* (1977), Lord Cross, in the House of Lords, stated that the insertion of such a term had to be 'necessary'.

Whether or not a term is implied into a contract as a matter of fact is decided using the 'officious bystander' test. This was developed following the case of *Shirlaw v Southern Foundaries Ltd* (1939), where MacKinnon LJ stated:

> '*Prima facie* that which in any contract is left to be implied and need not be expressed is something so obvious that it goes without saying; so that, if, while the parties were making their bargain, an officious bystander were to suggest some express provision for it in their agreement, they would testily suppress him with a common "Oh, of course!"'

Terms implied by statute: the Consumer Rights Act 2015

Since the rise of consumer society and the unequal bargaining power that consumers can encounter when making agreements with businesses, successive governments have introduced statutory terms that are implied into contracts to balance the parties' positions. In such cases, neither party can ignore or exclude such implied terms.

The main statute governing this area of law is the Consumer Rights Act 2015. The terms that are implied under this Act are specifically under ss 9, 10 and 11 for the supply of goods and ss 49 and 52 for the supply of services.

Table 7.3.3 **Key cases on implied terms**

Case	Facts	Element of implied terms
Grant v Australian Knitting Mills Ltd (1936)	C bought woollen underpants which contained traces of chemicals. These chemicals caused a painful skin disease.	Term does not cover every eventuality
The Moorcock (1889)	D owned a wharf and allowed the C to dock their ship at a jetty. Both parties knew the ship would be damaged at low tide if it were to remain at the jetty. The ship was badly damaged at low tide.	To preserve business efficacy
Poussard v Spiers and Pond (1876)	P was hired as lead actor in an operetta. When she was taken ill and unable to perform, her lead role was given to an understudy. P sued for breach of the contract.	Significance of terms

Types of term

When parties are negotiating before formalising a contract, some matters are left as mere representations and others form the terms of the contract. So, important matters will invariably become terms of the contract, which are either expressly incorporated or implied into the contract.

When the terms are incorporated into the contract, some may have more importance than others. Therefore, the law applies certain weightings to the terms.

The type of term breached dictates the type of remedy or resolution to which the injured party is entitled.

Table 7.3.4 Types of term

Type	Explanation
Condition	Fundamental in carrying out the purpose of the contract fully. Breach of a condition gives the injured party the right to reject the contract – see *Poussard v Spiers and Pond* (1876).
Warranty	Any other term of the contract. It is normally a term that is descriptive or 'ancillary' to the contract. Breach of a warranty does not allow the injured party to reject the contract – instead, they are allowed to claim damages to compensate them for any loss.
Innominate term	Neither a clear condition nor a clear warranty; it is decided upon by the courts, depending on the level of 'injury' following a breach.

Condition: contractual term which goes to the root of the contract.

Warranty: generally a descriptive term.

Innominate term: can be either a condition or a warranty.

Revision activity

Using the internet, find a contract for the sale of goods from a high-street shop and decide which of its terms are conditions and which are warranties.

Exam tip

In exam questions which include identifying terms, the decision on whether a term is a condition or warranty may be self-evident. However, where this may not be the case, ask yourself whether the term is integral to the contract (condition) or incidental to the contract (warranty).

Exclusion clauses

This section looks at how parties may wish to reduce or even exclude liability, and how the courts and statute law view such practices.

Exclusion or exemption clauses may be inserted into a contract in order to reduce or eliminate the liability of either party where certain events may occur. They can operate perfectly legitimately where both parties are of equal bargaining power.

However, it is common that the parties may have unequal bargaining power, particularly where consumers are involved.

Businesses will generally operate on standard form contracts. Here, the business will use a contract that is standard to its business purposes.

Exclusion or exemption clauses: clauses which seek to exclude from liability one party for a breach of contract, or even for a tort.

Revision activity

Identify an exclusion clause that might be written into a contract for the sale of a concert ticket.

Typical mistake

Do not assume that every exclusion clause will be invalid. In many cases, the clause will be valid and a show of tough or shrewd business acumen, rather than being unfair on the other party.

Common-law control of exclusion clauses

Where one party is more dominant and seeks to rely on an exclusion clause to the detriment of the other party, the courts have devised two rules which indicate whether to accept the clause's operation or deny it:

● the clause must be incorporated into the contract as part of the contract, and
● the clause will be constructed by the courts and must protect the party from damage caused and not seek to gain an undue advantage from it.

Incorporation of the clause

The exclusion clause is generally included in the contract either by signature or if the other party had knowledge of the clause:

● Where the parties sign the contract, then the maxim *caveat emptor* applies. Here, the general rule is that you agree to what you sign for – see *L'Estrange v Graucob* (1934), case details in Table 7.3.2.
● Where the contract is not necessarily signed but the clause should have been brought to the other party's notice (for example by a sign or on a document given to a party), the exclusion clause will only be binding if the parties had express knowledge of it at the time of the contract – see *Olley v Marlborough Court Hotel* (1949).
● A ticket with an exclusion clause on the reverse is generally insufficient – see *Chapelton v Barry* UDC (1940).

The general rules for knowledge of the exclusion clause to be enforced are:

● Did the party have knowledge of the clause (perhaps they had contracted before and were understood to have such knowledge)? or
● Were reasonable steps taken to bring the exclusion clause to the attention of the party?

Construction of the clause

The exclusion clause must be interpreted, or constructed, by the courts to see if it will achieve what it is meant to do without unduly penalising the other party.

The main rule of construction here is the *contra proferentem* rule: any ambiguity with regard to the clause must be interpreted against the party proposing or having drafted the clause and wishing to rely upon it – see *Hollier v Rambler Motors (AMC) Ltd* (1972).

Where an exclusion clause is held to be valid in situations where the claimant alleges negligence, very clear words must be used.

Unfair Contract Terms Act 1977

Before the enactment of the Unfair Contract Terms Act 1977 (UCTA 77), there was little statutory regulation of exclusion clauses, and the common-law decisions of judges were used to decide whether or not the exclusion clause should stand in a contract.

This Act was introduced to give consumers greater protection. It distinguishes between a consumer contract and one between businesses. Section 12(1) defines 'dealing as a consumer' where:

'(a) He neither makes the contract in the course of a business nor holds himself out as doing so; and

> **Revision activity**
>
> Collect five examples of exclusion clauses that can be found on the back of tickets, for example a bus ticket.

> **Revision activity**
>
> Collect five examples of notices that purport to exclude liability, for example 'Caution – wet paint'.

> **Exam tip**
>
> Remember that while a party may have signed the agreement, an exclusion clause may still be invalid. To be valid, the clause must be validly incorporated into the contract and stand up to statutory regulation.

(b) The other party does make the contract in the course of a business; and

(c) ... the goods ... are of a type ordinarily supplied for private use or consumption.'

The Act makes certain exclusion clauses void and makes others only valid if they satisfy the test for reasonableness.

Revision activity

Using your five examples from the activities above, apply the Unfair Contract Terms Act 1977 to each clause to see if it is valid or void under the Act.

Table **7.3.5** Void and valid causes under the Unfair Contract Terms Act 1977

Void exclusion clauses in UCTA 77	Section 2(1)	A party cannot rely on an exclusion clause that tries to exclude or restrict their liability for death or personal injury resulting from negligence.
Valid if reasonable in UCTA 77	Section 2(2)	In the case of other loss or damage, a person cannot exclude or restrict their liability for negligence except when the term or notice satisfies the requirement of reasonableness.
	Section 3	Where a consumer deals on a business' standard form of contract, the business cannot exclude its liability for breach, or provide a substantially different performance, or no performance at all, of the contract unless its actions satisfy the requirement of reasonableness.
	Section 11(1)	'The term shall have been a fair and reasonable one to be included having regard to the circumstances which were, or ought reasonably to have been, known to or in the contemplation of the parties when the contract was made'

Consumer Rights Act 2015

Table **7.3.6** Exclusion and limitation clauses and impact of the Consumer Rights Act 2015

Section of the Act	Definition
Section 31	Liability that cannot be excluded or restricted (goods): • A term of a contract under ss 9, 10 and 11 to supply goods cannot be excluded or restricted by a trader.
Section 57	Liability that cannot be excluded or restricted (services): • A term of a contract under s 49 to supply services cannot be excluded or restricted by a trader.
Section 65	The bar on exclusion or restriction of negligence liability: • Traders cannot rely on a term inserted into a consumer contract or notice which excludes or restricts liability for death or personal injury resulting from negligence. • Where a term of a consumer contract, or notice, intends to exclude or restrict a trader's liability for negligence, a person is not to be taken to have voluntarily accepted any risk merely because the person agreed to or knew about the term or notice.

Table 7.3.7 Key cases on exclusion clauses

Case	Facts	Element of exclusion clauses	Legal point
Olley v Marlborough Court Hotel (1949)	O booked into M's hotel as a guest. A sign in her room stated the hotel would not be held responsible for any articles lost or stolen. O left a fur coat in the bedroom which was later stolen.	A representation is not a term unless the parties are aware of it when making the contract.	Since the contract was made at the reception desk, the notice in the bedroom was too late to become a term of the contract.
Chapelton v Barry UDC (1940)	C hired a deckchair at the beach. He paid 2p and was given a ticket which said on the back the council would not be liable for any accident or damage. When the chair collapsed and C was injured, he sued for damages.	Incorporation of the clause	The court held that the clause was not incorporated into the contract since it was a mere receipt given after the contract was made.
Hollier v Rambler Motors (AMC) Ltd (1972)	C's car was damaged in a fire at D's garage. On previous occasions, the standard form contained an exclusion clause excluding liability for fire damage. On this occasion, the standard form had not been signed.	Construction of the clause	The Court of Appeal stated that the standard form was not incorporated into the contract simply because of previous dealings.

Now test yourself

TESTED ☐

1 Why are mere representations, statements of opinion or fact or trade 'puffs' not automatic terms under a contract?
2 Why was the *ratio decidendi* in *Oscar Chess Ltd v Williams* (1957) important in setting clear rules on incorporating representations into a contract?
3 Explain three ways in which terms are implied into a contract by fact.
4 How has Parliament, through statute law, created implied terms in a contract?
5 Explain the difference between a condition and a warranty.
6 What is an innominate term?
7 Explain what is meant by an exclusion/exemption clause.
8 What are the two common-law rules for whether an exemption clause will be accepted or denied by the courts?
9 How have the courts approached exclusion clauses that appear on notices, tickets or receipts?
10 How has the *contra proferentem* rule helped claimants in contractual disputes over exclusion clauses?

Answers online

Exam summary

In the exam, you MAY be asked to:
● respond to a scenario question based on contractual terms by advising a claimant as to the validity of specific exclusion and limitation clauses
● discuss and evaluate the topics of exclusion and limitation clauses in a full-length essay question.

These types of question will each be worth a maximum of 25 marks.

7.4 Vitiating factors

Many factors potentially invalidate (vitiate) a contract, meaning that the agreement is not enforceable. One of the most common **vitiating** factors is where one or both parties to the contract misrepresent one or more aspects of the agreement.

> **Vitiating:** invalidating; a vitiating factor makes a contract null and void. The two most common vitiating factors are misrepresentation and economic duress.

Misrepresentation

If a party is encouraged to enter into a contract because of factual statements which later turn out to be untrue, then the untrue statement or **misrepresentation** may provide a remedy to the injured party.

> **Misrepresentation:** a false statement of material fact.

A misrepresentation is a false statement of material fact and cannot be:
- a mere opinion – see *Bissett v Wilkinson* (1927)
- an expression of future intent – see *Edgington v Fitzmaurice* (1885)
- a mere trade puff – see *Carlill v Carbolic Smoke Ball Co.* (1893), case details in Table 7.2.2.

It is made by one party to the agreement to the other party, at or before the time of the agreement. The statement is intended to encourage the other party to enter the agreement and not intended to form part of the contract.
- A misrepresentation can arise from conduct rather than from a verbal or written statement – see *Spice Girls Ltd v Aprilia World Service BV* (2000).
- A statement made after the formation is not actionable – see *Roscorla v Thomas* (1842), case details in Table 7.2.7.

Misrepresentations cover many different types of statement. They may be blatant lies or innocent telling of inaccurate information.

Table 7.4.1 Types of misrepresentation and their remedies

Type	Remedy
Fraudulent	A statement is made knowingly or deliberately, or being reckless as to whether it is true or not.
	Remedy:
	• The injured party can sue in the tort of deceit.
	• The injured party is entitled to reparation for 'all the damage flowing from the fraudulent inducement' – see *Doyle v Olby (Ironmongers)* (1969).
	• The defendant is responsible for all damages and consequential loss where there is a causal link between the misrepresentation and the damage – see *Smith New Court Securities Ltd v Scrimgeour Vickers Ltd* (1996).
	• A loss of profit can also be claimed.
	• The injured party can still affirm the contract (insisting on its continued performance) or disaffirm the contract (and refuse any future performance).

Type	Remedy
Negligent	This can be actioned at common law where the loss is financial – see *Hedley Byrne and Co. Ltd v Heller and Partners Ltd* (1963). Liability for the misrepresentation will only arise where there is a 'special relationship' and the party making the misrepresentation owes a duty of care to the other party. Section 2(1) of the Misrepresentation Act 1967 allows an action where a misrepresentation is made and a loss occurs as a result of relying on the misrepresentation. That person will be liable unless they can show they had reasonable grounds to believe the statement. Remedy: ● Damages are available under the 1967 Act and at common law. ● Common-law damages are based on foreseeable loss under tort law. ● Contributory negligence can reduce the amount of damages.
Innocent	Damages to compensate the injured party are available if the other party makes an innocent misrepresentation which later turns out to be false (s 2(2) of the Misrepresentation Act 1967). Remedy: ● There is no automatic or absolute right to damages. ● There is a discretionary right to damages. ● Rescission is possible.

Exam tip

It is vital to appreciate the three main types of misrepresentation.

Omission in a consumer context

Misrepresentations in the form of false statements are not the only issue here. The opposite can be as problematic – that is to say, where unscrupulous traders deliberately leave out information or are 'economical with the truth'.

The Consumer Protection from Unfair Trading Regulations 2008 protect consumers from unfair or misleading trade practices, as well as banning deceptive omissions. The regulations make it an offence if a trader:
● omits material information that an average consumer would need to make an informed decision to contract
● hides, or provides material information in an unclear, unintelligible, ambiguous or untimely manner.

Any contractual information must also be displayed plainly, as any obscure presentation is equal to an omission.

Revision activity

Identify five statements that could be considered misrepresentations in the sale of a car, for example the engine size is 1.3 when it is a 1.1 etc.

Economic duress

REVISED

Threats to coerce a party into a contract have long been recognised at common law. **Economic duress** occurs where there is a threat to a person's financial situation. A contract agreed under economic duress cannot be recognised as a true or real agreement between the parties.

Economic duress: where one party makes threats of an economic nature to the other party in order to form or change an agreement.

Lord Kerr in *The Siboen and The Sibotre* (1976) described economic duress as 'such a degree of coercion that the other party was deprived of his free consent and agreement'.

Pressure to negotiate and enter into contracts are a fact of business life. Sometimes it may be difficult to identify the line between necessity to contract and coercion. However, several rules have been identified.

Revision activity

Identify five instances that could be considered economic duress in the formation of contract to supply football boots to an independent sports shop by a major sports label.

Table 7.4.2 Rules and remedies for economic duress

Rules	These are fairly *ad hoc* as cases arise: ● Courts will take into account whether the injured party protested, whether there was an alternative route available or whether they took steps to avoid it – see *Pao On v Lau Yiu Long* (1980). ● Threats by a union to blacklist a ship were decided to be economic duress – see *The Universal Sentinel* (1983). ● A threat to a small firm by a larger firm that it would breach a contract can be economic duress – see *Atlas Express v KafCo.* (1989). ● There was no economic duress in *Williams v Roffey* (1991), as the builders had made a reasonable choice.
Remedies	The effect of economic duress would be to make a contract voidable. An injured party will, therefore, be entitled to have the contract put aside, unless they have expressly or impliedly asserted it. The injured party must seek rescission as soon as possible after the original economic duress has stopped. As economic duress is similar to the tort of intimidation, a remedy for damages would lie in tort.

Table 7.4.3 Key cases on vitiating factors

Case	Facts	Element of vitiating factors	Legal point
Bissett v Wilkinson (1927)	A statement was made without expert knowledge as to how many sheep an area of land could hold.	A statement alleged to be a misrepresentation must be a statement of material fact.	The statement was speculation and mistaken so could not be relied upon.
Edgington v Fitzmaurice (1885)	Directors of a company borrowed money allegedly to repair buildings but paid off debts which was their intention from the start.	A statement alleged to be a misrepresentation must be a statement of material fact.	This was a false statement of material fact and a clear actionable misrepresentation.
Spice Girls Ltd v Aprilia World Service BV (2000)	In signing a contract to promote scooters, the group failed to notify the manufacturer that one of them was about to leave and did so.	Silence is generally not a representation since no statement is made, but there are exceptions.	The presence of the group member during filming and signing of the contract was a representation that no one in the group was about to leave.
The Siboen and The Sibotre (1976)	Charterers of ships during a world recession demanded renegotiation of their contracts with ship owners.	Definition	Economic duress is such a degree of coercion that the other party was deprived of free consent and agreement.

Case	Facts	Element of vitiating factors	Legal point
Pao On v Lau Yiu Long (1980)	C refused to complete the main contract unless certain subsidiary agreements were met by D. D was anxious for the main contract to be fulfilled.	Validity of claim	The validity of claims depends upon: whether the injured party protested, had an alternative course open to them, was independently advised or took steps to avoid duress.
The Universal Sentinel (1983)	The ship was blacklisted unless a release fee was paid to a shipping workers' federation.	Where was pressure from?	Economic duress can also include pressure from trades' unions or federations.

Now test yourself

TESTED ☐

1   What is a misrepresentation under contract law?
2   What are the three different types of misrepresentation?
3   Explain the remedies available for one type of misrepresentation.
4   What is economic duress?
5   According to Lord Scarman in *Pao On v Lau Yiu Long* (1980), what must be checked before the validity of a claim of economic duress can be established by the courts?

Answers online

Exam summary

In the exam, you MAY be asked to:
● respond to a scenario question based on vitiating factors by advising a claimant as to potential:
 – misrepresentation
 – economic duress
● discuss and evaluate in a full-length essay question the topic of:
 – misrepresentation.
 – economic duress.

These types of question will each be worth a maximum of 25 marks.

7.5 Discharge

Discharging a contract refers to the point at which a contract comes to an end. Usually, this would be the point at which all contractual obligations are fulfilled, called 'performance'.

However, there may be other ways that a contract comes to an end: frustration or breach.

> **Exam tip**
>
> Unless asked to do so by the question, you do not have to suggest ways that a contract can come to an end if your answer suggests there is a problem with the contract in a scenario.

> **Typical mistake**
>
> If a question clearly leads you to a particular type of discharge of contract, for example breach, it will be unnecessary for you to discuss all the other ways a contract can come to an end. Keep your answer relevant to the scenario.

Performance

REVISED

A contract is not discharged until all of the obligations are performed. This general rule requires that performance must match exactly and completely the contract's obligations – see *Cutter v Powell* (1795).

Modification of the general rule

The general rule can be modified or avoided in several ways:
- ○ Severable contracts are those where obligations are divisible, whereby each separate obligation can be singularly enforceable – see *Taylor v Webb* (1937).
- ○ Part-performance can be acceptable by both parties and payment for what is performed can be enforceable.
- ○ Where substantial performance is achieved and a party has largely performed their obligations, it may be possible to enforce the appropriate payment – see *Daken v Lee* (1916).
- ○ Acceptance of part-performance can arise if both parties agree, but the agreement must be genuine.
- ○ If either party is prevented from performing the obligations under the contract, then the general rule will not apply.
- ○ If one party has tendered performance which has been refused by the other, then the parties' obligations are discharged – see *Startup v Macdonald* (1843).

Time of performance

In many cases, a failure to perform on time is a breach of warranty, which then allows damages but not a repudiation of the contract.

Where time is of the essence, repudiation can follow from a breach if:
- both parties had made this clear
- the subject matter dictates such
- a time extension is given on the proviso that repudiation will occur if this deadline is not met.

Frustration

REVISED

A **frustrated contract** occurs where an unforeseen event prevents the absolute performance of the contract.

> **Frustrated contract:** where an unforeseen event prevents the absolute performance of the contract.

The doctrine of frustration was developed to provide a remedy for situations that arise during the duration of the contract which make future performance:

- illegal, or
- impossible, or
- fundamentally different.

Table 7.5.1 Doctrine of frustration

Illegal	Both parties are ready and willing to perform, but a change in the law prevents performance. This can be a change in the law in another country or the outbreak of war making trade with a hostile country illegal – see *Metropolitan Water Board v Dick Kerr* (1915).
Impossible	The contract ends in one of four ways: • subject matter is destroyed – see *Taylor v Caldwell* (1863) • subject matter is unavailable – see *Morgan v Manser* (1943) • one of the parties dies • there is a risk of the contract being unable to be performed completely.
Fundamentally different	The central purpose of the contract is destroyed by a frustrating event. This development essentially, and famously, arose due to the postponement of a coronation. The result of the frustration depends upon whether the commercial purpose of the contract is destroyed, as per *Krell v Henry* (1903), or if that purpose actually continued, as per *Herne Bay Steamboat Co. v Hutton* (1903).

> **Revision activity**
>
> Research online the cases of *Taylor v Caldwell* (1863) and *Morgan v Manser* (1943).

Limits of the doctrine of frustration

Certain restrictions or limitations are imposed by the courts, as it may be unfair on one of the parties to simply set aside the contract. Instead, obligations remain:

- where one party induces the frustrating event (then the contract will be breached)
- if the event is expressly provided for in the contract (then the frustration does not apply)
- where the actual event was or should have been foreseen.

Law Reform (Frustrated Contracts) Act 1943

This Act was created to address some of the unfairness of the common-law doctrine. It states the following:

- Any money already paid before the frustrating event is recoverable.
- Any money payable before the frustrating event is no longer owed.
- Where any expenses have occurred, payment can be ordered by the court.
- If any valuable benefit has been obtained, payment may be ordered by the court.

Breach

A breach occurs where a party fails to perform their obligations under the contract. It arises where there:

- is non-performance, or
- is a defective performance, or
- are repudiating obligations without any justification.

Table 7.5.2 Types and consequences of breach

Type of breach	Explanation	Consequence
Breach of a general term	Breach of a general term of the contract, allowing an action for damages	Where a general term is breached, an action for damages is available, but a party cannot repudiate a contract for breach of warranty.
Breach of a condition	Breach of a condition which is either expressed or implied, including an innominate term, where the breach is sufficient to allow the repudiation of the contract – see *The Hong Kong Fir Case* (1962)	A breach of a condition allows either an action for damages and/or for the party to repudiate a contract.
Anticipatory breach	An anticipatory breach, where one party notifies the other of an intention to breach their obligations under the contract – see *Hochester v De La Tour* (1853)	If there is an anticipatory breach, a party can either wait until the contract is unperformed or can sue immediately.

Revision activity

Research online *The Hong Kong Fir Case* (1962) and *Hochester v De La Tour* (1853).

Table 7.5.3 Key cases on discharge of contract

Case	Facts	Element of discharge	Legal point
Cutter v Powell (1795)	Correct goods were delivered in wrong size cases.	Performance	Part performance is no performance.
Taylor v Webb (1937)	A seaman died so performance was not complete.	Avoiding the strict rule on performance	If the contract has divisible obligations, a fair payment for each part completely performed can be expected.
Daken v Lee (1916)	A builder completed a contract but some of the work was unsatisfactory so D refused to pay.	Substantial performance	If performance is substantial, then recovery is possible.
Startup v Macdonald (1843)	The contract was to deliver at the end of March, which the seller did at 8.30 p.m. on 31 March (a Saturday).	Avoiding the strict rule on performance	If a party offers to perform and is refused by the other party, then payment is recoverable.
Williams v Roffey (1991)	Extra money was promised to builders if they would simply complete their contractual obligations on time.	Agreement to end a contract	Consideration must be provided to end a contract.

Case	Facts	Element of discharge	Legal point
Frost v Knight (1872)	D promised to marry his fiancé when his father died. D broke off the engagement before he died.	Consequence of an anticipatory breach	Fiancé successfully sued D, even though the actual breach had not yet arrived.
Metropolitan Water Board v Dick Kerr (1915)	A contract to build a reservoir was stopped by the government due to the outbreak of war.	Frustration of contract	This was a clear frustrating event, as it was impossible for the parties to continue.
Taylor v Caldwell (1863)	A music hall central to a contract was destroyed in a fire.	Frustration of contract	Frustration by impossibility
Morgan v Manser (1943)	An actor was contracted for ten years but conscripted into the army for six of those years.	Frustration of contract	Due to obvious and important frustration, both parties were excused performance.
Krell v Henry (1903)	A room was booked to observe the coronation procession of King Edward VII. The coronation was postponed due to the king's illness.	Frustration of contract	The central purpose was to observe the procession and therefore the contract was frustrated.
Herne Bay Steamboat Co. v Hutton (1903)	As part of King Edward VII's coronation celebrations, D hired a boat to watch the king review part of his fleet. The coronation was postponed due to the king's illness.	Frustration of contract	The central purpose of the contract (a trip around the Solent) remained, so there was no frustration.

Now test yourself

TESTED ☐

1 How does the case of *Williams v Roffey* (1991) modify the rule on discharge of contract by agreement?
2 Define the different types of breach.
3 What is meant by frustration of contract?
4 What are the main ways a contract can be frustrated?
5 Explain one of the limits to the doctrine of frustration of contract.
6 Why was the case of *Krell v Henry* (1903) decided differently to the case of *Herne Bay Steamboat Co. v Hutton* (1903)?

Answers online

Exam summary

In the exam, you MAY be asked to:
- respond to a scenario question based on contractual discharge by advising a claimant as to whether there has been a valid discharge through performance, frustration or breach
- discuss and evaluate in a full-length essay question the topics of performance, frustration and breach of contract.

These types of question will each be worth a maximum of 25 marks.

7.6 Remedies

Damages

REVISED

Compensatory damages

The main type of common-law remedy is damages. The two main types of damages available to the injured party are:

- liquidated, and
- unliquidated.

Table 7.6.1 Types of damages

Liquidated damages	Liquidated damages operate when both parties to the contract have, at the time of contracting, fixed an amount of damages in a clause in the contract that would be paid should there be a breach of contract – see *Dunlop Pneumatic Tyre Co. v New Garage and Motor Co.* (1914). However, the amount fixed could be ignored by the court unless it represents a fair and proper assessment of any loss: ● If the amount is a proper reflection of the loss, the courts will enforce the agreed amount of damages. ● If, however, the amount is seen as a penalty, that is to say an amount of money that far exceeds the breach of contract, this will be unenforceable. ● The court will not enforce a penalty clause where it seeks merely to punish the defendant for a minor breach.
Unliquidated damages	Where there is no fixed amount of damages, the courts can fix an amount based on the actual loss, called unliquidated damages. Here, the courts look closely at the principle of placing the party in the position they would have been in had the breach not occurred.

Causation and remoteness of loss

The main tests for unliquidated damages can be seen by looking at the issue of causation and the remoteness of loss in order to fix the amount:

- For causation, the courts will simply look at the breach to see whether it was factually caused by the actions of the defendant.
- For remoteness of loss, it is not practical to compensate for every consequence that follows a breach of contract. Here, the courts will look at what consequence should be compensated for and how much compensation should be paid.

In *Hadley v Baxendale* (1854), Alderson B stated in court:

'Where two parties have made a contract which one of them has broken, the damages which the other party ought to receive in respect of such breach of contract should be such as may fairly and reasonably be considered either arising naturally, i.e., according to the usual course of things, from such breach of contract itself, or such as may reasonably be supposed to have been in the contemplation of both parties, at the time they made the contract, as the probable result of the breach of it.'

This is known as the rule in *Hadley v Baxendale* (see Table 7.6.3 for the case details). The court decided that the carrier was not liable for the loss for two reasons:

- The absence of a mill shaft would not normally cause a loss, since the mill owner could have a spare.
- The carrier was not aware that the claimant could not restart production until a new mill shaft was made.

Mitigation of loss

Common sense should prevail that following a breach, the injured party should, as best as possible, try to lessen or mitigate any actual or potential loss – see *Pilkington v Wood* (1953).

The courts will take a dim view if the claimant simply sat back and allowed the consequences of the breach to get worse, when they could have done something to prevent further loss. The basic principle here is that the injured party must act reasonably in relation to the breach.

If the alternative is to take an unreasonable course of action, for example to buy substandard goods in replacement, then the courts will not require them to do so.

It is up to the defendant to prove that the claimant failed to follow a reasonable path to mitigate any loss.

Equitable remedies

There are many types of equitable remedy, all of which are not 'as of right' like common-law remedies but instead at the discretion of the courts. The most important are:

- specific performance
- rescission
- injunction
- rectification of a document.

Table 7.6.2 Equitable remedies

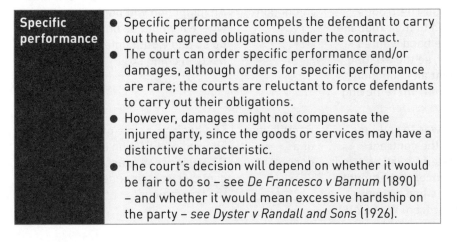

Specific performance	<ul><li>Specific performance compels the defendant to carry out their agreed obligations under the contract.</li><li>The court can order specific performance and/or damages, although orders for specific performance are rare; the courts are reluctant to force defendants to carry out their obligations.</li><li>However, damages might not compensate the injured party, since the goods or services may have a distinctive characteristic.</li><li>The court's decision will depend on whether it would be fair to do so – see *De Francesco v Barnum* (1890) – and whether it would mean excessive hardship on the party – *see Dyster v Randall and Sons* (1926).</li></ul>

Rescission	Rescission is an equitable right where a contract is set aside. The remedy is to bring the parties back, as best as possible, to the position they were in before they entered the contract.
Injunction	This is an order preventing or restraining another party from breaching obligations by: ● enforcing a restraint of trade clause ● protecting confidentiality ● enforcing compliance with a contract of personal service – see *Page One Records v Britton* (1968).
Rectification of a document	This is an order to redraft a written contract which is flawed and does not represent the original agreement – see *Webster v Cecil* (1861).

Revision activity

Consider five examples of a breach of contract, for example apples instead of oranges to an orange juice manufacturer, and decide the most appropriate equitable remedy to compensate the breach.

Table 7.6.3 Key cases on remedies

Case	Facts	Element of remedies	Legal point
Dunlop Pneumatic Tyre Co. v New Garage and Motor Co. (1914)	D supplied tyres to N, who under the contract would pay D £5 for any breach, for example selling under D's recommended prices.	Liquidated damages	This case set out a test to differentiate between liquidated damages and penalties.
Hadley v Baxendale (1854)	There was a delay in transporting a mill shaft. C sued D for the losses as a result of the delay	Remoteness of damage	The test was established for remoteness of damage
Pilkington v Wood (1953)	C sued a solicitor for damages after receiving negligent advice when buying a house. The solicitor said he should have sued the vendor to mitigate the loss.	Mitigation of loss	This argument was rejected. The court said that the duty to mitigate did not require C to 'embark on a complicated and difficult piece of litigation against a third party'.
De Francesco v Barnum (1890)	A young dancer entered into a contract of apprenticeship which paid her no money and disallowed her from taking on any paid employment elsewhere.	Specific performance	The contract was so disadvantageous to the dancer that the court would grant neither an injunction nor require specific performance of the contract.
Dyster v Randall and Sons (1926)	C, who had been made bankrupt, could not find the financial means to purchase a house he had agreed to buy.	Specific performance	The court refused an order of specific performance.
Page One Records v Britton (1968)	Sixties pop group The Troggs were contracted to their manager indefinitely. The band wanted a new manager, so the existing manager sought an injunction preventing them from removing his service.	Injunction	An injunction will not be granted where it would be unreasonable to do so and would unfairly restrain a party in doing so.
Webster v Cecil (1861)	An agreement was to sell land for £2,250, but the contract incorrectly stated £1,250. W tried to enforce the incorrect amount. C could prove he had already refused an offer from W of £2,000.	Rectification of a document	The basic principle of equity allowed rectification of a document – C's evidence was accepted and the contract was amended to represent the true amount.

Consumer remedies under the Consumer Rights Act 2015

The Consumer Rights Act 2015 provides certain remedies under s 19 if statutory rights under a goods contract are not met.

Table 7.6.4 Remedies under s 19 of the Consumer Rights Act 2015

Section 19(3)	If the goods do not conform to the contract because of a breach of any of the terms described in ss 9, 10, 11, 13 and 14, or if they do not conform to the contract under s 16, the consumer has the: • short-term right to reject (ss 20 and 22) • right to repair or replacement (s 23), and • right to a price reduction or the final right to reject (ss 20 and 24).
Section 19(4)	If the goods do not conform to the contract under s 15 or because of a breach, the consumer has the: • right to repair or replacement (s 23); and • right to a price reduction or the final right to reject (ss 20 and 24).

Now test yourself

TESTED

1 Using examples, what is the difference between common-law and equitable remedies?
2 How do the courts distinguish between a penalty and liquidated damages?
3 How do the courts decide whether to allow a claim for unliquidated damages?
4 For what reasons is a claimant expected to mitigate their loss following a breach of contract?
5 How would specific performance provide a remedy for a claimant, and in what circumstances would an order for specific performance be denied?
6 How would rescission provide a remedy for a claimant?

Answers online

Exam summary

In the exam, you MAY be asked to:
• respond to a scenario question based on contractual remedies by advising a claimant as to the types of remedies they would wish to be awarded by the court
• discuss and evaluate in a full-length essay question the topic of remedies.

These types of question will each be worth a maximum of 25 marks.

7.7 Evaluation

Evaluation of the formation of contract

Table 7.7.1 Evaluation of the formation of contract

Evaluative point	Evaluative explanation
Whether a contract exists depends on proper formation	Without the existence of a clear set of rules on formation, there can be no business efficiency in a contract.
Mutuality of offer and acceptance	An agreement only exists if a valid acceptance follows a valid offer.
Doctrine of consideration	*Quid pro quo* – this provides the basis of the proof of an agreement.
Intention to create legal relations	This provides a clear rebuttable presumption that not all agreements are enforceable simply because someone 'promises' someone else to do something.
The form, or documentation, required for a contract	Certain types of contract must take certain forms, e.g. sales of land, to reflect the seriousness of the contract, whereas other contracts with less importance can be made via 'simple' contracts.
Capacity of minors	Certain contracts are unenforceable against minors to reflect the bargaining position and protect the vulnerability of minors.
Privity of contract	Generally, a contract is only enforceable by, or against, the parties to it. Although, necessarily, certain third-party rights are now enforceable under the Contracts (Rights of Third Parties) Act 1999.

Evaluation of contractual terms

Table 7.7.2 Evaluation of contractual terms

Evaluative point	Evaluative explanation
Pre-contract/ formation discussion	Parties are able to identify the basis upon which they are prepared to contract.
Representations	Any discussion of a statement of fact at formation becomes a 'representation' and is expressly or impliedly incorporated into the contract.
Clear rules about representations under contract law	Representations are distinguished by type: terms, mere representations, misrepresentations, or mere opinions, expert opinions, trade puffs or reliant trade puffs – see *Carlill v Carbolic Smoke Ball Co.* (1893).
Tests for terms	Courts have established clear and distinct tests as to whether or not a representation is incorporated into a term of a contract.
Parole evidence rule	Generally, oral or similar evidence which adds or varies the terms of a written contract is not admissible. However, the Law Commission has argued exceptions to the rule exist, e.g. trade usage and custom.
Implied terms	Implied either: ● by fact – by the implied though unexpressed intentions of the parties, or ● by law – where the law prescribes certain provisions are included.
Exclusion clauses	Strict guidelines are established where a party is trying to remove or limit their liability through an exclusion or exemption clause.

Table 7.7.3 Ideas for reform of formation of contract

Evaluative point	Idea for reform
Rules on offer and acceptance using modern electronic means are vague and open to interpretation.	Specific EU or international legislation identifying rules on formation while using electronic means would greatly clarify the law.
The privity of contract rule prevents a sub-contractor from being liable to the original contracting party.	The Contract (Rights of Third Parties) Act 1999 could be expanded to cover this eventuality.
The privity of contract rule prevents a consumer from benefitting from consumer protection legislation if they did not purchase goods themselves.	The Contract (Rights of Third Parties) Act 1999 could be expanded to cover this eventuality.
The rules on revocation of a unilateral contract can be vague and difficult to identify the point at which acceptance begins and it becomes too late to revoke.	Legislation is required to identify and clarify the rules on the revocation of a unilateral contract.
A rebuttable presumption against an intent to create legal relations in domestic situations can be harsh.	Instead of a presumption against an intent to create legal relations in domestic situations, switch the presumption to there being an intent to create legal relations, unless it can be proved otherwise.

Table 7.7.4 Ideas for reform of contractual terms

Evaluative point	Idea for reform
A lack of damages available for innocent misrepresentation can lead to injustice, particularly where there is a bar to rescission.	Expand the Misrepresentation Act 1967.
Exclusion clauses and limitation clauses can be harsh on the party subject to them, particularly where that party is of weaker bargaining strength.	Expand judicial controls and allow greater protection for individuals under the Unfair Contract Terms Act 1977 and other legislation.
The contra proferentum rule operates very strictly against the party inserting the clause, unless they spell out precisely what the clause will cover.	Clear and specific guidelines are required as to what is and is not acceptable, to allow businesses to legitimately rely upon exclusion clauses and limitation clauses to protect their business.
Terms of a contract must be available to the contracting parties, but there is no insistence in law that the terms are read, leading to injustice.	Either the law should stipulate that a contracting party is made aware of the terms by evidentially reading the terms, or that a summary of the most divisive terms must be read to the parties.
The large amounts of correspondence before a contract is formed – the battle of the forms – can lead to uncertainty as to which terms were incorporated.	Instead of using the various common-law tests, legislation should be used to standardise contracts to provide business efficacy, rather than trying to get 'one over' on each other.

Exam practice

1 Adam is a student in the final year of studying A Levels. In his spare time, he designs and makes T-shirts. Adam can supply ready-made T-shirts from his catalogue and made-to-order T-shirts at the request of a buyer. Adam has just received an enquiry for 100 ready-made T-shirts and 100 made-to-order T-shirts from his father, who runs a shop.

However, Adam has told his father that he is going to give up his studies in order to concentrate on his business. Alarmed at this, Adam's father places the order for the T-shirts and says he will pay him £200 per month to finish his studies in six months' time. Adam says that this is not enough and he would need at least £500. His father says he will only pay Adam £300 per month: 'Take it or leave it'. Adam reluctantly agrees to continue with his studies and accepts his order for the T-shirts. Adam's father pays on time for the order for the T-shirts, but after three months he stops paying £300 monthly and refuses to continue to do so. In fact, his father says that he only had enough money for three months and had no intention of paying Adam after that.

Advise Adam whether an enforceable contract has been entered into. [25 marks]

2 Harry owns Harry's Autos. Sarah owns Sarah's Taxis. One of her taxis needed its annual service, so she went to Harry's Autos for it to be serviced.

As part of the service, the front brake pads were changed. Sarah collected the car but as she was driving it back to the office, she pressed the brake pedal, the brakes failed and the car was involved in an accident. Sarah suffered a broken collarbone, the front bumper of the taxi was damaged and an expensive, high-quality webcam that she keeps in the taxi for her own security was damaged beyond repair.

Sarah telephoned Harry when she was discharged from hospital to tell him about the accident. She said the accident could only have been caused by the service he provided being defective. He replied that he did not accept liability and that she should look at the clauses on the receipt carefully.

Advise Sarah on whether she can recover her losses from Harry. [25 marks]

3 Baroness Hale said in *Transfield Shipping Inc v Mercator Shipping Inc* (2008) 'Loss of the type in question has to be 'within the contemplation' of the parties at the time when the contract was made.'

Discuss how the law of contract restricts the amount of damages payable in the event of a breach of contract. [25 marks]

ONLINE

Glossary

Acceptance: unconditional agreement to all the terms of an offer.

Actus reus: the guilty act.

ADR: alternative dispute resolution, one of the key Woolf reform recommendations.

Appropriation: any assumption by a person of the rights of an owner.

Arbitration: a form of ADR where the parties to a dispute refer the case to an independent third party, known as an arbitrator, to decide.

Assault: where the defendant intentionally or recklessly causes the victim to apprehend immediate unlawful personal violence/force.

Attempt: if, with intent to commit an offence under s 1(1) of the Criminal Attempts Act 1981, a person does an act which is more than merely preparatory to the commission of the offence, they are guilty of attempting to commit the offence.

Automatism: an involuntary act such as a spasm, reflex action or convulsion, or an act performed while a person is unconscious (such as suffering from concussion or sleepwalking).

Autonomous: legally capable of making one's own decisions, and therefore legally responsible for their consequences.

Bail: a form of security, either a sum of money or a promise in exchange for the freedom of an arrested person as a guarantee that they will appear in a criminal court when required.

Balance of probabilities: the civil standard of proof which means the claimant must satisfy the court that their version of events is more likely than not.

Basic intent crimes: crimes where recklessness will suffice as *mens rea*.

Battery: the intentional or reckless application of unlawful force upon a victim.

Belonging to another: belonging to any person having possession or control of property or having any proprietary right or interest in it.

Bill of Rights: a document which sets out the civil rights of citizens.

Binding precedent: a case decision from a senior court that must be followed in future cases.

Breach of contract: when a party fails to carry out any of their obligations under the contract, or in carrying it out they fail to do what they are supposed to do.

Burden of proof: a defendant is innocent until proven guilty.

Burglary: where a trespasser enters a building (or part of a building) intending to steal, inflict GBH or do unlawful damage; or having entered a building (or part of a building), a trespasser steals or inflicts GBH, or attempts to do so.

'But for' test: the injury or damage to property must have been caused by the breach of the duty of care, i.e. it would not have happened but for the breach.

Civil courts: courts that deal with non-criminal matters.

Claimant: legal term for a person or organisation starting a civil claim in the courts.

Conciliation: a form of mediation where a third party is active in raising ideas for compromise between the parties in dispute.

Condition: contractual term which goes to the root of the contract.

Conditional fee agreements (CFAs): 'no win, no fee' arrangements.

Consent: express or implied permission from the 'victim' for the defendant to carry out the injury.

Consideration: 'an act or forbearance of one party, or the promise thereof, is the price for which the promise of the other is bought, and the promise thus given for value is enforceable'.

Constitutions: sets of rules which state how a country is to be run and the specific rights of its citizens.

Contemporaneity rule: the general rule in English law that the *actus reus* and the *mens rea* must occur at the same time.

Contract: an agreement between two parties which is binding in law and therefore enforceable in court.

Correspondence principle: the result which the defendant intends or foresees should match the result that actually occurs.

Criminal courts: there are two levels – the Magistrates' Court deals mainly with summary offences, and the Crown Court deals mainly with indictable offences.

Cyber-crime: criminal activity carried out by the use of computers, generally via the internet.

Damages: money calculated to return the claimant to their original position before the tort had taken place (in so far as it is possible to do so with money).

Data protection: the legal control of access to, and the use of, factual and statistical data generally stored in digital or paper-based systems.

Defendant: legal term for a person defending or responding to a legal claim (called a respondent in some aspects of civil law).

Delegated legislation: secondary legislation, i.e. laws passed in a specific area by a secondary body to which Parliament has passed its power.

Diminished responsibility: a special, partial defence to murder only, argued where an unlawful killing occurs due to the defendant's abnormality of mental functioning.

Direct intent: it was the defendant's decision to bring about the prohibited consequence.

Discharge (of a contract): the ending of a contract.

Duress by threats: a common-law defence whereby someone committed a crime because they were subject to a threat of death or serious injury.

Duress of circumstances: a common-law defence whereby someone committed a crime because of the circumstances in which they found themselves.

Economic duress: where one party makes threats of an economic nature to the other party in order to form or change an agreement.

Eiusdem generis: covering things of the same type.

Exclusion or exemption clauses: clauses which seek to exclude from liability one party for a breach of contract, or even for a tort.

Expressio unius eat exclusio alterius: the expression of one thing implies the exclusion of another.

Fair labelling: crimes should be defined to reflect their wrongfulness and severity.

Fault: there is some wrongdoing by the defendant.

Freedom of expression: being free to express ideas, views and opinions and share them with others without the state interfering.

Frustrated contract: where an unforeseen event prevents the absolute performance of the contract.

Golden rule: where judges decide that the literal rule produces absurd results when interpreting statute.

Green Paper: a consultative document issued by the government putting forward proposals for reform of the law and often inviting suggestions.

Gross negligence manslaughter: an offence requiring the death to have been caused by the defendant's gross negligence, rather than deliberately.

Guilty: legally responsible for a specified wrongdoing.

Horizontal direct effect: directives give an individual rights against other people, provided they have been implemented.

Human rights law: law governing fundamental rights and freedoms that exist in our legal system simply because we are human beings.

Immunity from suit: free from any legal action.

Indictable offences: the most serious, more complicated offences tried only and fully in the Crown Court, for example murder, manslaughter and robbery.

Information technology: the use of systems, especially computers and telecommunications systems, for storing, retrieving and sending information.

Injunction: a court order to stop; this is most common in torts such as trespass and nuisance.

Innominate term: can be either a condition or a warranty.

Intention: a decision to bring about the criminalised act.

Invitation to treat: the early stages of forming the agreement are often not considered to be offers but simply invitations for parties to make offers.

Judicial precedent: where past decisions of judges create law for future judges to follow.

Judicial review: process allowing certain decisions of government or other public bodies to be challenged by citizens to see if they are 'reasonable'.

Judiciary: collective term for all the different types of judge in the English legal system.

Juries: representatives drawn from the electorate who decide the guilt of offenders in the Crown Court.

Justice: the idea that the law is 'fair' in how it seems to punish wrongs and protect rights.

Lay people: in the criminal justice system, either magistrates or juries; 'lay' in this circumstance means legally 'unqualified'.

Legal moralism: immoral conduct is criminalised for better social cohesion.

Legal personnel: a collective term which includes barristers, solicitors and legal executives.

Liable: held to be legally responsible for a breach of the civil law.

Literal rule: where judges use the exact meaning of words when interpreting statute, no matter how absurd the outcome.

Loss of control: a special, partial defence to murder only, argued where an unlawful killing occurs following the defendant's loss of self-control.

Magistrates: volunteer citizens who work as unpaid (except for expenses) judges in the Magistrates' Court and the Youth Court. They deal with the vast majority of criminal cases.

Mediation: where a neutral third party attempts to resolve a dispute (possibly face to face) with both parties, without giving their opinion.

Mens rea: the guilty mind.

Miscarriage of justice: where someone is convicted and punished by the courts for a crime that they did not commit.

Mischief rule: a rule of statutory interpretation used to prevent the mischief an Act is aimed at.

Misrepresentation: a false statement of material fact.

Murder: the unlawful killing of a human being with malice aforethought.

Natural law: rules which are not necessarily written down as laws but are nevertheless followed by citizens.

Natural law theory: theory that maintains that the law should be used to enforce moral values.

Necessity: a common-law defence whereby someone committed a crime because it was necessary to avoid a greater evil.

Negotiation: where an individual attempts to resolve an issue directly, privately and possibly face to face with the other party.

Normative concepts: concepts which establish standards of normality or acceptable behaviour.

Noscitur a sociis: the meaning of a word can be gathered from its context.

Novus actus interveniens: where a subsequent intervening act breaks the chain of causation.

Obiter dicta: 'other things said'.

Oblique intent: the prohibited consequence is virtually certain, and the defendant realises this.

Occupiers' liability: the duty owed by occupiers to those who come onto their land.

Offer: an expression of one party's willingness to contract on certain terms, made with the intention that it will be legally binding upon acceptance.

Online dispute resolution (ODR): a contemporary method of using digital means, for example the internet, to resolve disputes without having to use litigation.

Original precedent: arises if the point of law in a case has never been considered before so judicial precedent cannot apply.

Paternalism: the state is justified in protecting individuals from harm.

Persuasive precedent: usually in the form of *obiter dicta*, persuasive precedent is part of the judgment that should be followed in similar cases but is not binding. However, a reason for deciding not to follow it must be given.

Positivism: theory that maintains that laws and morals should be kept separate.

Postal rule: the acceptance is valid and the contract is formed when the acceptance letter is posted, and not when it is received by the offeror.

Private nuisance: unreasonable interference with the enjoyment or use by the occupier of their land.

Procedural law: puts systems in place in an attempt to ensure justice, i.e. it provides a framework in which all should be equal before the law.

Property: includes money and all other property, real or personal, including things in action and other intangible property.

Prosecutes: legal term for bringing a criminal charge against a defendant.

Public nuisance: a nuisance which materially affects the reasonable comfort of life of a class of Her Majesty's subjects.

Purposive approach: where judges look to see what the purpose of the law is when interpreting statute.

Quantum meruit: a reasonable sum of money that is to be paid for services in contracts where an exact sum of money is not stipulated.

Ratio decidendi: 'the reason for the decision'.

Reasonable doubt: the criminal standard of proof which means the prosecution must provide sufficient evidence for the jury or magistrates to be certain of the defendant's guilt – if they are not, then they have reasonable doubt.

Reasonable person: an objective test, i.e. how a hypothetical person would behave sets a standard against which the defendant is compared; sometimes known as the 'man on the Clapham omnibus' or 'law's ghost God'.

Rebuttable presumption: a conclusion that a judge will take in court unless the contrary is raised and proven.

Regulation: a process whereby the actions of individuals or a collective are overseen and governed by an authorised organisation.

Remedy: in contract law, this is a way of providing a solution to a breach of contract.

Representations: statements made before the contract which may or may not become one of the main terms of the contract.

Restitutio in integrum: putting the claimant back in the position they would have been in if the tort had not been committed, in so far as it is possible to do so with money.

Restriction: a right or freedom can be limited where it is just and equitable to do so. Each restriction depends upon the exact nature of the right and freedom.

Revocation of an offer: the withdrawal of an offer.

Rights: rules or laws which are believed to belong to every person without discrimination.

Right to a fair trial: individuals charged with a criminal offence or involved in cases concerning a civil right have a right to a public hearing with an impartial and independent 'tribunal' or judge within a reasonable time.

Right to freedom of peaceful assembly and association: you are able to assemble (gather) with other people for peaceful purposes and associate with (be in the company of) others for the same reasons.

Right to liberty and security of person: no one without just cause can interfere with your right to live a free life. There may be exceptions, such as arrest or imprisonment.

Right to respect for private and family life: no one without just cause can interfere with your right to live a free life.

Robbery: where someone steals and subjects the person to force or fear of force.

Royal Commissions: temporary, *ad hoc* committees set up to investigate and provide a report on specific areas of law.

Rylands v Fletcher: where the escape of non-naturally stored material onto adjoining property damages or destroys that property.

Self-defence: using reasonable force in order to defend oneself.

Sentencing: any punishment given to an offender who has been convicted.

Separation of powers: the three main sources of power (executive, legislature and judiciary) must be separate and not held by one specific person or body.

Specific intent crimes: crimes where only intent will satisfy the *mens rea*.

Standard of proof: the defendant's guilt must be proved 'beyond all reasonable doubt'.

Stare decisis: 'let the decision stand'.

Strict liability offences: offences that require no fault for some or all of the *actus reus*.

Subjective recklessness: the defendant commits an act knowing there is a risk of the consequence happening.

Substantive law: legal rules which determine rights and obligations or how a society must behave, for example criminal, contract, tort or human rights law.

Sue: take civil legal proceedings against a defendant.

Summary offences: the least serious offences in terms of injury or impact, tried in the Magistrates' Courts, for example assault, battery and certain road traffic offences such as speeding.

Theft: the dishonest appropriation of property belonging to another with the intention of permanently depriving the other of it.

Theories of rights: systems of ideas proposed to explain the rationale of having rights based on general principles.

Tort law: an area of the law that allows a person to claim compensation when they have been injured or their property has been damaged.

Transferred malice: where *mens rea* can be transferred from the intended victim to the actual victim.

Trespassers: persons on the occupier's land who have no permission or authority to be there.

Triable 'either-way' offences: offences that can be tried in the Crown Court or in the Magistrates' Court, for example theft, s 47 ABH and s 20 GBH/wounding.

Tribunals: an informal method of dispute resolution developed for issues arising under the UK's 'welfare state', for example education, health and employment.

Ultra vires: a Latin term meaning 'beyond the powers', i.e. the secondary body has exceeded the powers given to it by the parent Act.

Unlawful act manslaughter: an offence requiring the death to have been caused by the defendant's unlawful conduct, rather than deliberately intending to kill.

Vertical direct effect: an individual can claim against the state even if the directive is not yet implemented.

Vicarious liability: a third person has legal responsibility for the unlawful actions of another.

Visitors: in law, adult visitors are those who have been invited or licensed to enter, or who have a statutory right to enter, or have contractual permission.

Vitiating: invalidating; a vitiating factor makes a contract null and void. The two most common vitiating factors are misrepresentation and economic duress.

Warranty: generally a descriptive term.

White Paper: a document issued by the government stating its decisions as to how it is going to reform the law; this is for information, not consultation.

Notes

OCR A Level Law